MANAGING GLOBALLY

MANAGING GLOBALLY
A Complete Guide to Competing Worldwide

Carl A. Nelson

IRWIN
Professional Publishing
Burr Ridge, Illinois
New York, New York

Reprinted by permission of Perigee Books, a division of The Putnam Publishing Group. *The Deming Management Method* copyright © 1986 by Mary Walton.

Permission to use excerpts from *Kyocera: A Bond of Human Minds* by Kasuo Inamori was given by Kyocera International, Inc.

© Carl A. Nelson, 1994

Sponsoring editor:	Cynthia A. Zigmund
Project editor:	Jane Lightell
Production manager:	Jon Christopher
Designer:	Jeanne M. Rivera
Compositor:	Montgomery Media, Inc.
Typeface:	10.5/12 Palatino
Printer:	Maple-Vail Press

Library of Congress Cataloging-in-Publication Data

Nelson, Carl A.,
    Managing globally: a complete guide to competing worldwide/Carl
  A. Nelson.
      p.   cm.
  Includes bibliographical references and index.
  ISBN 0-7863-0121-X
    1. Strategic planning.   2. International business enterprises-
Management.   3. International economic relations.   4. Competition,
International.   I. Title.
HD30.28.N45   1994
658' .049—dc20   93–24632

Printed in the United States of America
1 2 3 4 5 6 7 8 9 0 MP 0 9 8 7 6 5 4 3

To Barbara, my understanding wife.

Contents

Chapter Ten
INITIAL SCREENING: COUNTRY POTENTIAL   84

Profit, 224

Presence, 224

Getting Help, 224

Nonfinancials, 224

Financials, 224

Final Shot, 224

Appendix A
GENERIC CORPORATE-LEVEL STRATEGIC
ALTERNATIVES   225

Offensive Strategies, 225
Stable Strategies, 225
Defensive Strategies, 226
    Combination Strategies, 226

Appendix B
NUMBER CRUNCHING   227

    Traditional Ratios, 227
    Liquidity Ratios, 227
    Leverage (or Debt) Ratios, 227
    Activity Ratios, 228
    Profitability Ratios, 228
    Other Financial Analyses, 229
    Growth Ratios, 229
    Working-Capital Analysis, 229

Appendix C
TIME-FUTURE ANALYSIS   231

Pre-workshop Questionnaire, 231

Appendix D
FORECASTING TECHNIQUES   233

    Benchmarking, 233
    Critical Success Factors/Strategic Issues Analysis, 233
    Delphi Technique, 233
    Dialectic Inquiry, 233
    Environmental Scanning, Forecasting, and Trend Analysis, 233
    Experience Curves, 233
    Focus Groups, 233
    Future Studies, 233
    Market Opportunity Analysis, 233
    Metagame Analysis, 234
    Multiple Scenarios, 234
    Nominal Group Technique, 234
    PIMS Analysis, 234

Acknowledgments

This book pioneers a new approach: strategic management in the global setting. Needless to say the result must be shared with the many contributors who freely communicated their thoughts to me. I accept full responsibility for any faults this book might have and gratefully share any praise for its virtues with the following persons:

Graduate students of United States International University with whom I experimented: Ghazy Kamal R. Adnan, Choi-Ha Cheung, Jian Feng He, Yu-Yin Hung, I-Ru Kung, Eric Poncelet, and doctoral candidates David A. Anderson, Keith D. Brouthers, Temple Thomas Moore, Robert C. Moussetis, Jean R. Pearlman, Robert Edward Pottoff, Wu-Tien Tsai, James D. Underwood.

I am particularly grateful to the following executives who allowed me valuable interview time and gave freely of their views of the future: Harry Todd, former chairman and CEO of Rohr Corporation; Richard Cramer, founder and former president of IVAC and IMED; John S. Barry, chairman and CEO, WD-40; Dan Pegg, president of the San Diego Economic Development Corporation; Paul E. Humphrey, president and chairman of Humphrey, Inc.; Paul F. Mosher, president of Kelco, Division of Merck & Co.; David Hale, president of Gensia Pharmaceuticals, Inc.; Lawrence Emond, director of the U.S. division of Japan's largest business research firm, MDB; Patrick M. Boarman, professor, National University; H. Igor Ansoff, professor, United States International University; Jack Hayes, CEO of Global Strategies, Inc.; Kenneth J. Widder, M.D., Chairman and CEO of Molecular Biosystems, Inc.; William L. Everitt, vice president of communications, Kyocera International, Inc.; Oliver R. "Chris" Stanfield, vice president and chief financial officer, Echelon, Inc.; John Bowne, president and CEO, Software Products International; Greg Reyes, chairman of the board, Sunward Technologies; Gene W. Ray, Ph.D., president and CEO of The Titan Corporation; Michael S. Inoue, Ph.D., vice president of corporate technology and planning, Kyocera International, Inc.; James W. Owens, Ph.D., president, Solar Turbines Incorporated; David J. Conti, editorial director, Business McGraw-Hill; Hans Boars, director of marketing, Solar Turbines Incorporated; Cynthia Zigmund, senior editor, Irwin Professional Publishing; Jane Lightell, editing manager, Richard D. Irwin, Inc.; and Jane Crouse and Mary Beth Nilles of Montgomery Media, Inc.

Thank you!

Introduction

Trade is the currency of peace.

Clayton Yeutter

During the last quarter of the 20th century the good ship globalism sailed across earth like a tidal wave bringing a cargo of economic interdependence. That voyage is irreversible, and as the phenomenon continues to sweep across oceans and cultural barriers more nations and businesses worldwide are joining the expansion. As we approach the new millennium, the world business environment is in the throes of remarkable change.

- There has been an explosion of cross-border business and investment which will not quickly subside.
- Dramatic geopolitical shifts have redefined the global economic balance and have ushered in new political leadership.
- New markets have been created and the face of consumer demographics has been redrawn.
- Globalization and regional integration are creating a fiercely competitive world marketplace where the price of admission is a clear strategic vision.
- More businesses realize that 75 percent or more of their potential market lay beyond local borders.
- Superior management and global brand recognition will be major factors of success.
- Technological and scientific breakthroughs based on superior information networks will make or break manufacturers.

Modern leaders know the 21st century will be a quantum more complex, and they must control their own destiny or outside forces will control it for them. They know that only the organization that adapts itself continuously will survive and that they must utilize long-term thinking because short-term thinking spells death in the global marketplace. Leaders also know they need a framework that will help them focus on a winning direction for their organization in the new economic age.

It must be noted, however, that the average CEO does not know how to formulate and manage global strategy. This was confirmed in a recent joint study by Korn/Ferry International and Columbia University Graduate School of Business titled Reinventing the CEO . The results of data collected from 1,508 international respondents showed that the top area of expertise needed in the year 2000 by the ideal CEO was strategy formulation.

Managing Globally: A Complete Guide to Competing Worldwide pioneers the process called *global strategic management* which holds the key to economic survival in the new century. The approach explains how to make the paradigm shift from local to global through a strategic formulation process that takes advantage of global opportunities.

Audience

This *results-oriented* book has been structured to aid any organization—of any size, with any product or service—to formulate and execute winning strategies. It accomplishes this objective by serving as a guidebook which leads the reader step-by-step through a do-it-yourself process.

Of course it has always been the CEO's job to concentrate on the entire company, not just on its parts. But the modern CEO needs help. Shaping an organization's future is the responsibility of every manager and every employee who wishes to take advantage of the opportunities brought about by the new economic freedom.

Therefore, the audience for this book includes executives, boards of directors, senior- and mid-level managers, key employees, supervisors, sales personnel, and staff and support groups at every level of every size company. It is for those people who seek results by better understanding what is happening in international business and trade as we enter the 21st century.

This book works for companies in any country in the world. For instance, a Mexican company can use it to develop a European or American strategy and an Asian organization may use it to go global.

How this Book Was Written

Most authors come to their conclusions based on postmortem experiences or scholarly research. I did that, but in addition, I talked to business leaders to get their views firsthand. I interviewed more than a dozen CEOs of all sizes and types of organizations, as well as others who were skilled teachers and consultants in the field. I discovered that many were interested in and, in fact, were experimenting with a new, strategic approach to managing, but, for them, the material on the market was either too scholarly or too esoteric. I drew from leaders' experiences and then let them review the draft manuscript. Thus the process described in this book is a reflection of practitioners.

Special Benefits of this Book

Managing Globally: A Complete Guide to Competing Worldwide uses a general management approach which combines small doses of theory with large portions of practical information designed to gain results. It discusses every major element of the global strategic management process from formulation to implementation. The thing that is new—that differentiates this book from other books about strategic management—is the integration of an explanation of how to take advantage of global opportunities through the global screening and assessment process. Like an admiral or general in battle, if you do not understand the forces that surround you, you cannot win, let alone compete.

Another major feature of *Managing Globally* is its approach; it is a tool for each of the major elements needed to build a global strategy. To support this approach, the book is topical, logical, and touches every major aspect of global trade. As an example the book deals with the new Europe, that is, the 1989 peaceful revolution which is changing Marxism to market theory in central and Eastern Europe. This book shows how to analyze the impact of EC92, NAFTA, and the potential Asian trading blocs. It offers methods of doing business with changing national economies.

Other special features of *Managing Globally* include the following:

- A pioneering global strategic management process.
- Practical checklists, forms, questionnaires, flowcharts, matrices, and examples.
- Working tools for global expansion.
- A do-it-yourself strategic formulation process.
- Step-by-step solutions for global complexity.
- Identification of important global economic indicators.
- Introduction of a nine-step intelligence screening process.

- Tools to design a winning global strategy.
- A results-oriented implementation process.
- A discussion of how to establish a global corporate philosophy using the ideas of Deming and Inomori of Kyocera.
- Data base and data service providers.
- How to screen and analyze changing countries, markets, products, and industries.
- How to analyze a global product.
- How to match entry strategies and tactics.
- How to manage the integrated global business.

Organization

The need for strategic thinking has never been greater. The rules have changed and you must adapt to win! Therefore, the quest of this book is to take you beyond daily operations into the world of global strategy, which is a new approach to managing your firm.

By explaining how to use strategy in the global setting, this book offers a framework to think through, put in writing, and take action on a document which an organization can use to enter and compete on a worldwide basis.

To be realistic and useful in the workplace a book of this nature must be honest. To that end *Managing Globally* does not suggest you adopt blue-sky, naive, or out-of-touch ideas, but it does encourage creative thinking.

Using a step-by-step model which reviews the major influences of business, government, industries, and markets, this book offers a pragmatic technique to structure the resulting plan. Finally, it explains the technique of implementing the plan to make the vision come true.

As shown in Figure I–1, this book is organized into the five major tasks which explain the formulation and implementation of strategic management in the global setting.

Tasks

Tasks 1–4 are designed to give you the tools necessary to formulate the strategy. But it is one thing to dream up a shrewd plan, it is another to execute it in such a way that measurable outcomes give intended results. Therefore, Task 5 is about implementing that strategy.

Task 1: Understand the Strategic Process

By the time you finish Chapters 1–3, the concepts of strategic management should be securely imbedded in your mind. Don't hesitate to go back and review should there be doubts.

Task 2: Establish Time-Present, Baseline, or Current Position

Task 2 is the process of establishing the organization's current profile—what is the firm doing in time-present. Chapters 4–8 provide the necessary tools to do the prework steps, that is, institutionalize the global strategic management process and review how the firm got started, how it got to time-present, and what is going on today. This task includes understanding the firm's capabilities and problems.

Task 3: Map Time-Future

Firms use more than one method to screen for the future. Chapter 9 explains how to use the in-house Global Family Opinion Team to do ad hoc brainstorming. It also offers other methods such as wargaming and using the Delphi technique and focus groups. In other words, the organization uses multiple methods to gain a snapshot of time-future. In addition to the GFOT input, this book offers a method called global opportunity mapping which has nine screenings. As shown in Figure I–2 mapping includes need and political/economic screenings.

FIGURE I–1
Global Strategic
Management Tasks

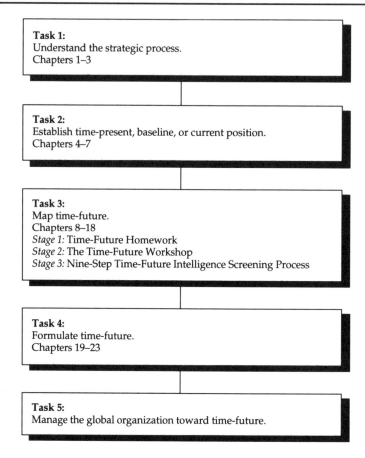

Task 1:
Understand the strategic process.
Chapters 1–3

Task 2:
Establish time-present, baseline, or current position.
Chapters 4–7

Task 3:
Map time-future.
Chapters 8–18
Stage 1: Time-Future Homework
Stage 2: The Time-Future Workshop
Stage 3: Nine-Step Time-Future Intelligence Screening Process

Task 4:
Formulate time-future.
Chapters 19–23

Task 5:
Manage the global organization toward time-future.

The precondition for Task 3 is intelligence because the challenge of going global is that complexity requires volumes of evaluated information. There are about 200 nations in the world, give or take 10 on any given day. Global expansion requires a mapping process which offers an orderly method to screen and prioritize each country by several characteristics. You cannot formulate a global strategy unless you screen the international economic system—in its parts and in its entirety. Therefore, the purpose of Chapters 10–18 is to provide you the tools for analyzing intelligence as it relates to your firm, its technology, and its products in the global economic setting.

The data collection and analysis phase should not be limited to the scenarios of the ad hoc sessions. If not constrained, it may uncover other promising arenas. Until now most organizations have been comfortable in the home market where culture, commercial code, business practices, and the many other elements which lead to successful business are well understood. From now on the world becomes complex because each sovereign nation presents an entirely new challenge of different economic conditions, cultures, and practices.

Task 4: Formulate Time-
Future (Diagnose and
Formulate Objectives
and Strategies)

In Task 4, developed in Chapters 19–23, one or more groups are assigned to analyze the information gathered from the ad hoc phase, and compare it with that which was developed during the mapping process. The expectations of the ad hoc opinions are compared with the results of the screening analysis to validate and to determine gaps and opportunities.

FIGURE I–2
*Nine-Step Global Time-Future
Intelligence Screening Process*

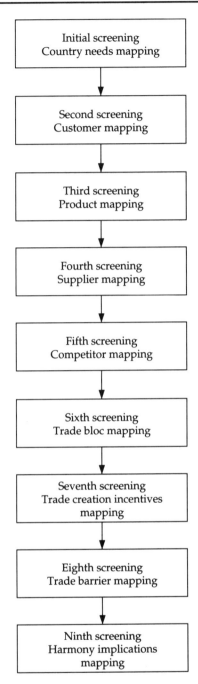

From these opportunities come new objectives. To choose future objectives from a list of alternatives is the purpose of the process. Obviously no firm can afford everything; resources must be identified and rationed.

Global business strategy must then be matched with country entry tactics to produce the best approach to managing the firm. The methodology for matching the various entry tactics with strategies is explained in Chapter 21. Needless to say, the new strategy must be linked to operating plans and budgets. Then the strategic plan must be approved. These processes are discussed in Chapters 20–26.

FIGURE I–3
Strategic Task Framework

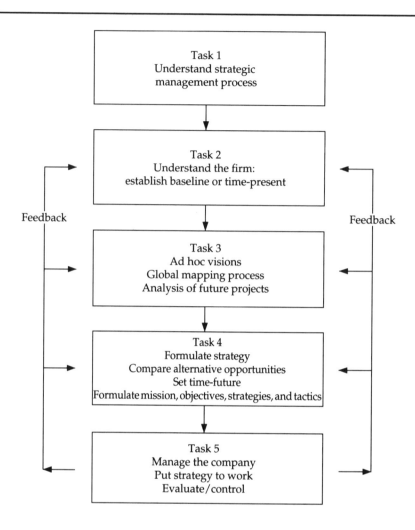

Task 1
Understand strategic
management process

Task 2
Understand the firm:
establish baseline or time-present

Feedback   Feedback

Task 3
Ad hoc visions
Global mapping process
Analysis of future projects

Task 4
Formulate strategy
Compare alternative opportunities
Set time-future
Formulate mission, objectives, strategies, and tactics

Task 5
Manage the company
Put strategy to work
Evaluate/control

Task 5: Manage the Global Organization to Achieve the New Strategy

This task is detailed in Chapters 24–27. Strategy does not implement itself. Leaders and managers must carry the results of the process through to a successful conclusion. Implementation not only means execution, but also feedback and results measurement. Task 5 shows the process of managing the new strategy.

To achieve the results of the global strategic paradigm, Figure I–3 shows the framework of the five tasks with the feedback loops necessary to ensure success. These tasks correlate with the way the book is organized into its five major parts. Refer to Figure I–1 to see the connection of the tasks to the book chapters.

How to Use This Book

Managing Globally is meant to be used on a daily basis and to be applied in the real world. Therefore, I suggest the reader first gain a grasp of the total process. As you read, apply the steps mentally to your own organization. Be particularly aware of the perquisites in terms of time, authority support, and resources before beginning implementation. This book provides the necessary tools to design a winning global strategy.

Note: Some have urged that the book include case studies. But cases are continuously changing and others become obsolete; therefore, if you learn best through that application I suggest any current casebook will amply serve you.

1

UNDERSTAND THE STRATEGIC PROCESS

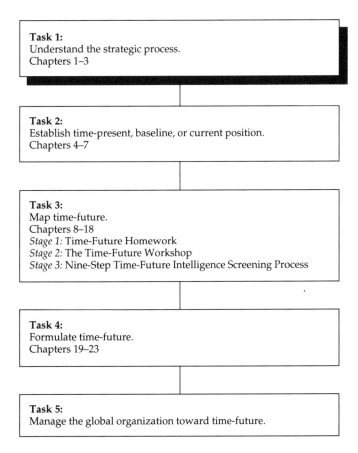

Task 1:
Understand the strategic process.
Chapters 1–3

Task 2:
Establish time-present, baseline, or current position.
Chapters 4–7

Task 3:
Map time-future.
Chapters 8–18
Stage 1: Time-Future Homework
Stage 2: The Time-Future Workshop
Stage 3: Nine-Step Time-Future Intelligence Screening Process

Task 4:
Formulate time-future.
Chapters 19–23

Task 5:
Manage the global organization toward time-future.

The purpose of this task is to establish the setting for the global strategic management process, to review its theoretical background, and to provide a transition for practical use of strategy, particularly for business.

Chapter 1 discusses the need for strategy based on the increased complexity of the global economy and the issues that must be addressed when formulating a global strategy. Chapter 2 presents the basic strategic paradigm and explains the transition from theory to practice. Chapter 3 describes the global strategic management process.

Chapter 1

Strategy in the Global Economy

If we could first know where we are, and whither we are tending, we could better judge what to do, and how to do it.

Abraham Lincoln

Why is the use of strategy the most powerful planning tool available to managers? Because it is the only method by which an organization can deal with modern complexity. But strategy is not new. Its use dates from before Christianity and its adoption for domestic business management dates from the mid-1950s. So what's new?

Using strategy in the global context is new and pioneering, and it is necessary because the economy of the 21st century will be a quantum more complex than previous periods and the use of strategy is the key to organizational survival.

CHANGED CONTEXT

By the late 1930s America had been a political and economic union for more than 150 years, yet most businesses were only local or regional. Things changed rapidly in the late 1940s when all businesses began to think national. It was the same in all industrialized countries. Today most major organizations worldwide have saturated the national market and every business is thinking international. Competition among domestic and foreign firms in local markets is dynamic.

The 21st century will be known as the century of the global business. All businesses must decide now how they intend to compete. In most cases that means changing the context of their long-term business strategy from domestic to global.

Don't misunderstand. The worldwide context has already changed. Most CEOs have seen the trend: global trade will continue to explode. They know they must reshape their firm to compete in the global marketplace. They also know they must have a strategy. If nothing else that strategy must include the seeds of a global beginning. Even if a firm has a foothold in other country markets, it must periodically revisit its external environment to ensure an integrated strategy is in place.

GLOBAL MANAGER

A new kind of manager has emerged—the global manager. This person must not only understand diverse country economics, cultures, and customer markets, but also understand how to deal with the international economic system.

Managers can no longer think one dimensionally—about only one national market or how trade is managed by only one country. Domestic business has become a plural term. Every company of the future will operate in more than one country, the home country being just one of the firm's many markets.

Do not get caught in the irrational syndrome that only companies that have a truly global product are going global. Not all smaller businesses will achieve true global business status, but it can become a target, a vision for incremental growth. After all, IBM was once a small business!

As Kenichi Ohmae described in his book *The Borderless World*, modern businesses attempt to visualize themselves equidistant from their customers and markets.

3

FIGURE 1–1
Equidistant
Global Strategic Vision

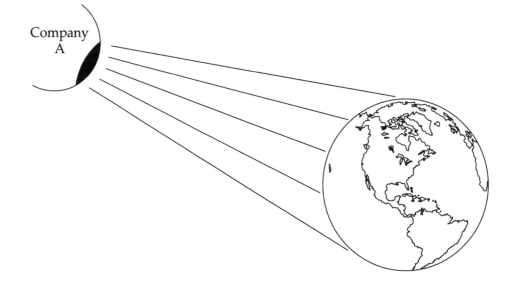

> Henry Ford's failure was not his original strategy. He took the simplistic approach to early mass production: "Give it to them (in any color) as long as it is black." His failure was that he didn't understand how to deal with complexity and didn't have a replacement strategy when the first one played out.
>
> Fortunately the industrial revolution and the mass production era went beyond Ford's myopia to trigger terms such as *competition, infrastructure, technology,* and *product differentiation*. Today, in the post-industrial age, our understanding of the boundaries of competition and opportunities has remarkably expanded.

Figure 1–1 shows this concept as if the firm had its eye suspended in space looking at the earth and all its country markets. The global firm no longer sees only a home market, rather it sees economic denationalization and multiple opportunities.

Competition in the New Economic Age

It is a misconception that only the largest firms in the world think about global strategy. To the contrary the availability of sophisticated intelligence and simplification of methods allow all firms to develop a strategy to enter and compete in global markets. Just as everyone seems to know about globalism, so do they understand the need for business strategy.

I asked American business executives about strategy. In personal interviews, they all responded with a positive theme—about the need for strategy. Here is what some of them had to say.

> *Does a modern firm need a strategy? Sure. It's figuring out what's going on. Understanding where you are...trying to figure out where I wish to go. Strategy becomes the plan or the road map—what moves do I make to get where I want to go. You start with the external thing and kind of work back to where you position yourself, time-now, then you jump time and say where would I like to be time-future. Like how many moves on the chess board am I going to get to get that guy in check? And then how do I execute that, which of course is the tactics of the thing.*

> Harry Todd, managing partner, Carlisle Enterprises, L.P. and
> former chairman of the board and CEO of Rohr Corporation

Does a modern firm need a strategy? It's important for a company to try to figure out where it's going, certainly. Rather than come in the morning and say what'll we do (today)? Not keep changing directions all the time. The old saying "plan your work and work your plan."

John S. (Jack) Barry, chairman of the board and CEO of WD-40 Company

Yes! If not it will fail.

Oliver R. "Chris" Stanfield, vice president of Echelon Corporation

COMPLEXITY

In the past, before the global boom, business was simplistic. As Peters and Waterman suggested in their book *In Search of Excellence,* just tend to your knitting—which was most often your own domestic market. Do that and business would take care of itself.

Today's problem is not whether there is complexity, but rather how to handle it. Businesses all over the world are entering the global marketplace. They bring new products, markets, technologies, and the need for new capital. Day-to-day operations are challenging. But even more challenging is the ability to look ahead, to have the vision to define a new strategy with objectives that are often complex and to keep a management handle on the complexity.

What Caused the Complexity?

The causes of increased complexity are apparent to even the most casual observer. Most nations, including the United States, have changed their provincial view of the world as evidenced by an increase in the volume of cross-border trade. The trade boom begot globalism and that begot interdependence and that begot complexity.

Cross-Border Trade Boom

As a matter of understatement, what began when ancient African gatherers exchanged their excess with neighboring foragers has greatly expanded. Over time the evolutionary process swelled as early humans formed tribes and sent adventurers beyond their forests, their land borders, and finally their shores. Eventually the pharaohs of Egypt sent camel caravans tramping the continent and the Persians sent buyers to China. Then the likes of Vasco da Gama, Columbus, and Magellan began crossing oceans. Before we realized it, 5,000 years of international trade history was behind us.

Figure 1–2 shows roughly the growth of gross global product (GGP) and international trade over time. The curve of gross global trade (GGT) was essentially flat until the late 1800s when the development of clipper ships changed the slope. The curve sprang to life about the turn of the century and took a dynamic upward bend as the technology revolution heated up. Faster steam-powered ships were followed by the innovation of international radio. The invention of the Otto and Diesel cycles brought trucks, then airplanes. Then came television and satellites, and the boom was here.

The Explosion

Although we have seen many revolutionary stages since 1945, the real explosion in international trade didn't begin until about 1965. Then, economies awakened from a sleep caused by the ravages of death and destruction. The boom came after production capability had been restored and when people wanted more of everything. Figure 1–3 shows the growth of world exports in U.S. dollars since 1950 and highlights the dynamic increase of the last 20 years. The curve would be even more dramatic except it does not include financial flows nor trade among the nonmarket countries. Even though there have been economic setbacks, such as recessions which caused flat periods, the trendline is dynamically upward.

FIGURE 1–2
Growth of Gross Global Trade

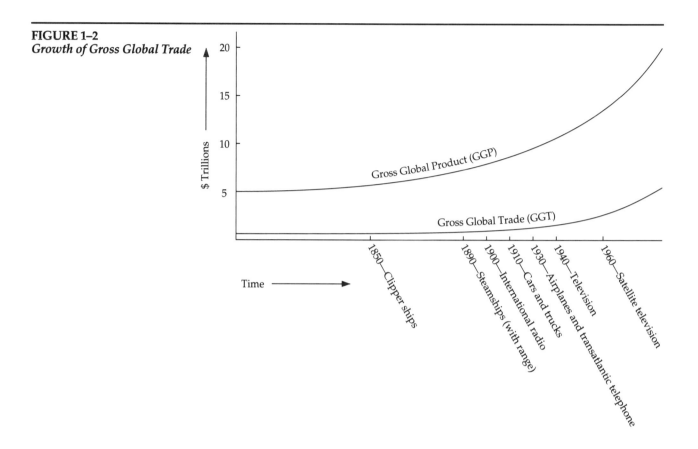

What Caused the Boom?

What brought about this revolutionary expansion? Was it consumer wants or was it caused by manufacturers who pushed new products by means of innovative promotion? Actually there were multiple causes.

The American experiment. This started a little more than 200 years ago by a group of disenchanted English colonials. Transplanted to the North American shore, they were determined to try freedom—to migrate across interstate borders, to sell across those borders, and to steadfastly build a market-oriented economy which became a model for the world.

Profit as a motivator. Worn like a badge of honor, the word *profit* is no longer a shameful thought in most of the world. Private, for-profit, free enterprise has shown itself to be a significantly stronger motivator than altruism. Capitalism works and being a successful person of commerce brings high esteem.

Competition as an energizer. Free markets and free enterprise beget competition and that stimulates energy. Everyone likes a winner and as the news of the success of the American experiment leaked across the world others wanted to try.

No world war. During the years since World War II, there have been many small wars on almost every continent. But for many reasons, not the least of which has been the strength of the United States and NATO, the Cold War never sparked. Therefore there has been a generally peaceful environment for commerce to grow.

FIGURE 1–3
Growth of World Exports

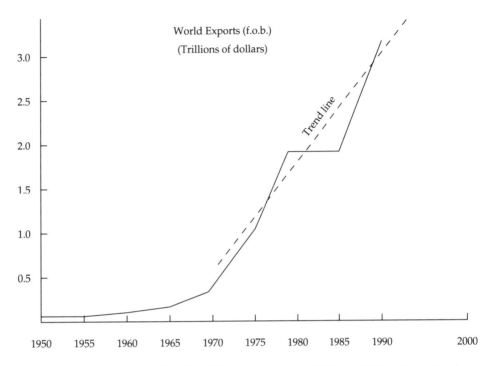

Source: Constructed by the author from United Nations annual reports 1983 through 1989 and International Monetary Fund statistics 1948 through 1989. Not adjusted for real dollars.

Marshall Plan. Unlike most victors, the Allies rushed to the aid of their fallen adversaries with imaginative economic growth programs. Those programs were, by most measures, extremely successful.

Supranational organizations. The same visionaries who developed the Marshall Plan also saw to it that the world had a basis for ongoing economic development. Organizations like the World Bank, General Agreement on Tariffs and Trade (GATT), and United Nations Conference on Trade and Development (UNCTAD), a major committee of the United Nations, are legacies of brilliant post-war thinking.

Then came Hollywood. It must be acknowledged that Hollywood and the motion picture industry had as much to do with the changing wants of the people of earth as any prior invention.

And Walt Disney. The genius of Walt Disney struck across borders taking Mickey Mouse and Donald Duck into the homes of children of all cultures and to all corners of the globe. When California's Disneyland opened in 1955 followed by the Disney theme parks of Orlando, Florida, Tokyo, Japan, and Paris, France, travelers became exposed to visionary ideas of what the world could be and they wanted their share.

Age of communications. Another cause has been the growing ability to communicate globally. The world has become a communications sieve. Instantaneously people know everything of importance that is happening. The technology of radio, telephone, facsimile, and satellite television brought about the age of aspirations. People learned about things and wanted more things. It brought the ability to communicate cheaply and rapidly. For instance, a 10-minute telephone call from the United States to England in 1950 cost $209.30, and there were only about 110,000 made. Forty years later, in 1990 a 10-minute call cost only $9 and 185,000,000 calls were placed.

Modern transportation. As trucks, trains, and airplanes developed, so did the ability to move the factors of production: management, labor, capital, and technology. This flexibility removed the rigidity of advantage one nation had over another in terms of products they had to offer in world markets.

Business schools. Developed by elite American business schools, the growth of management as a science is a recent phenomenon. Even more recent is the success of marketing as a science. These new disciplines have spread to every aspect of university and business life.

Sogo shosha. These giant, Japanese, general trading companies called *sogo shoshas,* such as Mitsubishi, Mitsui, and Sumitomo, developed over a period of about 100 years. They proved to be models of international marketing success.

New competition. Another cause of the expansion was the growth, after World War II, of Japan and the Four Tigers of Asia (Hong Kong, Korea, Taiwan, and Singapore). They demonstrated for the world a new trading model and established new methods by which nations could grow economically. They stimulated global competition and are now closely followed by other developing nations such as Thailand, Malaysia, and the Philippines.

Phenomenon of content. People's attitudes about product content changed. Once upon a time "Made in U.S.A." meant good old American know-how and quality, unsurpassed in the world. At another time, "Made in Japan" meant cheap, low-quality copies. Responding to pocketbook economics, women, who do most of the world's household marketing, introduced the phenomenon of content. They no longer inspected where a product was made. National content became less important than quality. The less expensive the better. In the 1970s and 1980s products with labels "Made in Hong Kong," "Made in Japan," "Made in Germany," or "Assembled in Singapore" began penetrating world markets, and content took on less importance to the consumer. The reality of today is that few products have the pure content of one nation. Product content is more often a mixture of labor, raw materials, capital, and know-how—whatever it takes to provide the best product, at the best price—for the consumer who cares little about how it was made. What does count is global name identification: Kodak, Fuji, Mercedes, IBM, Sony, Ford, Honda, and so on.

MNCs. Last but not least came the superstars, the giant multinational corporations (MNCs) that spread their tentacles around the globe. Before the MNCs, international commerce was largely conducted by trading companies acting as intermediaries. At first the MNCs were seen as the bad guys, but recently they are seen as the model to which small- and medium-sized businesses aspire.

Give credit where credit is due. It was the businesspeople of the world, particularly the professional managers of the MNCs, who first saw the wisdom of globalization by partnering, joint venturing, and forming market alliances which further stimulated global interdependence. Who would have believed that merchants, not politicians, soldiers, or philosophers provided the catalyst to bring nations together?

GLOBALISM

Globalism has several meanings. It is used in the sense of a path, a movement, or a trend, something in motion. Some people say "the world is getting smaller." Another use of the term has to do with businesses that view their market in a global sense as opposed to a national or domestic sense. Then there is its use in terms of competition; "foreigners are competing in my market." Finally there is its use as it relates to commonality or standardization of production practices, products, and services in many different countries. Incredible technological improvements of transportation and communications during the 20th century accelerated globalism's irreversible trend.

Do Today's Managers Believe in Globalism?

Everyone seems to know that the age of globalism has dawned. When asked, "Do you believe in globalism?" and "Has there been a global boom?" every American business executive I interviewed responded with a positive theme. None espoused even the slightest doubt. Here is what some of them had to say.

Believe in globalism? Absolutely. Well, just take a couple of examples. Automotives the most obvious with the Hondas and the Nissans and the Mercedes and the BMWs and the Volvos. Those are global products sold in their own country and also sold here in the United States. The same thing is happening in aerospace. Consider commercial airplanes. Boeing and Douglas were the domestic suppliers and 15 years ago there wasn't any Airbus. Now there is an Airbus and there's 30 percent of the market. Sewing machines, food, anything—clothing apparel. Products are produced globally and are distributed and sold globally. Any company or any business that doesn't think globally is going to lose relative position. It's only a matter of time!

Harry Todd, managing partner, Carlisle Enterprises, L.P. and former chairman of the board and CEO of Rohr Corporation

The world is shrinking, very, very significantly. First, the number of people that are traveling, communications, the whole thing, it's just incredible…I talk to people that were in Paris yesterday and we get faxes from all over the world. It's amazing; it's a much smaller world. We're selling our product in 125–150 countries.

John S. (Jack) Barry, chairman of the board and CEO of WD-40 Company

My business is involved in biotechnology and its application to health care. What we're seeing is a strong move toward globalization both at the large company level where companies are merging to try to take advantage of more global opportunities as well as small companies like Gensia which if you look at the cost of basic research, you've got to look at how you commercialize that on a worldwide basis to get the kind of payback you need to do the costly research.

David Hale, president and CEO of Gensia Pharmaceuticals, Inc.

Globalism is here and we can either wait and learn how to defend after other countries have honed-in and sharpened their skills or go out and carry the attack to these other marketplaces.

John Bowne, president and CEO of Software Products International, Inc.

Believe in globalism? Absolutely and the pace will accelerate. Just look at Europe—the blocs and the North American FTA—big impact.

Daniel O. Pegg, president of the San Diego Economic Development Corporation

Globalization is not something about to happen. It already happened. As world expansion grew so did business operations and awareness. Decision-makers in every nation now visualize the marketplace in multinational terms and are looking for opportunities.

INTERDEPENDENCE

Economic interdependence is the notion that individual businesses, products, and national economies are no longer independent in their operations but are reliant to some extent on the commingling of the economies, businesses, and products of other nations. Today there are no autarkies. No nation is self-sufficient. Businesses depend on other businesses. Profit knows no border.

The Difference Between Globalism and Interdependence

Globalism does not equate to interdependence because the latter implies a pervasive commingling that transcends control by political forces. Interdependence also implies greater cooperation. Globalism may simply be the act of independently extending business operations across as many borders as possible.

Irreversible Trend

The new economic age of the 21st century will bring even more interdependence of businesses and national economies, and the trend is irreversible. This is because interdependence is to Adam Smith as democracy is to John Locke, Jean Jacques Rousseau, and Thomas Jefferson. Interdependence is synonymous with economic freedom. It stands for freedom to select and work at something of one's own choice; freedom to do business anywhere in the world. In other words interdependence means industrial equality.

Nations left in destruction after World War II have made miraculous comebacks. The dissipated Cold War has been replaced with detente and even new alliances. The peaceful revolution of 1989 and the not-so-peaceful one of 1991 in central and Eastern Europe resulted in the crumbling of the Communist bloc and the opening of doors to the West. China, even if the pace is not always to the world's liking, is undergoing revolutionary change—it is adopting its own form of market economics. Cross-border mergers and acquisitions are on the rise. Exports have boomed.

The explosion has already been so powerful that some argue it was the success of free enterprise and international trade, not democracy, that influenced the fall of communism, reversed the threat of world war, and increased international business opportunities.

The success of global business has been the centerpiece, if not the major stimulus, for the historical process of integrating the global economy. Changes of viewpoints such as *perestroika* (restructuring) and *glasnost* (openness) were launched when world leaders saw the wisdom and results of interdependence. That is, they saw that the nations that flourished most were those that allowed businesses to compete under free enterprise, market theory.

Economic orders are disappearing as evidenced by the momentum of a single European market scheduled for 1993 and the North American Free Trade Agreements. Investment, products, and technological innovation know no borders.

Needless to say there are those whose ethnocentric fears see the bogeyman behind every business deal, but they are being swept away by the reality that interdependence has already happened. Never before have businesses and nations known such interdependence. *Kokusai teki* literally means *global viewpoint* or *internationalization* in Japanese, and it's the buzzword on the streets of Tokyo.

New World Business Paradigm

In recent years a *new world business paradigm* sprang onto the scene. It is defined as the growing interchange of goods and financial flows among international consumers, businesses, and governments. Modern manufacturing companies of all sizes adjusted to the realities of global competition.

This pattern showed that many global businesses put their capital wherever it received the highest return with little regard, except for tax consequences, of where the return was remitted. International capital flows blur the identity of companies. Sony builds televisions in southern California. Ford builds cars in Mexico. What is a U.S. company? A European company? A Japanese company? Frankly an accurate definition is difficult, because they have crossed suppliers, investors, employees, and markets. Investment moves rapidly—U.S. firms own German companies, Japanese have stakes in Mexican firms, and Brazilian businesspeople have alliances in the Far East.

The Global Business

Not too long ago an international business meant only giant MNCs or multinational enterprises (MNEs). By the broadest definition these were firms with production facilities in at least two countries. For many people the MNCs were the colonial-style companies of the 1960s and 1970s perceived to have raped and pillaged third-world countries of their resources and remitted shameful profits to their home base in industrialized nations.

That was when the world was linear, before globalization. That was before smaller firms all over the world began adopting the MNC model. That was before the definition of business included the expanded interchange of goods and financial flows among international consumers, businesses, and governments.

In my book *Global Success*, I defined a global business as "one that has an international viewpoint; its employees are often of every ethnic, religious, and national origin; and they market and source wherever it makes good business sense." In other words, it is a company that is thrusting toward globalness. My definition does not imply some minimum of international sales volume, only the intention to take advantage of the growing phenomenon.

Kenichi Ohmae, author of *The Borderless World*, suggests that the global business is one where managers attempt to see and think equidistant from their markets. He said, "Building a value system that emphasizes seeing and thinking globally is the bottom-line price of admission to today's borderless economy."

Lester C. Thurow, dean of the Alfred P. Sloan School of Management at the Massachusetts Institute of Technology, calls them "cosmopolitan companies. They are the ones where 50 percent of the managers are not from the home country."

Today's global business differs from the MNC/MNE in that it is no longer locked into the definition that explains it as a giant company born in an industrialized nation. More often today's global business is a smaller firm that has tailored an incremental strategy, country-by-country, adopting whatever tactic best suits the strategy. Firms in many industrialized nations, such as the United States, now realize that as much as 75 percent of their market is beyond their borders. Some global businesses, particularly those home-based in less-developed nations, sell hardly anything in their own country. They only export because they realize, for them, as much as 100 percent of their market lies in the global marketplace. Others have licensing agreements in multiple countries. Yet others production share or are partners in joint ventures. Many are not yet equidistant in the sense that Ohmae defines globalization, but their strategy has that direction.

However they are defined, global businesses are today's outstanding companies because they include small- (less than 250 employees), and medium-sized (250–1,000 employees), manufacturing or service companies which have adjusted to the multidimensional realities of global competition. These companies are home based in every nation and their leaders understand the international economic system because they know that in 1989 cross-border trade accounted for more than $4 trillion on a gross global product (GGP) of $20 trillion.

A company can be considered a global business and have only one or even no truly global products. A company that thrusts toward globalization may have a

---

Paradigm

The buzzword paradigm (spare-a-dime) has spread, some believe like a bad virus, such that it now has common usage in the business world as well as in scientific jargon. The origin has been traced to a book published over 30 years ago by Thomas Kuhn, now professor emeritus at MIT, titled *The Structure of Scientific Revolutions*. He used paradigm to describe archetypal scientific constructs, but over time it came to mean basically any dominant idea. Paradigm is used in this book as a synonym for model or concept.

---

portfolio in which some products are localized, some are regional, and some are truly global. For example, United Distillers had a portfolio of over 200 separate brands but only three could arguably qualify as global brands— Johnnie Walker Red, Johnnie Walker Black, and Gordon's Gin.

WHO'S INVOLVED IN GLOBAL BUSINESS?

International trade ranges from small service industrial firms, banks, and insurance companies to giant trading entities like the Japanese *sogo shosha* and MNs that sell capital equipment and build land bridges across entire continents.

Today's international commerce attracts the best graduates of Japan's university system and America's top business schools. Often they are bid like American football players, some going in the first round, some in the second. At the same time, people with no formal business training have gotten into the growing field. The knowledge that was once the mandate of only the elite business schools is now being digested by masses worldwide.

Manufacturers

Make something and sell it for a profit! Business is as simple as that, and manufacturers all over the world, particularly Asian firms with small domestic markets, have charged into markets by making something and selling it globally. Of course, a growing number of companies have developed overseas manufacturing and assembly operations. Technology has changed so rapidly that many firms have formed multiyear strategic alliances with companies which are experts at staying with the state of the art in their industrial specialty.

Service Industry

Modern service companies have adjusted to the realities of global competition. Service industries like McDonald's, Ernst & Young, and Sumitomo Bank have spread everywhere, fulfilling the wants and desires of consumers worldwide.

Global Marketing

Modern marketers have developed networks of international contacts by attending major trade shows and using strategically targeted advertising. Multilevel marketing firms such as Avon and Amway have extended their operations across multiple borders.

Global Sourcing

Despite local-content laws and protectionist measures, capital equipment and raw materials purchasers now search for the best value worldwide. Manufacturers' buyers no longer source only within the boundaries of their own country for component parts thus running the risk of being noncompetitive in the global market. When Japanese auto manufacturers could not locate suitable component suppliers

> Q: What does being a global company mean to you?
> A: Meeting the competition fully in every market. I define markets in a big way:
> Europe. That doesn't mean you have a factory in France, Germany, England, and
> Denmark. Scale economics, in most cases, means you have to pick a place or two in
> Europe and try to function. Same in Asia—you wouldn't have a place in every
> country—you would pick the major trading bloc and develop a presence in one or
> more countries. If you're thinking about establishing a global presence you
> shouldn't try to eat the whole elephant in one bite. You want to start, depending on
> your product, by establishing presence in, perhaps Europe first, then Japan, then a
> developing country. Go global one step at a time.
>
> James Owens, Ph.D.
> president, Solar Turbines Incorporated
> a subsidiary of Caterpillar, Corporation

overseas, they enticed their domestic component suppliers to locate manufacturing plants overseas near their own plants.

Third World

Third-world companies have also been seduced by the success of the MNCs and have adopted the new definition of global business. An example of a global company from a developing country is the UB Group of India. In 1986, Vijay Mallya, chairman of UB Group, assigned his managers his ultimate dream: become India's first global business by expanding worldwide. Called a superbrat, the 34-year-old Mallya likes subordinates with MBAs who bring him new ideas to assist in the company's diversification from the cash-cow business of alcohol and beer into electronics, petrochemicals, telecommunications, and biotechnology. Thus far UB's globalization has taken it into joint ventures in Germany and Sweden.

WHAT DOES GLOBALISM MEAN TO YOU?

Do you remember when doing business was simple? Just make something and sell it—whatever your neighbors needed. Today it's not good enough to only sell in your own hometown or even your own country. Global businesses must include an outward (beyond the shores) strategy in business plans and policy. Going global is about geographic expansion of markets, but it is more complicated than that. It is about doing what must be done to compete and survive in the emerging global game.

Discarding the F-Word

From now on forget the word *foreign* as if it never existed in your vocabulary! Think one world and one people, because that is where interdependence and globalism are headed in the 21st century.

A word of caution. It won't be easy for you to drop the word *foreign*. Feelings of superiority, inferiority, prejudice, and ethnocentricity cannot be easily erased by just deleting a word. Cultures take hundreds of years to change so expect to continue to hear the words *us* and *them* in the business place, but at a rapidly declining pace.

Discarding the D-Word

The word *domestic* must also be outlawed in the global marketplace. Where is the domestic market if the firm has an equidistant denationalized point of view? There may be a home base or headquarters, and even in the early stages of globalization, a home market, but over time that should fade and the headquarters may eventually be anywhere in the world that makes good business sense.

> Perrier, a global business home based in France, recalled its entire stock of product from California because of the introduction of a minuscule amount of a toxic chemical. The company's leadership stated that Perrier's reputation for high values and ethics gave it no alternative. It was also good global business.

Greater Ethical Responsibilities

During most of history it was the soldier, the politician, and the clergy who were held in highest esteem. The merchant was held in less regard. But all that has changed. The new world business paradigm has brought new respect. Today we find some companies with greater power than some nations. Presidents and CEOs of global businesses are among the most respected leaders of the world.

Thus global business expansion brings with it greater ethical responsibilities. The new world business paradigm requires business leaders to constantly ask themselves, what's the purpose of the enterprise? Short-term stock valuation? Immediate returns on capital invested? Profit at any cost? Or is it jobs, long-term social good, and environmental sensitivity? Who has the responsibility for the welfare of employees and consumers? Is it only the state or is it also private enterprise?

SUMMARY

To survive in the complex global context of the 21st century businesses must consider new methods of managing. Operations must never be allowed to drive the organization; therefore, the modern global manager seeks to forecast the future and formulate a strategy which takes a denationalized point of view and drives toward global operations.

The next chapter explains how strategy moves from theory to practice. It offers an achievable prescription to use in the global context.

Chapter 2

From Theory to Practice

Where there is no vision, the people perish.

Proverbs 29:18

What is strategy? Strategy is simply a method of managing with vision and is applicable to any endeavor. Strategy is not a new word nor is there anything mysterious about it. Nevertheless, it is just coming into vogue in the everyday lexicon of laypersons who already use it to conduct personal and household affairs. Strategy is used to manage children, the community, the tribe, the household, church operations, the military, businesses, and the administration of governments. Strategy is not new, in fact it is just another way of looking at the activity called management. Successful strategy implies creating and mastering a game plan in a world where the rules are continuously changing.

DEFINITIONS

The word *strategy* is often used incorrectly. People say *strategy* when they mean *tactics*. They confuse operations with transactions. Consequently, some definitions are needed.

Strategy. Strategy is the science of planning and directing operations into the most advantageous positions *prior to engagement.*

Tactics. Tactics is the science of arranging and maneuvering *during engagement.*

Operations. Operations is the condition of *being in action.* Operations are the everyday decisions which result in business transactions—the closing of sales upon which all matters of the firm rely.

Transaction. A transaction is a *business deal,* a sale.
But it is strategy that guides and drives operations. Therefore, from time to time, operations and tactics must be set aside to think. Operations assume nothing will change. Operations just plod along making transactions. Strategic thinking assumes things will change and looks for the change. When a firm gets into operational difficulty, it generally means that operations were never properly linked to a strategy.
When you use strategy to manage your firm, operations gets a new definition: Operations is the implementation of strategy on a day-to-day basis.

Planning

Don't be confused about the difference between strategy and planning. Strategy is not an extended operating plan. To plan is to decide, in advance, the order you are going to do a lot of things in the future, then setting about to do them sequentially. Planning is a serial process based on today's conditions. Planning assumes nothing will change.

Planning does not go far enough. Planning is obviously better than not planning, but strategy causes us to do things we would not otherwise do. Strategy assumes the future will change and sets about attempting to forecast those conditions based on the best intelligence available.

Figure 2–1 illustrates the generalized strategy paradigm which incorporates a time shift from a time-present or a benchmark to time-future. What sets strategy apart from planning is the thrust into the future which takes into account the most likely conditions.

Strategy is the process of establishing time-present, then analyzing and forecasting, then deciding *what* objectives need to be accomplished in time-future. *When* and *where* (location) decisions are also critical.

After the objectives are determined (what, when, and where), the manager returns to time-present to formulate what resources (*how*) are needed to accomplish the objectives and *who* will achieve them. The final step is to set up key result indicators (KRIs) and feedback loops that ensure the objectives are attained as well as to devise a schedule to revisit the strategy.

FIVE TASKS

In its simplest form, strategy has just five basic tasks which are as follows:

1. Understand the strategic process.
2. Establish time-present, baseline, or current position.
3. Map time-future.
4. Formulate time-future.
5. Manage the global organization toward time-future.

GET PRACTICAL

To help you grasp the concept of strategy, think about the achievements of one of the greatest strategists of our time: Walt Disney. In 1953, Disney described his vision of a place to be called Disneyland to his best artist, Herb Ryman, and asked him to sketch it. That sketch was then used by Walt's brother Roy to persuade New York financiers to loan Walt the start-up money. Disneyland opened in 1955 and the rest is history. Walt's Disneyland was his strategic destiny come true—he made it happen. Today at Disneyland you can ride Star Speeder 3000 to Endor, all created by Walt's wonderful imagineers.

Another Practical Example

Figure 2–2 shows another practical day-to-day example meant to illustrate the use of the strategy paradigm.

Suppose you are a ninth-grade student. One day you fast forward and decide that after finishing college (time-future) you wish to work as an engineer.

An engineering career is the ninth-grader's objective, so the strategy to achieve that objective is a series of tactics and operational transactions which must be completed. The tactics are as follows:

- Complete the right high school courses.
- Learn all about the colleges that offer an engineering degree.
- Seek out and attend the right college.
- Take the right college courses.

The operational transactions are as follows:

- Get the necessary high school grades.
- Get good college grades.
- Graduate.
- Get a job as an engineer.

FIGURE 2–1
The Strategic Paradigm

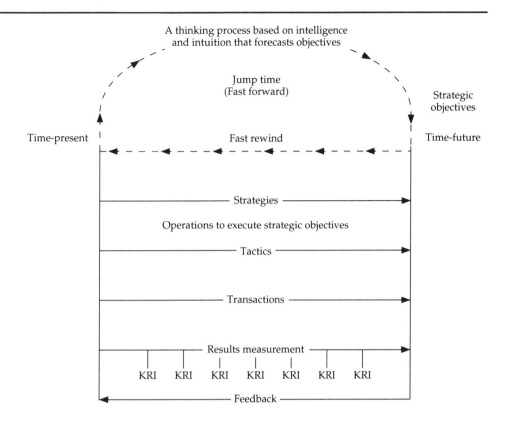

Mastering strategy means asserting control over your destiny

Strategy is behaviorally superior to planning because it concentrates on the positive achievements of the future and drives out negative thoughts of the past. Strategy brings clarity of purpose because it requires us to focus on the things we know best and provides for clear objectives. Above all, strategy adds discipline to our analysis and planning and allows a clear path to implementation.

Of course predictions of future conditions are often unstable. You may never end at the point originally selected. The best managers always take advantage of opportunities as they happen. Strategy must remain a flexible process. It even has room to incorporate intuition. Top leaders often throw in their instincts of the future based on their experiences of the past.

MAJOR USES OF STRATEGY

There are many practical uses of strategy, several of which stand out as the forerunners of its use for the complexities of global strategic management. The military, government, and domestic businesses practice strategy and their methods are companions to global strategic management.

MILITARY

The activity of strategizing was first developed by military thinkers such as Sun Tzu, a contemporary of Confucius, who laid the groundwork for Chinese military strategy thousands of years ago. It was Sun Tzu who in *The Art of War* (circa

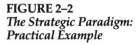

FIGURE 2–2
The Strategic Paradigm:
Practical Example

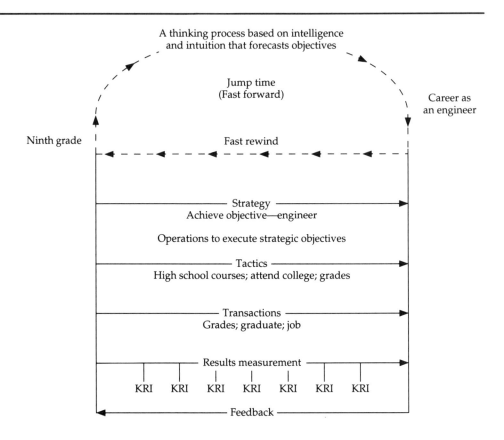

300 B.C.) made the first attempt to formulate a rational approach for military strategic theory and tactical doctrines. Among his quotations are the following:

- "Know your enemy better than he knows you."
- "One spy in the enemy camp is worth 10,000 foot soldiers."
- "We are not fit to lead an army on the march unless we are familiar with the face of the country—its mountains and forests, its pitfalls."
- "If you know the enemy and know yourself, you need not fear the result of a hundred battles. If you know yourself but not the enemy, for every victory gained you will also suffer a defeat. If you know neither the enemy nor yourself, you will succumb in every battle."

It is said that when the Japanese, especially those in business, want to learn about strategy, they don't turn to a Japanese military manual or to an American business text, but rather to the ancient Chinese philosopher Sun Tzu.

Another early strategist was Prussian general, Karl von Clausewitz, who was the first to make a complete study of warfare. In his book *On War*, he stressed the importance of strategy, which included political, social, and personal factors, as well as tactics and training to defeat an enemy. Von Clausewitz said, "Most battles are won or lost before they are engaged, by men who take no part in them, by their strategists."

A strategic plan is the integration of smaller pieces (tactics) into a larger purpose. But it was General Dwight Eisenhower who once said, "The plan is nothing, planning is everything."

Today strategy is used extensively in war games in the United States at the Naval War College in Newport, Rhode Island, the Army War College at Carlisle Barracks in Pennsylvania, and the Air University at Maxwell Air Force Base, Alabama.

Objective. Most military objectives are couched in the term *win.* Win the war or win the battle.

Grand strategy. This is the term used with the biggest of concepts. For instance the grand strategy of World War II was for the Allies to first contain the Pacific theater and concentrate on winning in Europe, then refocus to win in the Pacific.

Strategy. When used alone, the word *strategy* suggests a lesser notion than grand strategy, but larger in scope. The Pacific strategy of World War II was to island hop across the ocean to the Philippines then north until finally the Japanese islands could be attacked. An alternate strategy that President Roosevelt discarded after he met with General MacArthur and Admiral Nimitz at Pearl Harbor in 1944, was to bypass the Philippines, take Formosa instead, then attack the Japanese islands.

Tactics. The term *tactic* is the art or skill of employing available means or specific actions leading to the accomplishment of an objective. An example of tactics might be when General MacArthur took back the Philippine Islands from the Japanese. His tactics included the landing at Leyte, the bombardment of Manila, and the drive from the beaches to take the main island of Luzon.

Operations. One U.S. marine offered this interpretation of the term: "A military operation leads to a transaction when you are eyeball to eyeball with the enemy."

GOVERNMENT

Governments strategize and plan. And global business leaders should understand and maneuver to changing government strategies.

It is not clear which came first, military or government strategy. After all, governments from time immemorial have been attempting to stimulate economic development.

It was in 1981 when Richard Whalen of the Center for Strategic and International Studies at Georgetown University who first likened international trade to a game when he said the following:

> *The international struggle is actually a little understood contest among governing elites testing relative ingenuity and skill in devising new political and economic arrangements to offset mounting social and cultural obstacles to productivity.*

Comprehensive planning is a 20th century innovation. Virtually unknown before 1900, by 1975 planning had become pervasive in the world economy.

Prior to 1900 it was thought that Adam Smith's invisible hand would guide business to respond quickly to consumer demand with minimum government intervention. Over time, however, most nations have adopted either directed or indicative policies.

Directed Planning

Karl Marx never advocated central planning, but Frederick Taylor's Midvale work so influenced Lenin that he introduced it to Stalin who installed planning techniques in the public sector as a strategy for national industrial development. In 1928, the Soviet Union's Gosplan (State Planning Commission) developed three plans: (1) the general plan (10–15 years); (2) the perspective plan (five–year goals); and (3) the control plan (12 months). The Gosplan staff expanded from only 40 personnel in 1921, to 300 in 1923. In 1926, the staff grew to almost 1,000 people and became organized into 12 regions with 43 local planning committees reporting to it. By 1928, it implemented its first five-year plan.

> "Mankind measures a soldier's ability by his successes. As victory is the aim of all strategy and tactics, it is proper that generalship should be judged by the results attained. The immutable principles of war should be carried out whenever it is possible to do so, but when they conflict, the leader must carry out those which offer the greatest advantages."
>
> *Old Book on War Tactics*

Poland, Rumania, and Albania also adopted directed central planning. Hungary and Czechoslovakia chose a quasi-market road. East Germany and Bulgaria attempted the middle of the road. Yugoslavia used what it called guideline planning coupled with market theory. Other members of the Communist bloc established centrally planned economies.

In recent times the Soviet-directed system came up short in its goals, yet mixtures of planning and laissez-faire market mechanisms continue to flourish in other parts of the world.

Indicative Planning

Planning helped build Western Europe after World War II. The Organization for European Economic Cooperation was formed for the purpose of improved planning and distribution of Marshall Plan aid.

To attain its own growth strategies, France implemented an indicative planning process. The French solicited voluntary cooperation by using the persuasive powers of government—incentives such as preferred taxes and low interest loans. The aim of France's process was to improve per capita growth, develop investment priorities, and direct the flow of capital to advantageous sectors.

After World War II, Japan made the greatest gains using an indicative planning strategy. The government's Ministry of International Trade and Industry set rough general targets every two to three years. No exact details were given for most of the plan, but for a small number of high-priority industries it issued a comprehensive plan.

The Four Tigers of Asia followed suit by developing a model that established new methods by which nations could grow economically. As small island or insular properties, with low per capita incomes and commensurately small domestic markets, and without significant natural resources, they discovered that the factors of production moved easily across borders. Those factors—natural resources, labor, technology, management, and capital—could be controlled through a mixture of directed and indicative planning and industrial policy schemes.

Edwin Perkins, author of *The New World Economy in the Twentieth Century*, says,

Development planning or investment planning is thus a modern institutional innovation which, over the last 50 years, has been increasingly applied successfully to giant multinational business firms pursuing a strategy of diversified growth and almost equally to nation states to maximize returns on allocation of limited capital resources.

Even the U.S. government offers various tax and low-cost loan schemes to achieve its industrial aims.

Industrial Policy

Historically the term *industrial strategy* (policy) has been associated with at least some degree of centralized economic planning—directed or indicative. The underlying assumption is that market forces alone do not create the effect desired by a given nation. The need for strategic direction thus becomes the basis of government policy and interstate controls.

Industrial policy, or its alternate name, country-international strategic market planning, is a strategy used by a nation to strengthen its industrial base and develop competitive export industries to improve its balance-of-payments position. Masaaki Kotabe, a Japanese expert, explains it as "the sum of a nation's efforts to shape business activities and influence economic growth."

An American specialist, Chalmers Johnson, suggests that industrial policy is "the initiation and coordination of government activities to leverage upward the productivity and competitiveness of a whole economy and of particular industries in it."

All nations, including the United States, have some form of industrial and international trade policy, some written, some unwritten, some articulated to the public, and some not. Japan and France are the best-known examples of free world indicative planning. Executives of the Japanese Ministry of International Trade and Industry believe that although business and labor are conscious of world competitive challenges, they lack the credibility to speak from a broad, national point of view. Therefore government must concern itself with the strategic management of the economy by attempting to understand which sectors are likely to find better opportunities, and assist key sectors to achieve better positions in world markets.

Typically the industrial planning objectives of the nations which have adopted industrial policies are as follows:

- To improve a country's competitive position in key "sunrise" and high value-added industries as well as to rationalize its position in "sunset" or low value-added, and key linkage industries.
- To promote the shift of resources out of declining industries and into more promising sectors, which create new and higher value-added jobs.
- To intervene in a few key markets with the intention of helping domestic businesses establish or improve positions in new international markets.

Development of Strategic Industries

Sunrise and high value-added industries are industries growing fast relative to more mature or declining industries. Governments make wise use of factors of endowment by placing emphasis on higher value-added industries. This technique called *industry rationalization* adopts methods such as the following:

- Using the carrot-and-stick approach.
- Giving administrative guidance.
- Stressing a free enterprise environment.
- Ensuring a sound infrastructure.
- Developing standards.
- Encouraging economies of scale.
- Protecting domestic industries.
- Stressing market-driven business.
- Encouraging cooperation instead of competition, that is, the formation of cartels.

Simply put, each government, based on its chosen economic and social theory, adjusts its interstate controls, such as various tariff and nontariff barriers and incentive schemes, to keep its people working and its nation growing economically. In other words, international business is inseparably connected to economic development, and it is driven by interstate controls.

Nations today formalize their strategic vision in terms of industrial policy and announce the policy by focusing incentives on specific industries. Today's reality is that all governments formulate strategy at all levels: national, regional, provincial, and city.

DOMESTIC BUSINESS

Using strategy for business management is a phenomenon of the later half of the 20th century. The American historian Alfred P. Chandler of MIT in his 1962 book titled *Strategy and Structure* is given credit for being the first to conceive of the concept of strategy for business management.

Chandler defined business strategy as "the determination of the basic long-term goals and objectives of an enterprise and the adaptation of courses of action and the allocation of resources necessary in carrying out these goals."

Before Chandler's strategic revelations, businesses managed only adequately. From 1820 until about 1900, the period we now call the Industrial Revolution, two outstanding management thinkers emerged: Adam Smith and Frederick Taylor. In 1776, Smith published *The Wealth of Nations*, which led business thinkers along the path of creative management thought. Taylor's concepts of planning revolutionized forecasting for capital investment decisions.

During the mass production era, from 1900 to about 1950, the function of planning began to take shape. Business managers realized they must look ahead for changing economic and technological developments because decisions made today affected the future.

By the 1950s and 1960s most major businesses had adopted comprehensive planning, and the planning business management period was in full swing. Every large organization created planning departments to draft short-, intermediate-, and long-range plans which made the firm, in the words of Perkins, "a small economic system in its own right." Yet, firms were only planning; the strategy paradigm had not yet been adopted.

The era of using the strategy for business management began during the late 1950s and early 1960s and has expanded into the 1990s. By including the strategy in the concept of planning business management, the approach now incorporates external forces called *environment*.

H. Igor Ansoff, distinguished professor of strategic management at United States International University, expanded and elaborated on Chandler's strategy-structure hypothesis. Ansoff, now considered one of the gurus of industrial strategic planning, developed the first and one of the most elaborate models of strategic management. His theme is to develop new ways to manage in a *turbulent future*.

Michael Porter of the Harvard Business School argues that strategy is about *competitor behavior* which disrupts existing equilibrium and thereby changes the pattern of forces in the firm's environment.

Henry Mintzberg, another professor, takes the position that *strategy emerges* as the company grows.

James Quinn, yet another guru, believes in *logical incrementalism*, that is, that the next product will be better than the past.

Peters and Waterman, on the other hand, said "stick to your knitting and sit in the laps of your customers."

GLOBAL STRATEGIC MANAGEMENT

It is well understood by modern managers that a firm should develop some sort of a strategic plan, which is simply the measurement of its company, its products, and the likely prospects for future success. They need, however, a results-oriented search process to assist them in formalizing a vision into specific activities, programs, and projects in the global setting.

Strategy has gone through many ups and downs. In its early stages it was no more than an intellectual activity. In the later half of the 1970s and even into the early 1980s, strategic planning fell out of grace. Instead, buzzwords like *entrepreneurship, intrapreneurship, corporate culture,* and *quality circles* became fashionable. But because of the complexity of going global, strategy's value has had a revival as the dominant, if not the only, tool for managing the modern organization.

Global strategic management is about shifting from local to global and previous strategic management processes failed to embrace cross-border business. For them international was only an add-on, not a context change for the domestic or home-based firm.

In practice, though, the major multinationals left nothing to chance. Their strategy has always been that the conscious formulation of global strategy should drive the firm rather than letting the firm respond. In other words, the MNCs forecasted a strategic paradigm which advocated a globalization assumption.

The Old Questions

In the past, the kinds of strategic questions asked were as follows:

1. What business am I in?
2. Is there free entry into my industry?
3. What about the product markets?
4. Do the buyers have the money to buy my product?
5. What are the capital incentives and opportunities?
6. How great is the threat of a new entrant?
7. How captive is the firm to the power of suppliers?
8. How vulnerable is the firm to the power of strong customers?
9. How vulnerable is the firm to competitors offering substitute products?
10. What is the state of competition in my industry?

Those were the old questions and they still pertain, but today's strategy must anticipate globalization, not react to it. Today's strategy must be purposeful, deliberate, conscious, and mindful of global customers as well as competitors. It still includes mission statements, objectives, and decision rules, but the difference is that strategy no longer begins with the domestic or home market assumption and internationalization is no longer an add-on.

What's Different About Global Strategic Management?

No longer can a manager think one dimensionally. The process of global strategic management assumes the globalization context. *Domestic* becomes an obsolete term because the company will eventually operate plurally, in more than one country. The home country is only one of the firm's many markets.

The New Questions

Today's managers must address all of the old questions, but also come to grips with these pivotal new questions.

1. What will the business, economic, and political landscape look like in the 21st century?
2. On which customers, industries, and country markets should I focus?
3. What are the critical success factors for top-performing firms beyond the year 2000?
4. How should I reengineer my strategy, organization, and product mix to maintain and improve our competitive position in the 21st century?
5. How can I improve our global management processes?

Differs from Planning

What is the difference between global strategic planning and the old term long-range planning? The difference is explained in terms of viewpoint, that is, when you do long-range planning the domain of the firm is fixed, but when you do strategic planning the firm's domain is open and unending. Therefore, to grow and profit today you must learn how to play the game by understanding the global economic system and government's role. If your firm is not, in some way, expanding into global business, it may not survive.

Differs from Other
Empowerment Processes

Global strategic management is an empowerment process. But it is concerned with *external* management of the organization. Organizational development (OD) and total quality management (TQM) are *internal* management processes. It is not unusual that weaknesses in internal management are discovered during the strategic process, and it is not unusual that the same data are used for the OD and/or TQM processes to correct those weaknesses.

Grand Strategy

The ultimate target of the global business is presence, that is, to become an insider in home markets all over the world. Thus the grand strategy is to act *glocal* (a contraction based on the saying: "think global and act local"). That does not mean globalization must happen overnight. Rather global strategic management has long-term vision and embraces planned incrementalism as good business sense. Recognize that the concept is more complex because it requires defining the environment in terms of the international economic system. Remember also that complexity requires powerful, yet sensitive managers who are secure enough in their own intellect that they seek input, collaboration, and participation at all levels.

Customer Driven

The global business is a customer- or market-driven firm rather than a competitor-driven one. This is not just the result of the distinctly differing cultures faced by the international marketplace which drives the glocal concept, but the nature of the strategic paradigm, that is, being proactive instead of being reactive.

Differs from the
Domestic Paradigm

How does global strategic management differ from the hallmarks of the domestic strategic paradigm?

Figure 2–3 shows a simple example that illustrates the shift from a local to a global strategy. Suppose in the start-up of your organization (time-present) you intend to expand on a global basis. Expanding globally is an objective.

Your strategy is to achieve that objective by learning all about the international business, selecting the right countries (not necessarily your own), and taking the right entry tactics. You seek out experts and attend the right seminars (tactic). As you went along you checked your progress against a set of predefined KRIs.

SUMMARY

Today, everyone uses the word *strategy*. But the modern organization must ask if it is a global strategy.

The grand strategy of global strategic management is the world viewpoint, while strategy is the vision of glocal and of the country-business unit. Tactics to achieve global ends are the various methods of entry into other domestic markets.

For the giant MNCs the process of global strategic management has been in place for decades. For the small- and medium-sized firm the concept is still in its infancy, yet it is the approach for the 1990s and the new century.

Begin with the external, global viewpoint and instead of generalizing the environment be specific. Define unambiguous international management criteria.

Earlier uses of the strategy paradigm for business used return on investment as its bottom line. But as Kenichi Ohmae suggests, sales are the objective for the global firm because they must amortize their fixed costs over a much larger market base. This new logic contributes to driving managers toward globalization.

To assist you in understanding the four dominant uses, Table 2–1 shows one way to put strategy, tactics, and the operational transaction in perspective.

FIGURE 2–3
Global Strategic
Management Paradigm

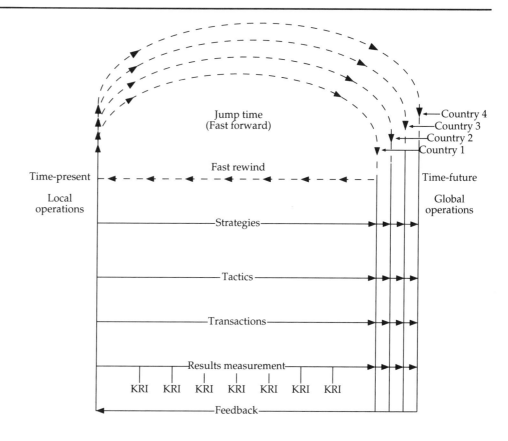

"Being competitor-driven is reactionary and [means] to look backwards. I think it's important to keep up with competition and what they're doing and to try to understand strategically where they're headed so you can counter their moves. But it's important to understand what's really important to you: what are your core competencies; what are you good at; and build on your strengths. You need to understand what competitor's strengths are and need to attack his strengths. I'd say our focus is the customer: what does the customer want and how to satisfy that, and what does he want in the future and how to position to satisfy that."

James Owens, Ph.D.
president, Solar Turbines Incorporated
a subsidiary of Caterpillar, Corporation

CHECKLIST

Here is a checklist of today's issues which begin with the global dimension.

- Is the firm a global business?
- To what degree is the firm already a global business?
- Does my firm have presence in global markets?
- What is the next step in the globalization process?
- What is the best match of tactics to strategy?

TABLE 2–1
Matrix of Strategy Uses

	Military	Government	Domestic business management	Global strategic management
Grand strategy	WW II: Europe first, then the Pacific	National economic policy	Corporate/local	World presence
Strategy	WWII Island hopping	Industrial policy	Business unit	Country/ corporate/ business unit
Tactics/ administration	Frontal assault	Barriers and incentives	Operations	Entry: export, joint venture, use trading intermediaries
Operational/ transaction	Eye to eye: gun to gun	Jobs and personal income	Return on investment	Sales

- When can I take the next steps?
- What will be the cultural impact of those steps? (Instead of dealing with only the original home-based culture, you must deal with many diverse cultures.)
- What is the geography?
- What are the governmental implications? (Before the global business explosion, it was tough enough dealing with home-country regulations; now you must contend with the commercial rules of other countries.)
- What are the ecological implications?
- How do I get global intelligence?
- How do the supranational organizations impact my strategy? (Every GATT negotiation brings fewer barriers. Everybody is now at your doorstep; therefore, you must consider being at their doorstep.)
- How can global capital markets be tapped?

The next chapter offers a step-by-step process for formulating and implementing such a strategy.

Chapter 3

The Process: Step-by-Step

More businessmen in all countries should seize the opportunities of the market—it is the entrepreneur who must initiate production and trade that leads to greater welfare.

Jan Pen, *former professor of economics and director of economic policy, the Netherlands*

Global strategic management is the results-oriented process of developing a thrust into the international arena which produces a set of globalized organizational objectives. These are supported by a pattern of activities called *tactics* and *operational transactions* which result in the implementation of the strategy. The global dimension makes formulation more complex and requires new methodology.

This chapter is designed to take the mystery out of formulating and implementing strategy in the global setting. It jump starts the process by explaining who does what and when they do it.

WHO

The best executives are known for taking risks but not wild gambles. Their chances are most often based on analysis and prudent judgment. Yet many of these excellent executives object to exposing their inner thoughts and risking their egos in an exchange of ideas with others in the organization. These leaders have strategic objectives but do not articulate them, believing that if they are not achieved no one will ever know the difference. In this regard, the entrepreneur who has committed time, resources, and a lifetime to his or her business is often most private. Some say, "What right do others have to formulate the strategy for this company? Who understands it better than me?"

It Starts at the Top

What is the leader thinking about in terms of the thrust of the company? If no one knows, no one can help. But initiating an open strategic management process can be risky. Leaders gamble their professional reputation and perceived loss of control. If, however, the executive has reasonable intellect and believes that the most able leaders are those who surround themselves with equals or better, then he or she should trust the strategic formulation process. In this day of enlightened leadership, where the only thing that works is teamwork and collaboration, the more people who participate in the development of the organization's vision, the better.

The decision resides at the top. If top management denies globalness and the changes in world economics that have taken place, obviously any attempt to mold a vision that includes a global approach will die before it gets started. But the basic truism of the 1990s and beyond is the interdependence of the nation-states. International trade is an area of business driving toward new horizons. The most important strategy to winning the trade game and reversing any dangerous trends toward inward thinking is to understand that globalism is a reality.

Of course, there will be barriers in your decision-making path. You could be faced with a formidable list of apprehensions, some perceived, some real. Despite the perceived stones in their path, many small- and medium-sized firms have overcome the obstacles. Aggressive companies search for alternative business arrangements. The misinformed will think of every conceivable reason not to get started, but this book is about reassuring you and assisting you to overcome the real barriers.

The Role of the CEO

The CEO, like the captain of a ship, is ultimately responsible for the firm's success and therefore for its strategy. The first task of the CEO is to declare the start of the process, that is, move strategy to the top of the priority list. But he or she must also commit resources, both financial and human.

Commit Resources

Committing resources to a long-term strategy to maintain long-term competitiveness is the only way to win the global trade game. It's a misconception that the only successful international businesses are those that have their own branch offices and plants in other countries. Certainly many do, but the vast majority of importers and exporters are just successful domestic manufacturers or service companies.

The Role of the Board of Directors

The involvement of the board of directors varies from company to company. Some boards function as working boards while others serve only to bring prestige and influence to the generation of new business. For most companies the board's function is to oversee the entire process, not by micromanaging, but rather by ensuring the CEO has the capacity and does a good job of seeing the strategic process through to its successful conclusion. The board should be briefed at selected, major steps, but unless it has special skills, it should scrupulously avoid taking part in the process. If the board is in the ratification loop, the firm's new strategy may either be negotiated as a step-by-step process, as a final approval, or left to the CEO.

The CEO and/or board of directors of any organization gets the final vote. So if some of the results of the strategic process seem to be naive and out of touch, the leaders of the firm have ample opportunity to expose the weaknesses and adopt only the ideas that are feasible.

Strategic Planning Staff

The use of a special staff section to coordinate strategic planning varies from company to company. In the 1960s and 1970s planning staffs got out of hand—planners devised complex corporate blueprints and handed them over to operating people to execute. Some called it "paralysis by analysis," others called it "death on the shelf." According to Roger Smith, chairman of GM, "Plans were put on a shelf and the firm marched off to do what they would do anyway." Today those firms that have a staff-planning function place less emphasis on sophisticated analytical forecasting and more on intelligence gathering and coordination of a collaborative planning style.

Some companies perceive that planning specialists get too far removed from reality and lose their effectiveness. If this is a problem, the solution is to move people from functional departments in and out of the special staff section for the purpose of maintaining effectiveness. Other firms select a functional department, usually marketing or finance, to serve as the coordinating group.

Regardless of the organization, responsibility must rest with a coordinating person or group to pull the entire process together. Some firms hire outside consultants to coordinate and facilitate the strategic planning process.

Functional Departments   The functional departments of any firm embarking on strategic planning must play a big part in the effort. All of the financial data must be prepared by the financial department. Marketing, operations (production), and research must also be players.

Participation   In general, if more people are involved in the process, there will be less resistance to change, and the results will more likely be adopted. Empowerment, collaboration, and ownership are major factors in the success of any strategic planning process. (The institutionalizing process is discussed in greater detail in Chapter 4.)

The Global Family Opinion Team (GFOT)   The outcome of the formulation process will be guidance that affects policy, tactics, and transactions at every level of the firm. Therefore, the players who participate must be representative of every level. I recommend forming what I call the global family opinion team (GFOT). Some companies call it the strategic council group (SCG). The label is inconsequential, but all managers should participate, as well as selected key employees from all major business units and functional areas. Remember, strategy does not implement itself. It is essential that ownership for strategy be accepted throughout the firm; and the key to that is collaboration and participation.

Certainly the vice presidents of production, marketing, finance, human relations, and other functional departments should be a part of the GFOT. Be sure to include managers of business units, divisions, plants, district offices, overseas offices, and so on. The formulation team must include those who are business smart and have influence, whether that's defined by an organizational chart or not. The GFOT is discussed in greater detail in Chapters 8, 9, and 19. As shown by the inverted pyramid in Figure 3–1, the intent of the GFOT is to instill bottom-up inclusion in the formulation process.

Do not exclude a player from the process who has informal influence, because that person can derail months of conscientious effort. One of the intents of this process is to enhance the firm's collaborative experience related to its external strategy. Early signals may expose the need for strengthening internal management. Organizational development and total quality management processes may be carried out simultaneously with the formulation of the global strategic management process.

Mind-Set   Mind-set is an important ingredient in the strategic process. Although top management must be on board from the beginning of the process, it is just as important that the entire management team get into it. Not everyone will see the global strategic process in the same way. A positive approach may not ensure success, but less than that will certainly deliver failure.

Impact on Operations   There are costs to strategy formulation, some real, others perceived. Most managers and employees object to anything that keeps them from operations. Time lost from day-to-day transactions due to involvement in the strategic process is often a perceived cost. Actually it should be viewed as an investment in survival.

Strategy must carry the torch! There is pain, but the stronger the research and commitment to strategy formulation, the better the long-term prospects of the firm.

Needless to say, the process should never begin as a surprise. People in the organization must have sufficient lead time to organize their work. After the process becomes a routine part of the company's operation, it becomes less painful.

FIGURE 3–1
Global Family Opinion Team
(GFOT)

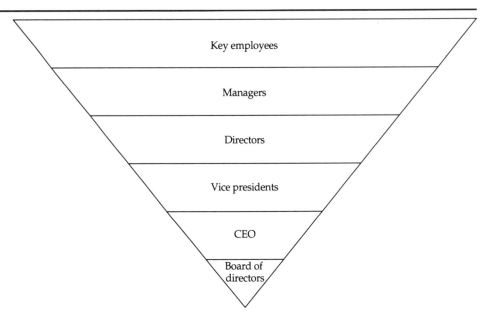

Key employees

Managers

Directors

Vice presidents

CEO

Board of directors

Rule of Thumb

Strategic formulation should never take more than 10–15 percent of anyone's time on an annual basis. Implementation of the strategy should be the most demanding aspect of managing the company.

WHAT

Organizations vary in size and sophistication. Large firms with multiple products and complex organizations attack the problem differently than an entrepreneur. No doubt each will adjust this model to his or her own situation.

Methods of Planning

In practice there are three planning methods: bottom up, top down, and iterative.

Bottom up. The Japanese typically use the bottom-up method, attempting to always gain consensus throughout every level of the firm. The advantages of bottom up is less-perceived coercion from the top, and those responsible for attaining goals are the same people who formulate them. The disadvantage is that each segment of the organization pursues the objectives it perceives as important with no insurance that the result will equate to the total perceived by headquarters.

Top down. For the top-down method, headquarters provides guidelines, including definitions of the business with mission statements and objectives to subordinate divisions. Employees, in turn, explain how they can achieve what is expected of them. The advantage is that headquarters is probably in the best position to see the global perspective and optimize corporatewide resources. The obvious disadvantages are that this method restricts creativity and initiative and does not take into consideration local conditions and opportunities.

Iterative. I recommend the iterative method because it allows for diverse national environments and offers the best opportunity for success of the global strategy. Start with the bottom up, collate the results, and add to them the corporate perspective. Gain acceptance by allowing comment before finalizing the strategy. By using this method the firm takes advantage of the best effects of both bottom up and top down.

WHEN

Strategic planning has a beginning, but it has no end (unless management does its job so badly that the firm does not survive). It is a process which is revisited on a regularly scheduled basis with feedback loops built in to ensure success. The intent is to *routinize* the process in such a way that global strategic management is institutionalized and accepted as a natural way of doing business.

Span of Strategy: How Far?

By span of strategy I mean how far into the future should an organization look. How visionary should the plan be? The answer depends on the level of strategy, such as corporate, business unit, or functional. Span also relates to size, complexity, and industry. Each organization will face this issue differently and there are no wrong answers. As an example, the corporate grand strategy might span an extremely long time, 30–40 years, but subordinate business-unit strategies might only be in the eight–10-year range and technological strategies might only be two–five years.

Table 3–1 gives several span-of-strategy estimates. Other guidelines include the following:

- The span for a start-up firm should be short term, that is three–five years.
- A small organization with multiple products that is stable and expanding should look a bit farther into the future, maybe a five–10-year expansion.
- The large complex firm that has many subsidiaries can take a deeper look into future expansion like 10–15 years, but its subsidiaries may take a shorter view.
- Super large, complex, worldwide organizations, like giant transportation firms, may need to look very far into the future. A span that looks as much as 30 years into the technological future would not be unusual.
- A large organization in the oil industry may need to look 40–50 years into the future.
- A company in the garment industry might concentrate on a six–12-month span for product styles, but 10–15 years for global expansion.

Revisit Frequency

Here the debate rages. Some believe that strategy should be revisited every year, while others believe that strategy must be allowed to play out over an extended period. Most true strategists believe that some major happening must occur before strategy is changed. Tactics, on the other hand, should be flexible, and operations (transactions) are in constant change.

Don't let the organization bounce off walls while formulating strategy and never getting anything else done. Strategy is not a continuous formulation process. It does require continuous feedback and operational corrections, but the people of the organization must be allowed to play out the hand.

I recommend that corporate strategy be cast firmly, but revisited at some agreed-upon frequency to be certain that the broad choices are still sound and that all players continue to understand the long-term thrust of the firm. Logical strategy should remain valid even with an organizational change of command. New CEOs, however, should revisit this strategy early on to either bless it or make changes so that the organization firmly understands the vision. Subordinate strategies may be revisited on an annual basis or as feedback dictates.

TABLE 3–1
Span of Global Strategy

Years in business	Size/type of business	Scope of business	Span of strategic planning	Span of tactical planning
1–5	Entrepreneurs	One or more products	3–5 years	1–3 years
5–10	Small, expanding	Multiple products	5–10	3–5
10–20	Large, complex	Multiple businesses	10–15	5–8
20–25	Super large	Complex	10–30	5–8
Any	Oil and gas company	Small	25–30 / 40–50	3–5 / 5–8
Any	Garment industry	Large	5–10	6–12 months

Scheduling

Typically the strategic planning process is linked to the firm's fiscal or operational cycle. For some it is the tax year, for others the calendar year. The strategic process can begin for the first time at any point in the business cycle; however, once started it should be repeated at an agreed-upon frequency to coincide with the firm's operational planning schedule.

If the firm's cycle is on a tax-year basis, operational planning should begin shortly after the end of last tax year. In the United States, since the tax year typically coincides with the calendar year, the cycle would begin in January or February. For Japan, because its tax year always begins on April 1, strategic planning sessions would begin in April or May.

American Examples

Solar Turbines Incorporated, headquartered in San Diego, California, and a division of Caterpillar, Inc., is the manufacturer of gas turbine systems and 70 percent of its market is outside its American home market. One of the first things Dr. Jim Owens did when he took over as president was install a strategic management process. Knowing that his own responsibilities included making an annual presentation in March to Caterpillar about the profitability of the Solar organization, Owens determined to have his strategy worked out no later than February. His first step was to form a team of the top 42 people in the company. He labeled them the Operation Council Group (OCG). Since the firm was already globalized, the OCG included key personnel from all over the world.

To put the plan together, Owens decided to have two strategic planning meetings a year: one in the summer and one in the fall. This way, by February, he could review the strategy and be ready to brief Caterpillar in March. He called the OCG together for three days in August to talk about the year-to-date performance, to formulate the firm's mission statement, and to discuss those factors which might be critical in a 10-year span of strategic vision. (Solar has learned that although operationally three–five years is measurable, a five-year strategic horizon is not adequate. Thus, theirs is a 10-year vision.)

At the conclusion of the August session Owens asked the OCG to provide, by October 1, a written critique of the August session and any new ideas they may have. In early October the CEO mailed to his vice presidents a copy of the consolidation of their thoughts for review prior to the next meeting which was to be held off-site during late October. During that meeting the vice presidents re-edited the strategic input, prioritized the next business planning cycle, and made capital resource allocation decisions. The Solar leadership also holds a meeting in February to review the operational plan for the existing year and a final review of the strategic plan. Figure 3–5 shows Solar's planning cycle.

Minnesota Mining and Manufacturing (3M) was founded in 1902, but it did not export or establish an international division until the early 1950s. It was not

FIGURE 3–2
Solar Turbines, Inc.
Planning Cycle

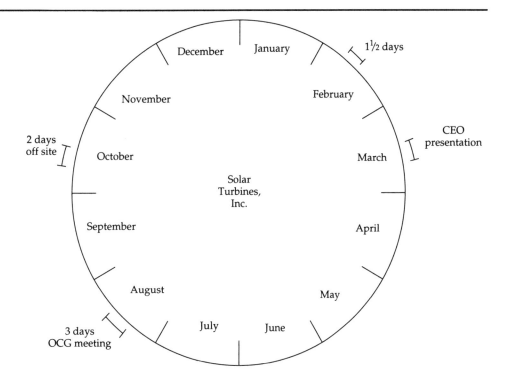

until 1988, after Allen Jacobson became CEO, that structured strategic planning was adopted. He felt that although cross-functional teams were making good decisions, they were of a short-term nature. The result was a reorganization of over 200 worldwide units into 20 strategic business centers (SBCs).

Figure 3–3 shows the 3M strategic planning cycle. Corporate starts the planning cycle in January by having the SBCs ask their operating managers to analyze internal and external forces. Their plans then go to the SBCs for review and consultation. SBC plans then go to a strategic planning committee consisting of vice presidents at headquarters who represent the four sectors into which the 20 SBCs are organized. In July, a 34-member corporate headquarter management committee reviews the plans, votes on spending priorities, and feeds direction back to the operating units who then prepare operating plans and budgets by December. These final plans are submitted back to headquarters and finalized into corporate worldwide plans.

The span of strategy for 3M is 15 years. Each year prior to the December operating reviews, the management committee holds brainstorming sessions to discus trends and developments over that span. These sessions include presentations by business-unit managers who offer their picture of the industry for that period. The outcome is a broad guide for strategic planning.

Japanese Example

For the Japanese company Kyocera, the fiscal year 1991 began on April 1, 1990. The operational year 1991 extended from April 1, 1990, until March 30, 1991. Every year Kyocera does a one-year operating plan which has, according to William L. Everitt, vice president, "absolute accuracy of numbers and goals." Therefore, the plan for operational year 1992 had to be finalized no later than March 1, 1991, in order to be placed into effect on April 1, 1991. In order that the one-year operational plan be ready, it follows that any strategic planning processes had to be completed well in advance of the annual process so that line managers had time to take into account any changes in thrust.

FIGURE 3–3
3M Strategic Planning Schedule

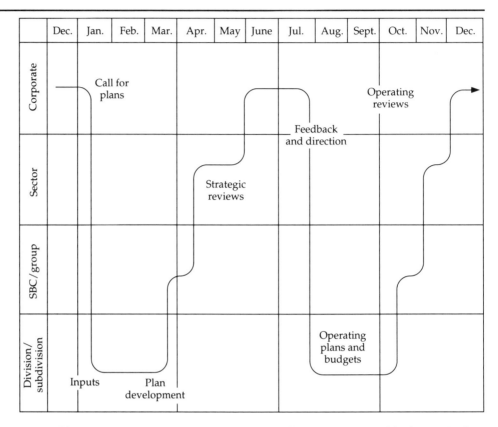

Reprinted from *Long-Range Planning*, "Planning Global Strategies for 3M," p. 15, 1988, with kind permission from Pergamon Press Ltd, Headington Hill Hall, Oxford OX3 0BW, UK.

In 1988, Kyocera completed its 10-year strategic plan which it called "The Vision" or "Green Trillion" (more is explained in Chapter 8). This long-term plan was not written in great detail, but it was Kyocera's vision of what it would like to be and do by the year 2000.

In 1991, Kyocera adopted a worldwide five-year subordinate tactical plan. The firm's five-year planning cycle overlaps the annual planning cycle. Beginning shortly after the new calendar year, the five-year plan was written in quite a bit more detail than the 10-year vision plan. It was completed in time for the next one-year operational planning process which began on April 1. Kyocera believes the Green Trillion plan should be allowed to play out, that is need not be revisited immediately. Shorter term plans, however, may be adjusted often to make the vision come true.

Generic Example

Strategy drives operations, but operations execute strategy. To lay out a strategic planning cycle, back off from the operational cycle sufficiently to have the strategy formulated in time to develop short-term operational business plans. If the organization is a start-up, design the planning cycle from inception to include strategic formulation. This reduces the pain of having to introduce the process at a later date. If the firm already has a history of operational planning, but is just beginning the strategic process, fit the strategic cycle around in-place operations. Figure 3–4 shows a typical strategic scheduling process.

FIGURE 3–4
Generic Strategic Planning Schedule

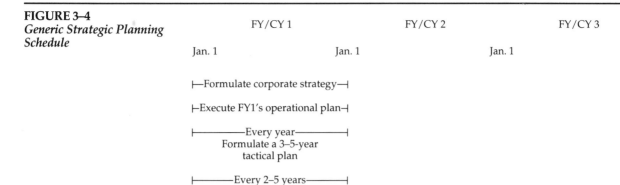

FY = Fiscal year
CY = Calendar year

SUMMARY

The global strategic management process assumes there is the intent to take the firm into the global marketplace. Some international markets will not be as rich or as promising as others. But the potential for even modest sales gains outweighs the associated costs or risks. An increase in volume usually means rising profits as well as an opportunity to utilize excess production capacity. For some products it can often extend the life cycle that was otherwise declining.

Before attempting to formulate an organizational strategy you need to understand the entire process, but you will waste your time if top management is not on board. After leadership gives the okay, the process requires lead time to set up a schedule, initiate participation, and secure the necessary resources. Having the right mind-set and a prospective GFOT is essential to success.

CHECKLIST

- Does the CEO and the board of directors support strategic planning?
- Do they support it in the global setting?
- Are they willing to commit resources?
- Does the firm have a planning staff?
- If not, who will coordinate the strategic plan?
- Has the firm formed a GFOT?
- What method of planning will be used? Bottom up, top down, or iterative?
- What will be the span of strategy?
- Has the firm adopted a planning schedule?
- Is the schedule well understood throughout the firm?

The next chapter introduces Task 2 and explains how to institutionalize the strategic management process.

T A S K

2

ESTABLISH TIME-PRESENT, BASELINE, OR CURRENT POSITION

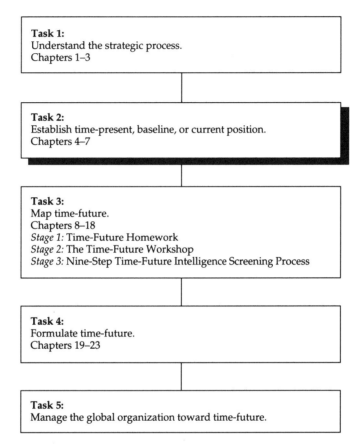

Task 1:
Understand the strategic process.
Chapters 1–3

Task 2:
Establish time-present, baseline, or current position.
Chapters 4–7

Task 3:
Map time-future.
Chapters 8–18
Stage 1: Time-Future Homework
Stage 2: The Time-Future Workshop
Stage 3: Nine-Step Time-Future Intelligence Screening Process

Task 4:
Formulate time-future.
Chapters 19–23

Task 5:
Manage the global organization toward time-future.

The second task of the formulation process is about establishing a baseline or time-present. It includes a review of the past and an analysis of the firm's current position. It answers the question: Where are we today?

Chapter 4 describes the need to implant and institutionalize the strategic process and offers two examples of corporate philosophies

Chapter 5 shows how to gather and incorporate the organization's historical background.

Chapter 6 covers the process of filling in the trends and influences from the firm's beginning to its current position.

Chapter 7 describes the process of establishing the firm's current or time-present position.

Chapter 4

Institutionalize Global Strategy

[Global corporations are the] most powerful human organization yet devised for colonizing the future. . . . [They are] exporters of dreams.

Richard Barnet and Ronald Mueller, *well-known critics of multinationals*

There are three elements to institutionalizing the global strategic management process. The first is to establish the strategic planning process as an ongoing routine of the firm. The second element is to implant globalism in the corporate culture. The third, and possibly the most important, is to instill a global corporate philosophy.

None of these elements can be installed overnight. In fact, you should expect the complete institutionalization to take at least five years. Nothing of value happens in less time. Even after the processes and philosophies are in place they must be continually reinforced through an internal training program. I recommend a series of short face-to-face meetings with employees to explain the global strategic management process and to allow feedback.

INSTITUTIONALIZE THE STRATEGIC CONCEPT

Even after the firm has successfully been through the global strategic formulation process, it is possible that it will backslide to its old ways.

Problems

From the beginning, the strategic team involves many people in the formulation process, yet there may still be those within the organization who will resist any future use of the system. Their thoughts will run the gamut of those who always resist change.

- The strategic process wastes time.
- Long forecasts cannot be accurate.
- Expanding markets internationally is really only an add-on to the local problem. It doesn't need a different strategic process.
- Ignore it and it will go away.
- Globalism will die of a natural cause called nationalism.

Causes

- Frustration will impact on business time.
- The old ways were okay; we made enough money.
- Belief that one iteration of the strategic process is enough.

Solutions

One of the first things to ensure the ongoing growth of the strategic process is to imbed it in the firm's long-range schedules. This means that on an annual, biannual, or triennial basis the firm revisits the process. Obviously if the company has had successful results from its first attempt, the institutionalization process is more likely to take hold.

39

"There is nothing more difficult to take in hand, more perilous to conduct, or more uncertain of success than to take the lead in the introduction of a new order of things, because the innovation has for enemies all those who have done well under the old conditions and lukewarm defenders in those who may do well under new."

Machiavelli from *The Prince*

How to Institutionalize the Strategic Process

Rather than blame those who implement strategy, there is a danger that the process itself will be blamed if immediate success is not realized. Chapter 24 discusses implementation in greater detail, but keep in mind what Dwight Eisenhower said: "The plan is nothing, planning is everything." Take that one step further—the plan implementors are as important as the formulators for only they can turn strategy into profit.

- Get support and influence from top management from the beginning.
- Train new employees from the beginning.
- Strive for inclusion at every level of the firm
- Talk the process up as good for the organization, especialy during long-range schedule discussions.
- Develop a persuasive argument. Ask dissident employees about globalism. Do they think it is an inevitable process? If not, what do they think is happening in the world?
- Point out that the strategic process is also a method of self-analysis and, if nothing else, results in a healthier organization.
- Strive to schedule strategic planning with other organizational improvement techniques such as OD and TQM. This minimizes the impact on key employees' time.
- Reinforce that strategic planning is better than crisis management.
- Explain the difference between strategic management and operational management.
- Explain that the resultant strategic plan is flexible.

CHANGING CORPORATE CULTURE

Strategy does not implement itself and it is not immune to the age-old disease called resistance to change. It is one of those things that must be accounted for from the beginning.

Causes

Those who resist change are not just troublemakers. Their reasons are real for them, yet what is expressed is not always the root cause. In many cases their arguments of dissent evaporate just by listening. Here are some of the underlying causes.

- Global strategy can cause employees to struggle with old morays about the word foreign and about their prejudices of other cultures. "They" are all lazy or "we" are superior to "them."
- Dissentient employees often fear losing their jobs.
- Secure in what they do now, they don't want to change.
- Some individuals will perceive their position of power threatened.
- Dissentient employees often fear losing money or other organizational rewards.
- Dissentient employees often are "don't-rock-the-boaters."

- Group leaders defend the group power position.
- They might lose organizational resources.
- Some individuals might perceive they will lose face, pres
tion with peers if they join in the change.

Problems

The most unsuccessful results from strategic planning are in those firms where the leadership applies pressure from the top without trying to strengthen the firm's threshold of collaboration. These firms generally get what they want—employees comply, but then the new strategy dies. There are many other problems related to the heavy-handed use of strategy.

- Absenteeism increases.
- Sick rates increase.
- People search for new jobs and tell others to do so.
- Quality degrades.
- Attitudes sour.
- Morale drops.

Solutions

To reap the intended results, this chapter develops the idea that no matter where they are in the world people need leadership. This chapter also explains a practical method of institutionalizing and managing change caused by new strategies.

Important Things to Remember

- *Leadership:* Remember how leadership differs from psychology and management. The latter have developed into sciences. Leadership is inspirational—even spiritual.
- *Leaders:* Look for secure leaders who continue to learn and who welcome change.
- *Slugs:* Avoid anxious, overly proud, rigid follower types.
- *Accommodate:* Take away fears before they happen.
- *Control:* Control is a good management word and is best achieved by making problems transparent to employees. The open, bottom-up, top-down organization is a healthy organization.
- *Visibility:* This is like shining a light on strategy. Explain what it is all about. Strive for as many persons in the organization as possible to understand the process.
- *Facilitation:* Facilitated participation such as the global family opinion team leads to team building even when organizations are decentralized. Open and objective management leads to goal accomplishment.
- *Discovery:* Let the discovery process about other cultures happen. Let the players learn that people from other countries are okay. Bring in people from the other countries to live and work. Soon you will hear that "they" must not be so bad.
- *Search:* Monitor and find the causes of resistance. Treat the symptoms immediately. Don't let the problem fester into a disease.

INSTILL A CORPORATE PHILOSOPHY

In order to compete in the marketplace of the 21st century, the global organization must have a philosophy upon which to build a survivable enterprise. This philosophy should be culturally neutral; that is, it should extend across borders and be accepted throughout your future worldwide organization.

Communications

Leaders must not only believe in the philosophy themselves, but they must also frequently articulate it throughout the organization. Spread it like a religion. Think about how armies and navies indoctrinate their recruits. From the beginning they

> Articulate your philosophy with missionary zeal.

instill their corporate culture, and the song is played over and over until the soldiers and sailors believe it even after they return to their civilian occupations.

Every organ of communication should be considered. Train new members from their first day on the job. If possible, the firm should have both an internal and external public affairs person whose major function is the dissemination of the message. Newsletters, company meetings, and personal offerings from the top executives should be used. Don't hesitate to preach your philosophy to all within earshot. Some will criticize you, but most will accept it in the way it is meant and be grateful that at least you have an unequivocal statement in a world of wishy-washy leaders.

This book offers two examples of corporate philosophies. The first, based on W. Edwards Deming's TQM, is drawn from *The Deming Management Method* by Mary Walton. The second corporate philosophy is that of Kazuo Inamori drawn from the book *Kyocera: A Bond of Human Minds*.

You could have your own equally sound philosophy or you may wish to adopt a mixture of the two models presented. Most important, as a leader, you must verbalize your ideas for the good of the organization.

TOTAL QUALITY MANAGEMENT (TQM)

The first philosophical model offered here did not begin as a philosophy and unfortunately, to this day many people do not think of it as such. The root of the TQM philosophy is the work of Dr. W. Edwards Deming, the statistical quality control genius who revitalized Japanese industry.

Deming was born in 1900 and earned his doctorate in physics from Yale in 1924. He was not introduced to statistical control until the mid-1930s when he met Walter A. Shewhart, a statistician at Bell Telephone Laboratories in New York. The techniques that Shewhart developed defined the limits of random variation in any aspect of a worker's task, setting acceptable highs and lows, so that any points outside those limits could be detected. Then the causes of the out-of-control point could be studied. Workers could be trained to do this charting themselves, giving them greater control over their jobs and allowing them to make adjustments on their own.

Shewhart's work, as well as that of Ronald Fisher, a famous British statistician, became the basis for Deming's own growth in the field. Over the years his reputation grew, and using the new sampling techniques in the U.S. Department of Agriculture was the basis for being asked to take charge of the 1940 census.

In 1946, Deming left the Census Bureau to establish a private practice as a statistical consultant. In 1947, he was recruited by the Supreme Command for the Allied Powers to help prepare for the 1951 Japanese census.

When Deming arrived, two years into the Allied Occupation, only the city of Kyoto, which had escaped widespread damage from aerial bombardments, was intact. All of the other heavy industrial areas between Tokyo and every other big city were nothing but twisted steel and broken concrete. Unknown to Deming as he worked on census matters, a group of Japanese known as the Union of Japanese Scientists and Engineers (JUSE) had organized to help the reconstruction of their nation. These men knew that the phrase "Made in Japan," at the time, was a synonym for junk. Learning of Deming's work with Shewhart, JUSE, in 1950, invited Deming to give a lecture on quality control methods. He accepted and, as the story goes, even refused any remuneration.

Beginning on June 19, 1950, Deming gave more than a dozen lectures throughout Japan. Later, on July 13, he met with the *Keidan-ren*, the 21 presidents of Japan's leading industries. He told them: "You can produce quality. You have a method for doing it. You've learned what quality is. You must carry out consumer research, look toward the future, and produce goods that will have a market years from now and stay in business." He emphasized: "The consumer is the most important part of the production line."

What started out to just be a series of lectures about statistical quality control turned into the Deming philosophy. The Japanese embraced it.

By channeling the energy that made them such a fearsome World War II military opponent into quality production, the Japanese reversed their field and became a formidable economic competitor. "Made in Japan" became synonymous with quality.

In 1951, to show their appreciation, the Japanese established the Deming Prize—a silver medal engraved with his profile. Given in two categories; Individual, for accomplishments in statistical theory; and Company, for accomplishments in statistical application, the Deming Prizes are highly sought, extremely prestigious awards.

Thirty years after he gave his first lecture in Japan in 1980, Deming was finally discovered in the United States by an NBC television producer. In one of the most successful documentaries in television history titled, "If Japan Can . . . Why Can't We?" Deming had the following exchange with Lloyd Dobyns, the narrator:

Dobyns:

Is there an attitudinal difference between the United States and Japan?

Deming:

They are using statistical methods. They have not only learned them, they have absorbed them, as Japanese absorb other good things of cultures. They are giving back to the world the products of statistical control of quality in a form that the world never saw before.

Dobyns:

Would the same methods work in the United States? Could we do the same thing?

Deming:

Why, of course we could. Everybody knows that we can do it.

Dobyns:

Why don't we?

Deming:

There's no determination to do it. We have no idea what's the right thing to do, have no goal.

Immediately after that nationwide broadcast Deming's telephone began to ring and his philosophy began to sweep across the United States and much of the rest of the world. In 1982, Deming published a book, *Quality, Productivity, and Competitive Position,* for use in his courses. Later it was retitled *Out of the Crisis.* In it Deming articulates his philosophy as "Fourteen Points," the "Seven Deadly Diseases," and "Some Obstacles." They are synopsized here for your consideration as a workable corporate philosophy:

Fourteen Points

The theory behind the 14 points is that management should be focused on improvement of processes instead of being focused on judgment of results.

1. *Create constancy of purpose for improvement of product and service.* Deming suggests a radical new definition of a company's function. Rather than making

money, the function is to stay in business and provide jobs through innovation, research, constant improvement, and maintenance.

2. *Adopt a new philosophy.* People are too tolerant of poor workmanship and sullen service. We need a new religion in which mistakes and negativism are unacceptable.

3. *Cease dependence on mass inspection.* Firms typically inspect a product as it comes off the line or at major production stages. Defective products are either thrown out or reworked; both are unnecessarily expensive. In effect, a company is paying workers to make defects and then correct them. Quality comes not from inspection but from process improvement. With instruction, workers can be enlisted in this improvement.

4. *End the practice of awarding business on price tag alone.* Purchasing departments customarily seek the lowest-priced vendor. Frequently, this leads to low-quality supplies. Instead, buyers should seek the best quality and work to achieve it with a single supplier for any one item in a long-term relationship.

5. *Improve constantly and forever the system of production and service.* Improvement is not a one-time effort. Management is obligated to continually look for ways to reduce waste and improve quality.

6. *Institute training.* Too often workers have learned their jobs from another worker who was never trained properly. They are forced to follow unintelligible instructions. They can't do their jobs because no one tells them how.

7. *Institute leadership.* The job of a supervisor is not to tell people what to do or to punish them but to lead. Leading consists of helping people do a better job and of learning, by objective methods, who is in need of individual help.

8. *Drive out fear.* Many employees are afraid to ask questions or take a position, even when they do not understand what the job is or what is right or wrong. People will continue to do things the wrong way or to not do them at all if they are afraid. The economic loss from fear is appalling. It is necessary for better quality and productivity that workers feel secure.

9. *Break down barriers between staff areas.* Often staff areas—departments, units, and so on—compete with each other or have conflicting goals. They do not work as a team so they cannot solve or foresee problems. Worse, one department's goals may cause trouble for another.

10. *Eliminate slogans, exhortation, and targets for the work force.* These never helped anybody do a job. Let people put up their own slogans.

11. *Eliminate numerical quotas.* Quotas only count numbers, not quality or methods. Quotas are usually a guarantee of inefficiency and high cost. A person, to hold a job, meets a quota at any cost, without regard to damage to the company.

12. *Remove barriers to pride of workmanship.* People are eager to do a good job and distressed when they can't. Too often, misguided supervisors, faulty equipment, and defective materials stand in the way. These barriers must be removed.

13. *Institute a vigorous program of education and retraining.* Both management and the work force will have to be educated in the new methods, including teamwork and statistical techniques.

14. *Take action to accomplish the transformation.* It will take a special top management team with a plan of action to carry out the quality mission. Workers can't do it on their own, nor can managers. A critical mass of people in the company must understand the 14 points, the seven deadly diseases, and the obstacles.

Seven Deadly Diseases
The theory behind Deming's seven deadly diseases is that we, as students, need reinforcement to understand the 14 points.

1. *Lack of constancy of purpose.* A company that is without constancy of purpose has no long-range strategy for staying in business. Management is insecure and so are employees.

2. *Emphasis on short-term profits.* Looking to increase the quarterly dividend undermines quality and productivity.

3. *Evaluation by performance, merit rating to annual review of performance.* The effects of these are devastating—teamwork is destroyed, and rivalry is nurtured. Performance ratings build fear and leave people bitter, despondent, and beaten. They also encourage mobility and management.

4. *Mobility of management.* Job-hopping managers never understand the companies for which they work. These managers are never there long enough to follow up on long-term changes that are necessary for quality and productivity.

5. *Running the company on visible figures alone.* The most important figures are unknown and unknowable—the multiplier effect of happy customers, for example.

6. *Excessive medical costs.*

7. *Excessive costs of warranty, fueled by lawyers who work on a contingency fee.*

Obstacles

Although a lesser category than his 14 points, Deming lists these obstacles to productivity.

1. Neglecting long-range planning.
2. Relying on technology to solve problems.
3. Seeking examples to follow rather than developing solutions.
4. Developing excuses such as "Our problems are different."

KYOCERA: A BOND OF HUMAN MINDS

Twelve years after Deming first visited Kyoto, Japan, in 1959, a new company was born in that city. Originally called Kyoto Ceramic Co. Ltd., but now called Kyocera Corporation, it did $3.4 billion in sales in 1992. In four surveys over the past several years—most recently in a sampling of 15,000 Japanese executives—Kyocera was given top honors as the company most admired for entrepreneurship and technological progress.

Analysts believe Kyocera will continue its sales growth of about 11 percent a year, with an average after-tax net of about 8 percent of sales—well above that of a typical Japanese company. All of this is accomplished with only about $558 million in long-term debt. In an environment of high leverage, Kyocera's equity stood at about 85 percent of capitalization.

In the early 1970s, Kyocera expanded its production base outside Japan. In 1989 it added to its plants already in the United States, Mexico, Brazil, and eight facilities in Western Europe.

Kyocera's founder, Kazuo Inamori, believes, "When a company is no longer on the offensive, that company is already beginning to go downhill." To back up his argument, Inamori is turning Kyocera into a worldwide, vertically integrated company that will not only make components but also expand into larger products and systems, which already include business communications equipment as well as hard disk drives, laser printers, and personal computers. Inamori expects Kyocera's annual sales to reach $8 billion in five to seven years.

In his book *Kyocera: A Bond of Human Minds*, Kazuo Inamori expresses his philosophy which may serve as model for your global business. The book begins by articulating the company's official global motto: *Kei-ten Ai-jin* which translates as "Respect the Divine and love people" taken from the writings of Nanshuu Saigo, a renowned 19th-century politician from Japan's Kagoshima prefecture.

In his book Kazuo Inamori lays out nine major points to his complex philosophy which are a rich mixture of Zen Buddhism and zealot-like exhortations. They are synopsized here for adoption by those who agree that there is universality in their logic.

Point 1: The Human Mind as the Basis

Kazuo Inamori never attended business school. What he knows about business he learned the hard way. He believes, however, that his ignorance of conventional business ways contributed to Kyocera becoming the efficient manufacturer and money-maker it is. Inamori recounts an anecdote from the firm's early days. At the time, he knew little about management, but solved a personnel problem by persuading a group of employees to trust him and believe in each other. If that happened, "In the future, I think we shall be able to do even better than the demand you are now making." They trusted him, went back to work, and today those people are Kyocera's top managers and executives.

This and other incidents convinced Inamori that the root of the firm's ability to perceive the world's needs in electronics has been fueled by belief in the human mind as the most dependable thing in the world. A trusting relationship became the basis for management and growth.

Point 2: Management Based upon Truth

This point of Inamori's philosophy reasons that management should be logical and based upon truth. The firm cannot succeed if management is contradictory, illogical, or contrary to conscience and moral values. When in doubt, always go back to basic truths.

Point 3: Amoeba Management and the Hourly Efficiency System

Conceptually, the amoeba management system (discussed in Chapter 24) is the essence of entrepreneurship. By dividing large organizational structures into small units, the firm avoids inefficiencies that are inherent in large systems and promotes an entrepreneurial environment. Inamori calls these small cellular units amoebas. There is no set pattern to forming amoebas. Sometimes they are based on various product divisions; in other cases they are created around process stages; yet in other cases small amoebas do everything from beginning to end. Amoebas are pretty much their own manager, except that they must have permission to make a purchase.

Though there may be bonuses, the amoeba system discourages rewards based on profit alone. Rather the philosophy uses an evaluation system computed on added value by the workers of each amoeba. Thus individuals feel a part of the accomplishments of the whole and benefit in the following ways.

- Each amoeba earns the satisfaction of knowing how much added value their group generated for each hour of each individual's time.
- Each group's outstanding contributions and each individual's contribution to the group are recognized and praised.
- As human beings, we want to operate at a high moral level and create an environment that brings out the noble spirit of the human race. Thus we have the ability to set goals higher than for our own personal benefit.
- The true meaning of humanity's own happiness is to lead a life that is meaningful, one in which we can honestly say that the world is better for the contributions we have made to society. The organization should be a place where individuals can accomplish, as a group, something that we cannot do as individuals.

Point 4: Management as a Response to Customer Needs

Serving the customer is the root of the firm's business philosophy.

- Sales personnel must be willing to be servants to customers.
- Management must totally and thoroughly respond to the needs of all customers.
- A customer's offer should be accepted and responded to immediately, even with an offer of precise delivery date.

- The customer's demands should be met with quick R&D support.
- We cannot succeed if products are poor in quality.
- A product that does not meet the criteria of dependable quality and supply is not marketable.
- The best quality must be offered regardless of production costs.
- After the prototype is built, the secondary problem of how to profitably mass produce it must be considered.
- Products should be supplied at competitive prices.
- The challenge to those who manufacture goods in the industrial sector is to offer a product at a price that is fair and advantageous to customers, and to maximize such prices through engineering efforts.
- Profit is not something we can obtain by demanding it.
- Price is determined through the market mechanism.

Point 5: Challenge the Future

In this point, Inamori deals with the offensive thrust of the successful person as well as the company. He argues that "success is multifaceted, but includes our attitude for business; the mental and spiritual state we have developed for creative research and invention; our engineering resources; and our ability to look ahead to market needs and technological development."

- Believe in the eternal growth of industries.
- When a company is no longer on the offensive, but rather on the defensive, that company is already going downhill.
- Don't seek employees who look at our past accomplishments and want to join the company for security and safety of its size and stability.
- Welcome only those who want to join the company to face new challenges.
- To continuously challenge the future means continuously exposing this foundation to risk.
- Financial strength covers risks and withstands each new challenge.
- Perseverance is a major ingredient for being able to challenge the future.
- Patience is another ingredient to challenge the future.
- The 21st century is an era of incredible opportunity.
- The prerequisite for development is to have employees who are willing to run at the head of the pack.

Point 6: Envision and Make It Come True

"Make goals that continue limitlessly into the future," says Inamori. "Strong desire must penetrate deep into our subconscious mind." To further his point Kazuo Inamori goes on to offer the following:

- The ideal individual is one who is full of hope.
- Only an individual who is willing to challenge the accepted beliefs and is willing to put in the efforts to break such barriers can open the door to the future.
- Making a vision come true will require undaunted willpower and a zeal for accomplishment.
- Success depends on how strong the desire is to accomplish and succeed.
- The willingness to encourage oneself is what I call willpower.
- Be conscious of a higher purpose.
- Faith is a very important virtue for human beings.
- To believe that this project will make people happy is to give real and true purpose to the work.
- If purpose and aggressiveness is due to a twisted self-interest, the same zeal that led to early prosperity will also lead to an early demise.

> "Let us each set our goals and make them come true through continuous desire, a desire so strong that it penetrates down to our subconscious mind. In my opinion, 'lucky' people are individuals who not only have burning desires and a determination to visualize and reach their goals, but, additionally, they are people whose subconscious inspirations are not clouded by selfish desires, and whose conscious actions are not biased by self-serving motives. As such a person's visions become reality, one after another, onlookers will stand back and marvel at his or her incredible 'luck'!"
>
> Kazuo Inamori

Point 7: Be Creative

Inamori exhorts others to

- Do what no one has done before.
- Avoid imitating others.
- Have faith in yourself.
- Have self-confidence not only technically but also as a human being.
- Be creative. Demand perfection from oneself.
- Accept a basic outline of this hypotheses.

Point 8: Reality Is a Reflection of Your Mind

This point reflects Inamori's belief in motivating the subconscious mind. He points out that true achievement (research) most likely happens when we are so committed that the subconscious as well as the conscious works for the solution to a problem.

- Visualization is to see the product even when it is still on the drawing board.
- Purity of heart brings good fortune.
- *Buts* and *ifs* cloud the image we draw in our minds and detract from our vision.

Point 9: The Formula for Success

Inamori illustrates this point with the formula

$$\text{Success} = (\text{Ability}) \times (\text{Effort}) \times (\text{Way of Thinking})$$

Thus our life's work can be synergistic; that is, the whole can be bigger than the parts. For instance, when average ability is multiplied by an extraordinary effort, the result is much more striking than that of an unmotivated genius. One can guide the work using the formula and achieve great things regardless of disadvantaged roots.

SUMMARY

The global strategic management process cannot be installed then expected to sustain itself. The institutionalization process could take five years and even then it must be reinforced periodically. The organization's philosophy should complement the global mission, and every employee in every country should be made conscious of it through various communications methods, especially in direct relations with top management.

CHECKLIST

- Is the first element of institutionalizing the global strategic management process in place? Is the strategic planning process an ongoing routine of the firm?
- Do you have a cycle schedule?
- Does everyone know when the process will start and when it routinely happens in the future?
- Have you taken steps to manage change?
- Have you implanted globalism in the corporate culture?
- Does the firm have a corporate philosophy?
- Is it understood in every country?
- Which elements of Deming's philosophy work for you?
- Which elements of Inamori's philosophy work for you?
- Is the leadership of the firm instilling a global corporate philosophy?

Chapter 5

How We Got Started

Demographics are revolutionizing our strategies for the world's consumer goods markets. We are big-brand people; however, if we forget the importance of local selling and marketing we will rue the day.

Mike Heron, *European regional director of Unilever*

One of the fundamentals of using strategy as a management tool, for any purpose, is establishing a starting point, a baseline, or "time-present." Three questions must be answered to establish the firm's current position.

1. What was our origin? How did we get our start?
2. How did we get from there to here?
3. What is going on now? What is our baseline?

The purpose of this chapter is to provide the tools needed to establish, in writing, the first point—how the organization began.

A NEW BUSINESS

You may be one of the fortunate who used the global strategic management process before starting a new organization. If you used this process to write the original business plan you may be surprised to find that your home market is not the best place to compete. For some, especially companies home-based in the third world, the best start-up market is in a wealthier, industrialized country. Even companies in large industrial nations may find that a market other than their own country is the best place to start. As an example, some biomedical firms are often better off getting a foothold in a country that has the most compatible food and drug laws. The firm that starts right is one which will have a high probability of survival in the long run.

THE MATURE BUSINESS

In the past most firms were not global nor did they have global aspirations. Most were happy to just get a foothold in their home country. Therefore, the first time the global strategic management process takes place there should be a complete review of the company's history.

History

Why is it important to recover and set down in writing the organization's history? First, it's important to understand the roots before beginning the visionary process. Second, the entrepreneurs who pained through the start-up process need to know that their brainchild will live on after them. Third, and more important, companies and future employees need heros.

The Heros

Everyone needs heros, and entrepreneurs are the heros of the free enterprise, free market, capitalist economic system. We know a great deal more about entrepreneurs today than in the past. We know they are often mavericks and they have a special fire-in-the-belly that pushes aside risk. We also know that

50

Coca-Cola Company's Mission Statement

"The Coca-Cola Company is the worldwide soft-drink leader, as well as one of the world's leading producers and distributors of filmed entertainment and the leading U.S. marketer of orange juice and juice products."

Solar Turbines Incorporated's Mission Statement

"Focus on customer needs to strengthen our position as the world's leading manufacturer of mid-range industrial gas turbines and turbomachinery systems."

---

they are not always professional managers, and therefore their time runs out when the organization has grown so big that professional management is needed. Typically they don't give up the reins of change easily and the process is often messy. Nevertheless, give them credit for what they did and let them be honored.

Origin of the Company

Every company had a beginning. Some of the greatest firms in the world were once mom-and-pop operations. Many started in a garage, a kitchen, or a small corner in someone else's warehouse. Every firm had a core idea. Most of the time the entrepreneur had the concept locked in his or her head. Later the idea may have been written. More often than not a generation passed before someone decided to put it in writing for posterity.

On the other hand, the CEO might decide that the firm has outgrown his or her original ideas and wants to develop a strategic analysis such as this book describes. It might be during just such a process that you are called upon to write, for the first time, the firm's original mission statement. To do so you must pick the brains of the founders or the people who were on board from the beginning and know what was intended.

Mission Statement

A mission is a description of what the organization intends to do, the purpose that sets a given company apart from other firms of its type. A mission identifies the scope of a firm's operations in terms of countries, markets, products, and technologies. It is a broad statement that provides focus and communicates to the organization's stakeholders (such stockholders, employees, customers, and suppliers) where the organization is going.

Feel free to interchange the word *mission* with *purpose*. Some refer to the mission as the driving force.

The mission is the foundation upon which everything of and in the firm is built. The words of the mission statement should be simple and straightforward. They should be framed in such broad terms that the mission will be an enduring explanation of the firm's intent. From the mission's words, anyone should clearly understand the firm's credo, philosophy, and image.

Goals and Objectives

What is the difference between a goal and an objective? None! For purposes of this book goals and objectives are the same.

Objectives or goals may be financial as well as nonfinancial. Objectives can be long term or short term, such as annually. The difference between long- and short-term goals has to do with specificity. Long-term goals typically refer to going global, gross sales, profitability, return on investment, employee relations, or leadership attainment in technology or products. Short-term objectives often specify target numbers of units to be sold or a percentage increase in after-tax income.

What Were the Firm's Original Goals and Objectives?

Back then, in the time when the firm was just getting started, the owners had some goals. Maybe they were any of the following:

- Make a living.
- Put the kids through school.
- Expand a technology.
- Carry on a skill.
- Make a better mouse trap.
- Sales of $10,000 in the first full year of operations.
- Sell 1,000 units of a new product in the first six months.
- Be my own boss.

Strategies

Don't be surprised if the founders did not use strategy as a management method. Most start-up companies did not but a few leaders did. If you can, write the firm's original strategy. Refer to Appendix A for a list of generic corporate-level strategies.

Markets

What were the firm's original markets? Were they local or regional? Or, from the beginning, was there an attempt to sell across borders?

Products

What were the company's original products? Do you still have a few units or copies for your company museum? Were they owner-invented or was the technology brought in from somewhere else.

Countries

In what countries did the firm originally operate? If it traded across borders, how did it learn and how long did that process take?

Sales

What was the firm's early sales record? State it in both currency and units sold in the first partial year and the first full year of operations.

Profitability

When did the firm break even? When did it become profitable? How much did the owners risk?

SUMMARY

All companies have a starting point and that is the foundation for the strategic formulation process. Over time, employees come and go but the strategic process will continue. Knowing your company's roots is the first step in establishing time-present.

CHECKLIST

- Is your organization a start-up or has it been in business for some time?
- Is your organization using the strategic management process for the first time?
- Who were the founders of the organization?

- Why did the founders start the company, and what were their original resources?
- What were the original goals of the organization?
- Have you stated the original mission in words?
- What was the original strategy?
- What were the company's original markets?
- What were the products?
- Have you established an organizational museum with copies of the early products on display?
- What countries did the company sell in?
- What were the first year's sales?
- When did the company become profitable?

Chapter 6

How We Got Here

I have but one lamp by which my feet are guided, and that is the lamp of experience. I know no way of judging the future but by the past.

Patrick Henry

Maybe your company has only been in business a few years or maybe it has been around for 10 or 20 years. No matter how long, firms have life and they change over time.

Continuing the process of establishing the organization's current position or time-present, this step of the global strategic process addresses more of the firm's history; that is, how we got from there to here. After establishing the facts of the company's birth, put down in writing the major elements that took place between that time and the present.

The Heros

An organization can have heros other than the founder(s). Men and women make remarkable contributions, and those special people, inside and out, should be revered just as highly as those that got the firm started. Maybe it was a secretary who loyally served the firm every day for 40 years. Or that effervescent salesperson who never wanted to rise to a top management position, yet continually set new sales records and established the key elements that drove every market plan.

At one point in IMED's history, the mother of vice president Doug Rumberger loaned the company funds to make payroll. She's a hero!

Management Structure

In the beginning the firm may have been only a two- or three-person proprietorship, but over time it changed to a partnership, then to a corporation. In its early years it may have had only two departments, but in stages it grew from two management layers to five. Draw some graphics and show the changes year by year. Explain the reasons for differing management styles as the company grew.

Outside Influences

Companies are affected by outside as well as internal influences. Try to identify those things that caused change and explain what was done to counter the influence. Were new products developed? Were prices changed because of new competitors or a rise in the cost of raw materials or components? Did a traditional source go out of business causing the firm to backward integrate and become a manufacturer of those parts?

Competition	Over the years who were the firm's competitors? How many of those are still in business?
Sales/Marketing Direction	Did the firm expand its markets over time? What were the phases of the expansion and what were the results? Show the annual sales success and failures and explain the causes of setbacks. What were the major customer trends during the intervening years? Did the products change and did the methods of selling change?
Financial Trends	Companies need money from time to time in order to stay in business or to expand operations. What were the sources of funds and from whom did they come? Who risked what? What have been the company's cash-flow trends?

SUMMARY

It is not enough to understand the organization's beginning. Over time a company changes, and therefore, to establish the current position, your analysis should attempt to capture the major influences of that change. Examine the bends in the road and why the organization changed.

CHECKLIST

- Besides the entrepreneurs who started the firm, who were the other heros of the organization?
- How has the organization structure changed over time?
- What were the major influences?
- What competition came and went? Who remains?
- What was the history of sales and marketing?
- What were the organization's financial trends?

Chapter 7

Baseline: What's Going on Today?

Reform must come from within, not from without.

Ralph Waldo Emerson

To this point you have established the origin of the firm and reviewed its growing pains. It is now time to answer the third question postulated in Chapter 5: What is going on today? It's possible that the organization is still in the learning curve phase, that is, just getting started; but more likely your company is established and ready to go global.

DATA COLLECTION

This step could pose problems for oversensitive or insecure management, because leaders open themselves to learning things they may not want to hear. The purpose of the analyses, however, is to establish the gaps between where the organization thinks it is and where it really is, and the effect the gap has on strategy.

It's surprising how much an organization thinks it knows about itself, and how little is really understood. This is particularly true of large firms. Strategic formulation causes an organization to take a pause from its operations and in many ways have new beginnings.

Capabilities

Every firm has a set of capabilities, that is, the things it is able to do or not do vis-à-vis the current company mission and objectives. These range from the effectiveness of employees and equipment to produce and sell, to the ability of corporate headquarters to raise funds to support new ventures.

Understanding today's capabilities is a major step in understanding the organization's current position and launching the strategic formulation process. The analysis of capabilities should be comprehensive and synergistic, that is, it should be done business unit by business unit. For large firms the picture should be pulled together into a corporate capability. Figure 7–1 shows the natural flow of this information-collection process.

STAGE 1: INTERNAL STRENGTHS AND WEAKNESSES

After the data are collected, write a list of your firm's strengths and weaknesses. Make certain that each has a note of explanation. For purposes of formulating a new strategy, the firm is most interested in the following key elements.

Current mission. Today's mission statement could be quite different than the original mission statement. Today's mission could also be very different from the eventual mission statement developed as a result of this global strategic management process. Explain why today's statement is different than any earlier versions.

Current objectives. Write the firm's current objectives. If not clearly defined, ask the leadership what it perceives the objectives to be. Are they stated in terms of

FIGURE 7–1
Capabilities: Corporate,
Company, and/or Unit

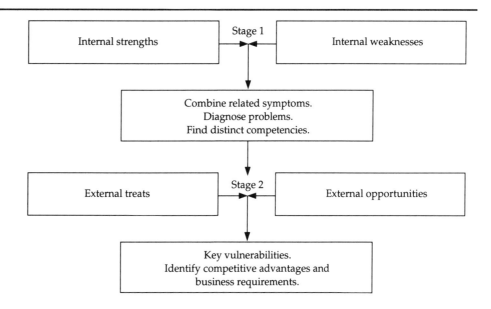

sales goals or percentage increases in profits? Are there nonfinancial objectives as well as financial ones?

Current strategies.   Outline the strategies top management is currently using to attain the objectives it has established. Is it going head to head with the competition or is it satisfied to have a niche?

Philosophy.   State the firm's philosophy regarding people, growth, the environment, human capital, and any other aspect of business and social life.

Markets.   Where are the current markets? What is the distribution network? What works and what does not? Who are the decision-making units for your product(s)?

Products.   List your firm's products. What are the best-sellers and what are the dogs? When were they ready for market and where are they in their life cycle?

Countries.   Does the firm operate in any countries other than the home country? Name them and explain their importance.

Sales.   Lay out today's sales picture. What is the trend and what have been the biggest successes?

Financial resources and assets.   By understanding the capital base you will learn the financial underpinnings of the firm which will allow it to expand or which will prevent the expansion. The finance department should crunch all the numbers as described in Appendix B.

Physical plant and equipment.   Are the plant and equipment modern or obsolete? What are the expansion capabilities? Consider cost versus benefit. Is location a strength? Does the equipment have flexibility and alternative uses? What is the maintenance record?

Distribution and communications. To what degree does the firm control distribution and communications? What are the cost, speed, and reliability?

Technical experience. Where do the strengths and weaknesses of your technology lie? What is your core technology and who is able to convert that technology into products? Are your technical people motivated to conduct strong searches? What are your connections to universities and other research and development centers?

Product/customer/service. This is the area of serving your market. What are the strengths and weaknesses of your product and/or services and their acceptance by customers.

Suppliers. What is the nature of the firm's buying decisions? How important are suppliers? What is the availability of substitutes and alternative sources? How good is the service of your suppliers?

Marketing experience/alliances. How good is the firm's marketing capability? Is this a strength? Are there significant weaknesses? Has your firm established any alliances which set you apart from your competitors?

Intellectual properties. To what extent does your firm rely on protection of intellectual property? Do you have significantly valuable intellectual properties? Do they represent a strength?

Internal organization and management. How is your organization working? Is there something special that brings strength to the firm? How do decisions get made—quickly or painstakingly slow?

Personnel resources. How strong are managers and key employees? Could the organization use people with some new specialties? What about morale and motivation? Do the directors and key shareholders have special connections? Does the firm have access to a specific consultant that fills an important gap?

Problem diagnosis. List the organization's strengths and weaknesses. Search for opposites. This analysis usually shows that many problems can be combined into a set of common or related symptoms which can be further sifted to one or more core problems. Look for customer complaints, absenteeism, rework, excessive overtime, product returns, or criticisms of service. What are the meanings of companion protests?

Distinct competencies. A distinct competence is something a company does especially well compared to its competitors. On the other hand, there may be some areas of incompetency which need to be corrected. Look for competencies in these areas.

- Personnel resources.
- Facilities and equipment.
- Technology.
- Product markets.
- Distribution and communications.
- Financial assets.
- Managerial skills and processes.
- Special relationships.

- Legal relationships.
- Special skills and synergies.

STAGE 2: EXTERNAL THREATS AND OPPORTUNITIES

Threats and opportunities emerge from many quarters. New technologies and products come on the scene. Competitors drop in to replace one that has dropped out. The government issues new regulations. Demographics change or there is a significant political upheaval. The intent of this analysis is to review what's going on today.

Country positions.   If the firm is already operating in more than one country, what are the strengths and weaknesses of the firm's markets? Should they be expanded? How valuable to the firm is the experience of operating in another country?

Current strategy.   How well is the current strategy working? Is it consistent? Does it have a global viewpoint? Has it been implanted in the firm's culture? How well is strategy implemented and monitored?

Key vulnerabilities.   These are the things that can impact the survival of the firm. It could be a weakness in converting technology to product or a vacant key marketing manager position. It could be skills, knowledge, or certain resources needed for a special project that keeps the firm in the competition and extends its life.

Competitive advantages.   These are the basic business elements which determine the firm's position relative to its competition. Is the firm an overall cost leader or niche player? Does it have specific technological strengths or is it especially strong in marketing?

Business requirements.   Either a key vulnerability or a weak competitive position may reveal a need to fill a new business requirement. A partnership with another firm may be a possibility or in some instances another company may need to be acquired that provides just the strength to continue in the current arena.

DATA SOURCES

I recommend the GFOT approach which has been successfully developed by WD-40 and many other firms. This superior method is inclusive and serves multiple purposes. It seeks the opinions of executives, key salespersons, customers, and other key personnel. Figure 7–2 shows the human being at the center of the strategic process. The organization succeeds or fails on its ability to get the most from it human resources.

The outcome of the formulation process will be guidance that affects strategy, tactics, and transactions at every level of the firm. Therefore the players who participate must be representative of those levels. It is essential that ownership for strategy be accepted throughout the firm. Implementation requires inclusion, and inclusion fortifies the institutionalization of the global business strategy process into the firm's culture.

I recommend three data sources to collect the information necessary to determine the organization's current position: functional managers, employees, and top management.

Don't worry that the questions asked each group are redundant. It is better to get more information than not enough. The process may expose symptoms that certain aspects of internal management require strengthening. In that case OD,

FIGURE 7–2
The Center of Strategy

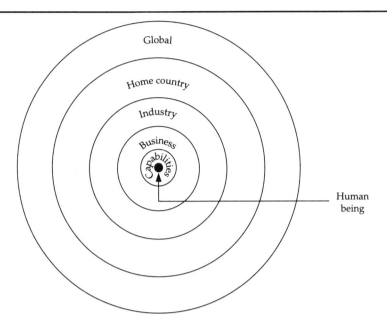

TQM, and/or empowerment processes like the General Electric workout program may use the same data.

Functional Managers

The functional managers of any organization are the traditional keepers of corporate information. Except for special projects that cut across functional lines, all collection and reporting is done through the line organization.

Employees

Typically these data are gathered in several ways. The first method is to circulate a form to all employees asking them to list what they think the strengths and weaknesses of the company are in several specific areas. Always allow employees an opportunity to express general concerns beyond those in which you are primarily interested. Sometimes the results of the questionnaire tell more about what employees don't know about the organization than what they do know. This is also useful. If they prefer to, allow employees to remain anonymous for this survey.

Figure 7–3 is a typical questionnaire used to get as much information and collaboration from employees as possible. Use all or some of these questions to format a letter to key employees.

Top Managers

These same questions can be used for top managers, but their responses should not be fill-in-the-blank statements. Rather they should either outline their thoughts in a letter or in an open, free-flowing but directed discussion.

In 1972, when John S. (Jack) Barry was the new president of WD-40, he called just such a meeting. While not using the precise format of Figure 7–1, the data shown in Figure 7–4 are examples of how this successful company developed its capabilities and ultimately improved its growth from a free-flowing discussion.

FIGURE 7–3
Time-Present Questionnaire

The purpose of this questionnaire is to get your opinion as to where the company is today.

1. Is the company growing behaviorally? Qualitatively? Quanitatively?
2. What are the company's internal weaknesses?
3. What are the company's internal strengths?
4. What are our human resources?
5. What are our financial resources?
6. Conceptually, what is the underlying value of our company?
7. State the current strategic thrust of the company as best you can.
8. What are our present objectives, financial and nonfinancial?
9. Where are we with respect to our present objectives?
10. What are today's critical issues?
11. What is our core technology?
12. What is our core strategy?
13. Do we need to eliminate any goals?
14. Do we need to change any goals or add new ones?
15. What are our strongest products?
16. What are our strongest services?
17. What are our weakest products?
18. What are our weakest services?
19. What are our external threats? Products? Competition?
20. What is the current scope of products? Markets? Users? Cutomers?

Editing and Collating

In preparation for the next task the data should be edited and collated by staff so that they can be offered to the GFOT for review and comments in the next task. This will be the jumping-off point for future ideas.

SUMMARY

1. Before the organization can visualize the future it must have a understanding or baseline of what is happening today.
2. The process has two stages.
3. Stage 1 is an assessment of today's internal strengths and weaknesses.
4. Stage 2 looks at the external situation in terms of threats and opportunities.

CHECKLIST

- Has the GFOT been formed? Do they know who they are?
- What kind of special recognition have the GFOT been given?
- Does the organization have a questionnaire similar to Figure 7–3 for its employees?
- Does each functional department have guidance to answer questions during both stages?
- Is there a letter that guides top management in their responses?
- Have the data been edited and collated in preparation for Task 3?

FIGURE 7–4
WD-40 Marketing Meeting
11/19/69

Facts

1. One-product company.
2. Small.
3. Marketing company.
4. Easy and quick to expand manufacturing—no or little capital required.
5. Product has broad use and application.
6. Both industrial and consumer market: $1/3$ consumer; $2/3$ industrial.
7. Packaged: aerosol and bulk.
8. Excellent performance (multiple uses): rust preventative; penetrant; lubricant; moisture displacement.
9. Demonstration needs "problem."
10. Preventive maintenance—problem solving—uses not self-evident.
11. Consumable.
12. Low–moderate cost.
13. Very low unit cost of application.
14. "Package" cost (unit) is higher than other units: 3 In 1, Graphite, Liquid Wrench.
15. Least expensive WD-40 = 98¢.
16. Education is necessary for this product.
17. Aerosol—ease of application.
18. Ease of entry—competition can come in.
19. Trademark—brand name critical.
20. Brand name long way to go—brand awareness regional.
21. Brand loyalty—highest in customer.
22. Multiple-use product, replacing single, special-use products.
23. Competition: Direct—CRC, LPS, Sprayon; Indirect— 3 In 1, Liquid Wrench, Graphite.
24. CRC "good" penetration in eastern market.
25. Relationship jobbers to sales.
26. Many trade channels.
27. Brand awareness—word of mouth.
28. Not seasonal.
29. Not geographic related.
30. Takes in wide branch of income.
31. Male vs. female—today—male buyer.
32. Frequency of purchase: Consumer = low = 2 to 3 times/year; Industrial.
33. Unit purchase low—consumer.
34. Typhoid Mary.
35. WD-40.
36. Impulse purchase—remote possibility today.
37. Sporting good "point of entry."
38. WD-40 "better mouse trap."
39. Industrial and consumer markets cross-feed each other.
40. Divine intervention welcomed.
41. "Brand loyalty" of direct competition high at consumer.
42. Auto trade channel—extra stop—price structure problem.
43. Today—not trade channel.
44. Today job is to sell against indirect—consumer.
45. Today job is to sell against direct—industrial (product superiority); depends upon which industry.
46. Question consumer appeal of present graphics on package.
47. Have great and continuing need for application—engineering. Technical needs for industrial.
48. "Big" industrial application still to be developed.
49. Price competition bigger problem in industry—specific use okay, won't pay for multiple users.
50. WD-40 small value to jobber and dealer.
51. Product has "sex appeal" when they get hooked!!
52. Good door opener for jobber.
53. General must force distribution.
54. No after-sale service.
55. Few returns.
56. Shelf life fine.
57. Exclusivity not problem (trade channel-wise).
58. Education—pioneer problem throughout trade channels.
59. Not sophisticated or highly technical problem.
60. WD-40 Company will focus on one product.
61. Product has no storage—handling (breakage) problem.
62. Penetration in Zone I overall still low.
63. Jobbers often don't sell—they do warehouse and bill.

FIGURE 7–4 (continued)

| | Percent total | Percent Breakout | |
		Consumer	In-house
Sporting goods	22.0	100%	—
Hardware	9.1	"	—
Chain	4.7	"	—
	35.8		
Auto and marine	18.1	85%	15
Service (locksmith, vending machine)	2.6	10%	90
	20.7		
Industrial fabrication	39.7	5	95
Other	3.8	5	95
	100.0		

Marketing tools available to us

1. Packaging design.
2. Shows and exhibits.
3. Trade ads.
4. Literature.
5. P.O.P. material.
6. Sampling.
7. Consumer ads—End user } General public
                          } Special interest end use
8. TV.
9. Radio.
10. Outdoor advertising (billboards).
11. Salesmen (company).
12. Product publicity (editorials).
13. Incentive (all levels).
14. Remembrance material.
15. Field supervision and training.
16. Market research.
17. Price of product = terms and conditions of sale, freight, cash discounts, etc.
18. General public relations.
19. Direct mail.
20. Sales aids—merchandising A & SP program.
21. Continuing communications to troops.
22. Traveling display—truck, VW type.
23. Bus advertising.
24. Home office people.
25. Sales "programs."

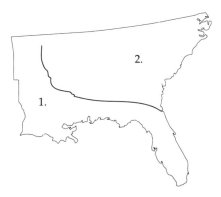

FIGURE 7–4 (continued)

Aerosol	Consumer			Industrial	
				Fact	Service
1.5 oz. sample					
3 oz.	5%	$1.10	99	0	1
·12 oz.	60%	$1.95	60	35	5
16 oz.	35%	$2.35	40	55	5
Bulk					
1 gallon		$7.00/gal.	5		95
5 gallon				} 100%	
55 gallon drum					

Independent stores	Chain	Industrial

Printed with permission of John S. Barry, Chairman, WD-40

3 MAP TIME-FUTURE

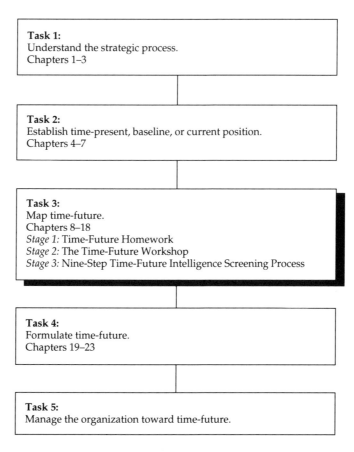

Task 1:
Understand the strategic process.
Chapters 1–3

Task 2:
Establish time-present, baseline, or current position.
Chapters 4–7

Task 3:
Map time-future.
Chapters 8–18
Stage 1: Time-Future Homework
Stage 2: The Time-Future Workshop
Stage 3: Nine-Step Time-Future Intelligence Screening Process

Task 4:
Formulate time-future.
Chapters 19–23

Task 5:
Manage the organization toward time-future.

This task presents an explanation of the nine-step global intelligence screening process.Global strategic formulation jumps off from the baseline of time-present. The time-future mapping process consists of three stages: (1) a homework stage, (2) a workshop phase, and (3) an intelligence-screening phase.

Stage 1, described in Chapter 8, explains how to do the homework needed prior to the time-future workshop. Stage 2, also explained in Chapter 8, develops the details of the time-future workshop including a description of the desired results. Chapter 9 introduces stage 3 which is the intelligence-collection process. Chapters 10–18 explain what information should be screened during the global-mapping process.

Ad Hoc Visions

The leader who would create a vision sufficiently compelling to motivate associates to superior performances must draw on the intuitive mind.
Ultimately, vision gets translated into sales and profit growth and return on investment, but the numbers come after the vision.

John Naisbitt

To this point in the process you have established a baseline of time-present, in other words, a jumping-off point. But you know the future will not be like the past or the present. The objective of the global strategic formulation process is to explore time-future.

The purpose of this chapter is to explain stages 1 and 2 of the global strategic forumulation process. These stages allow the organization to scan the future based on what the firm already knows today.

Span of Strategic Thinking

How far in time-future should you think? Refresh yourself by rereading the appropriate sections of Chapter 3.

For purposes of unrestrained, creative thinking the boundaries should not be restricted. So that stages 1 and 2 sing from the same sheet of music, I suggest the input be requested in blocks of time, such as five–10 years, 10–20 years, 20–30 years, and 30–50 years. Five-to-10-year strategic thinking should be rigorous. Ten years and beyond may be less specific. Twenty to 30 years may only be described in short paragraphs which outline very long-term objectives, and beyond 30 years may just be blue-sky. You will experience resistance from some who cannot conceive of thinking beyond a few years, but have them take a stab at the process anyway.

Kyocera's Green Trillion plan is a 10-year plan which includes nonfinancial ecology (green) strategies while achieving the corporate financial objective of one trillion yen (gross volume worldwide) by the year 2000. Kyocera has more general strategies based on various scenarios extending as much as 50 years into the future. Review "Kyocera: A Bond of Human Minds" in Chapter 4 for the underpinnings of the long-term strategy of this dynamic firm.

At no time during any task should the global strategist be bound only by economics or any other single discipline. Rather he or she must use a multidisciplinary approach. The strategist is most interested in meanings—how customers, competitors, and governments will act in the future.

STAGE 1: TIME-FUTURE HOMEWORK

Every organization has an intuitive understanding of strategic planning and unique experience about its business. Needless to say this information should be tapped in advance of the final formulation process.

Strategic Input

Typically key members of the GFOT are asked to submit their input, in writing, in advance of stage 2. This way the information can be collated and presented during the workshop.

Executive Opinion

For large companies, in addition to bringing outlying executives together for stage 2 (ad hoc visions), the corporation should send a questionnaire to the CEOs of subsidiary companies. Those CEOs, in turn, are asked to gather a jury opinion of their key managers and submit the results to headquarters. This is an inexpensive method that boosts top management's participation. Hard data which support opinions are necessary, but intuitive input is just as valuable. Appendix C offers a pre-workshop questionnaire suitable for time-future analysis.

Sales Force Opinion

Many firms base their strategic opinions on the input of the sales team. The sales force is the firm's traveling arm. It is in constant contact with customers. Sales teams that are selling across borders know foreign countries and their cultures. They are also excellent sales forecasters. But this method is limiting because sales personnel are often too narrow in their viewpoint, they seldom stay in tune to government events, and are sometimes protective of anything that smacks of change. Nevertheless, their opinion should be gathered for presentation during stage 2.

Customer Opinion

Most firms ask their customers about the future. Sometimes by questionnaire and sometimes by interview, the opinions of key customers are pooled then synthesized into a forecast. This method is sometimes flawed because all too often customers are not interested in your problems, and the people who do respond are not those who have the knowledge and best view of tomorrow.

Supplier Opinion

Suppliers, like customers, often bring startling news about the future as they see your organization. Be careful because they may tell you what you want to hear.

Supplemental Input

To supplement the opinions of the GFOT, many firms also seek the thoughts of outside experts. A forecast is a prophecy, an estimate, or a prediction of the future. To obtain desired results, firms go about this using differing techniques. Most select what works best for them.

A comprehensive list of as many as 20 different forecasting methods is in Appendix D. Only those methods most practical for small business will be discussed here: focus groups and the Delphi technique.

Focus groups.   This is a method of bringing together qualified and recognized experts to develop, evaluate, and synthesize their points of view.

Delphi technique.   The Delphi technique solicits, in writing, points of view on a particular subject from a cross-section of experts. By collating the answers, then again asking opinions of the same group about the collated responses, an answer can eventually be extrapolated.

STAGE 2: THE TIME-FUTURE WORKSHOP

For stage 2, I recommend a three-to-four-day, off-site workshop. I call this the *ad hoc visions phase*, others call it *what if, let's try*. The Germans call it *gestalt* which is defined in *Webster's New World Dictionary* as "a structure, configuration, or pattern of physical, biological, or psychological phenomena so integrated as to constitute a functional unit with properties not derivable from its parts in summation." Gestalt allows the thinker to synergistically visualize the whole greater than the individual parts of a problem.

Whatever it is called, don't run from the activity because this is where the right side of the brain finds freedom from the left side. It's an exercise in creativity.

This phase has several purposes. Foremost, it is an opportunity to take a stab at formulating the firm's strategy without the encumbrances of too much hard data and research—just think in the blue-sky. Later, in Chapter 19, you will learn how to compare these ideas with the analyzed data developed from Chapters 10–18 to determine gaps which then become short- and long-term objectives.

Agenda

This stage is acted out in a workshop atmosphere during which key players participate in pursuing an agenda that first reviews then gains agreement on time-present. Then, without the pressures of daily operations, the participants press on from the baseline to think about the future.

Day 1

- Review the homework of time-present.
- Discuss the collated strategic input gathered from the GFOT during stage 1.
- Discuss the collated input gained from supplemental opinions.
- Expected results: gain agreement on the time-present position of the organization.

Day 2

- Review mission statement.
- Establish spans of strategy.
- Discuss possible scenarios.
- List and explain assumptions.
- Desired results: choose and rank scenarios.

Day 3

- Discuss objectives.
- Discuss strategies.
- Discuss the appropriateness of matching various tactics to strategies.
- Desired results: tentative agreement on objectives, strategies, and tactics.

Global Family Opinion Team (GFOT)

Who formulates the strategy and policy that get done? Operators do! For the operators to take ownership of the new organization strategy they must participate in the process. Therefore those people who are in the actual day-to-day transactions of the firm must be involved. For this phase, the size of the GFOT may be reduced, but no one in a key position should be excluded.

All top-level business-unit managers and selected key employees from all major functional areas should participate. The formulation teams must include those who are business smart and have influence whether or not that is defined by an organization chart. You want the eventual plan to have every chance to succeed. If you exclude a player from the process who has informal influence, that person can derail months of conscientious effort. One of the intents of this process is to enhance the firm's collaborative experience related to its external strategy.

The participation of country managers is also essential. They bring to the formulation process a viewpoint of their culture and business methods, and an understanding of their market. This stage is also an opportunity for top management to display its motivation for the global strategic management process. It is a chance to show that strategy is not the exclusive terrain of the CEO and a small limited group.

GFOT Size

Team size is a variable. Each organization will tailor it to fit its practical setting. As a minimum the GFOT should have 10–12 regular members plus staff support. Subteams may be formed to certain aspects of strategy.

The Right Environment

Creativity is spontaneous. Little is known why or how it happens. It can take place on the noisiest New York subway or it could be a revelation in total seclusion.

Thomas Edison said that genius is 10 percent inspiration and 90 percent perspiration. Nevertheless, most people agree that physical environment and attitude have something to do with the process.

Physical Setting

Let's face it, the office is an unlikely place to think about strategy. The telephone rings, subordinates want solutions, and customers expect answers. Some preliminary work must be done in the office beforehand, but most firms have learned that the kind of thinking and open discussions leading to the best strategy takes place off site. Some go to the mountains, others to the seashore, while some small firms sequester the GFOT in a local hotel. The location need not be plush—in fact, it is better to trade off the cost of an expensive setting in order to have more people participate. To avoid the appearance of a home country or office, meetings should be moved around the world.

There are two times during the strategy formulation process when it is essential to have the undivided attention of the GFOT. The first is during the ad hoc visions phase. The second time is during Task 4 when the final mission, objectives, strategies, and tactics are established. During these two periods, in some creative way, key personnel should be out of their traditional work environment and allowed to participate in the strategy process. The payoff will be downstream sales and profits for the firm.

Mind-Set

Mind-set is an important ingredient for the process. Not everyone will see the global strategic management process in the same way. Some may make light of it, referring to it as a waste of time. Some may think it premature. Others may use time away from the office to spruce up their golf swing. But most will see it in the serious vein it is intended and give the process a fair chance.

Facilitation

Someone must direct the music to be played by the strategic formulation team and that person should *not* be the CEO. This is because the CEO will not get what he or she wants, and that is creative thinking. What the boss doesn't want is "me tooism." CEOs are, by definition, strong-willed people with high self-esteem and strong company orientation. The CEO must ensure that his or her dominance does not unduly influence the formulation process. This is typically done by allowing managers at all levels to participate and by selecting someone other than the CEO to facilitate the process.

By the same token do not try self-facilitation. It does not work! A facilitator is a must.

Some companies are large enough to have a planning staff at the corporate level. That department head can act as the facilitator. Most small firms appoint a key line or staff manager who not only understands the facilitation process, but also has the accommodating, patient nature required for the temporary duties. He or she also must want to do it. Obviously multiple teams require multiple facilitators, one per team. Many organizations invest in training in-house facilitators. Other firms hire an outside consultant who, for a fee, comes aboard for the duration of the formulation process and may stay through the implementation phase as well.

> *Consultant Checklist*
>
> - Must have a general management approach, not just human resource or financial management. (A former CEO would be ideal.)
> - Must have a methodology for assessing the level of motivation of individuals and groups.
> - Must be a pro at conflict-resolution techniques.
> - Must understand the levels of competition within the company.
> - Must contribute to the degree of cooperation in the organization.
> - Should make verbal reports every two weeks.
> - Should make written reports at end of every two months.

The facilitator's job is to keep the train on track, no more, no less. People who are accustomed to operating a business on a day-to-day basis can be overcome by detail at times when blue-sky thinking is needed. At other times, when detail is required, those same operators can be diverted into dreaming about big ideas that have already been cast off by the formulation team.

The job of the facilitator is to keep the process moving in productive directions and not get bogged down by one person's diatribe or misdirected thinking. This must be accomplished with the nicest sense of the players' feelings.

The process is not a high school exercise where popularity is important, yet we know that influence does play a part. People's feelings can be hurt and they can drop out of the participation process. No one should feel cornered in the sense that they feel they cannot, without undue chastisement by top players, give their free opinions.

The first job of the facilitator is to review the entire strategic process for the team. It is not sufficient to give the team only this chapter or an outline of it. There is no certainty that everyone will read the material. Therefore everyone may not get off to the same start. Certainly the team should have an outline of this material in advance of team sessions, but the facilitator must present the steps and be prepared to answer questions before the process begins.

Rules of the Game

One way around hurt feelings is to agree to a set of rules early in the process. Although not exhaustive, here are a few rules.

1. Speak only for yourself or for your business unit or department.
2. Let all ideas be freely entered into the process.
3. Agree to a cast-off rule; that is, a decision rule for which ideas eventually are recommended to top management and those which are cast off are given low priority.

Let the juices flow freely. Think in broadbrush, blue-sky terms. Get things out in the open. Think big. Think super. Think where you would like the firm to go in one, five, 10, 20, 50, or even 100 years as appropriate for your situation. Think about those who come after you. What can be done now to ensure the survival and growth of the firm they will inherit?

Results

Although not the final task of global strategy formulation, this ad hoc vision effort should at least be the first step at focusing the firm's direction. Everyone in the firm has a copy of the written agenda, but most also have an unwritten agenda of

FIGURE 8–1
Pyramidal Structure

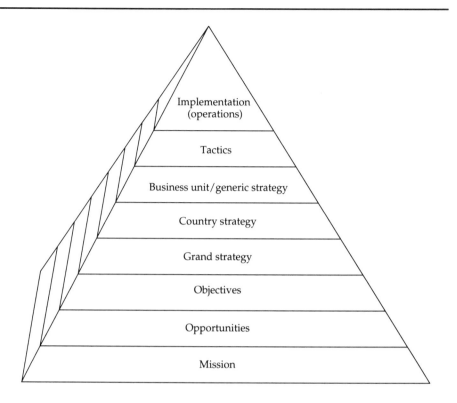

their own. The major result of this phase should be to get all views on the table and resolve any conflicts. Clarity of company thrust will result from reviewing and defining the company's global mission statement, stating tentative goals and objectives, thinking through strategies for various scenarios, and matching entry tactics with strategies.

Global Mission Statement

Company mission statements are usually fixed and seldom reconsidered; however, in the case of a firm going global it is not unusual to tear up the old and rewrite the new. Visualize the mission as the foundation of the firm's pyramidal structure. Figure 8–1 shows that without the foundation layer, the company's organization will crumble. The mission statement must be carefully worded so that it reflects the enduring direction of the company.

The global mission statement can be as simple as the one-paragraph model or it can have four paragraphs as shown in the following examples. Include any synonym you like: *worldwide, global, international,* and *cross-border* all establish the thrust into globalism.

SEARCH FOR OPPORTUNITIES

In its quest for a long-term strategy, the global organization is attempting to find the opportunities of the future. They will be discovered in terms of the factors of endowment: land, capital, labor, technology, know-how, intelligence, and market opportunities.

Examples of Opportunities

Opportunities are often exposed without the need for unusual analysis. For instance, it may be clear that there are only two products like yours in a given country or entry into a country is particularly easy.

Caution! Remember this process is about strategy; therefore, it is about future opportunities. That is not to say that something should not be done about an

---

One-Paragraph Model (Hewlett-Packard)

Hewlett-Packard is a major designer and manufacturer of electronic products and systems for measurement and computation. HP's basic business purpose is to provide the capabilities and services needed to help customers worldwide improve their personal and business effectiveness.

Multiparagraph Model (World Corp)

Preamble

We, the management of World Corp., here set forth ourt belief as to the purpose for which the company is established and the principles under which it should operate. We pledge our effort to the accomplishment of these purposes within these principles.

Basic Purpose

The basic purpose of World Corp. is to perpetuate an investor-owned company engaging in various phases of the computer software business, striving for balance among those phases so as to render needed satisfactory products and services and earn optimum, long-range profits.

What We Do

The principal business of the company, through its international representatives and subsidiaries, is the provision of computer software to meet the needs of ultimate consumers. To accomplish the basic purpose, and to ensure its strength, the company will engage in computer software related activities, directly or through subsidiaries or in participation with other persons, corporations, firms, or entities.

Where We Do It

The company's operations shall be worldwide. We impose no regulatory or geographical limitations on the acquisition, development, processing, transportation, or other ventures the company may engage. The company will engage in such activities in any location where, after careful review, it has determined that such activity is in the best interest of its stockholders.

---

immediate opportunity that is revealed. On the contrary, depending on company resources action should be taken immediately if it supports the organization's vision.

Opportunity Drivers

Chapters 10–18 explain a nine-step screening process and in-depth analysis of the global opportunity drivers: country needs, customers, product, suppliers, competitors, trade blocs, trade creation incentives, trade barriers, and harmony implications. Figure 8–2 shows a decision matrix useful for prioritizing the opportunities, country by country.

Strategic Visibility and Trend Analysis

Some options may seem overly simple. There is a tendency to shuffle away these alternatives. Be sure to identify and understand all options and the assumptions upon which the analysis was made. In some instances gaps will not be observable;

FIGURE 8–2
Global Strategic
Decision Matrix

Target countries	Country needs	Customers	Product	Suppliers	Competitors	Blocs	Trade incentives	Barriers	Harmony	Priority Go/No go
Home country										
Country 2										
Country 3										
Country 4										
Country 5										

however, don't overlook identifiable trends which can be converted to future opportunities.

Examples of Trends

1. Per capita income in Country A is increasing 15 percent a year.
2. Country B will be a market economy country in five years.
3. The political climate in Country C is stabilizing.
4. Technology is trending toward a particular direction.

Scenario Development

Several phases of strategy building require scenario building. This is the process of asking what if. Because you are trying to project into the future, nothing can be stated with certainty. Often the best we can do is develop scenarios based on our estimates and assign probabilities. The prioritized scenarios then become the basis for the firm's strategy.

Visualize scenarios upon which to base your strategy. What are the major issues? Revisit those developed in Task 2, time-present homework. Do they still hold? Do new scenarios come to mind? This is the time to refine scenarios. Think of regional as well as global scenarios. As shown in Figure 8–3, look for branching points for your scenarios. For each country, list the assumptions on which your scenarios are based.

Examples of Scenarios

1. The EC meets its goals for 1992 and one year later agrees to admit Turkey.
2. The ASEAN bloc forms and establishes subsidies for conversion of space technology into commercial products.
3. If a certain technology proves valid, Products A, B, and C will be competitive in Countries X, Y, and Z.

FIGURE 8–3
Scenarios

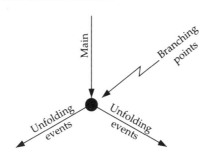

Assumptions

Scenarios are pictures of the future considering certain conditions. Those conditions should be listed in the form of assumptions associated with each scenario and objective developed during this task.

Recommendations

Now have the GFOT try its hand at defining some strategic objectives. Remember, for the purposes of this book, goals and objectives are synonymous. Based on the mission statement and goals the GFOT should offer strategies to accomplish those objectives. Near-term objectives, should be specific; long-term goals can be general.

SUMMARY

From the baseline of where the organization is today, the formulation process begins with a homework phase during which the opinion of in-house talent is gathered through questionnaires in advance of an off-site workshop. In addition to these opinions, many organizations use one or more methods to gain supplemental opinions, such as the Delphi technique and focus groups. All of the opinions from the homework phase are then collated and presented to the GFOT participants during the workshop.

The desired results of the workshop include a review of the organization's mission statement, various scenarios of the future, potential objectives, strategies, and tentative tactics that match the strategies.

CHECKLIST

- Have all aspects of Task 2 (time-present homework) been completed prior to the scheduled off-site workshop of Task 3 (mapping time-future)?
- Have the pre-workshop time-present questionnaires been collated for presentation during the ad hoc workshop?
- Have all aspects of phase 1 of Task 3 been completed and collated prior to the off-site workshop?
- Have the homework results been developed in such a form that they can be presented to the GFOT in a professional way during the first day of phase 2?
- Does the agenda for the workshop allow sufficient time for groups to discuss scenarios and gain tentative agreement about the organization's mission statement, objectives, strategies, and appropriate tactics?
- Has a nonpartisan facilitator allowed all GFOT members to fully participate in the workshop by getting early agreement on a set of rules?
- Is the site conducive to strategic thinking?

Chapter 9

Intelligence

The time has come to build a new world economy based on today's realities.

Lester C. Thurow, Ph.D., *Dean, Alfred P. Sloan School of Management, M.I.T.*

This chapter discusses the third stage of Task 3, mapping time-future. This chapter explains how to fulfill your strategic intelligence needs by providing a methodology and by defining the various data sources including HUMINT (primary human intelligence) and the many computer banks available.

One of the things that has certainly altered the way we work and do business is the evolution of intelligence technology. Stage 3 is about a systematic means of monitoring the international economic system in such a way that intelligence needed by top management about threats and opportunities can be collected and analyzed.

Intelligence is so vital to the global strategist it has become the sixth factor of production, that is, land, labor, capital, technology, management, and intelligence. For the strategist the concept of intelligence goes beyond just information gathering. Picture in your mind stacks of books, periodicals, technical journals, government records, and reports. Anyone can fill a room with information. But intelligence must complement the global strategic management process—it must be focused toward the long-term strategy of the organization.

Intelligence Mapping

Like the military, modern business intelligence not only gathers, it maps. It surveys, explores, and analyzes, then it makes an assessment of the information from all available sources. Intelligence is action information that goes beyond simple collection into estimating the implications related to intentions and vulnerabilities, as well as to the bottom line.

Global intelligence is more complex because it incorporates additional volumes of information related to other countries. The problem grows when you add language, cultural differences, and multiple markets. It can also be illusive, because some countries have less resources available to expend on gathering data and making it available. Nevertheless, data sources are available and tapping that data is an art form in itself.

Ethics

Even though it conjures thoughts of CIA, spies, and dirty tricks, intelligence is not a dirty word. The intelligence process is quite ethical; it's the users who sometimes lose their sense of values. At the outset I wish to stress the need for even stronger ethical behavior in the international setting, because trust is the foundation of all business relationships.

The half-life of secrets is very short, so intelligence is not about secrets. You can't run a business on secrets. Besides virtually all intelligence is public information. What you need is the right stuff for an analysis so you can use your brain to minimize or avoid risk and to make the best forecast of the future.

Time

Management must realize that the intelligence collection and analysis process takes time. It is not an event that can be turned on instantaneously. It is a growing necessity in most organizations and should be ongoing in support of operations as well as strategic planning. Developing an in-house intelligence function also takes time to grow. Some believe it takes three to five years to mature. The organization may not get an instantaneous return on its investment, but eventually the results will make a difference.

Management can assist in the timeliness of good intelligence by identifying issues early on and by ensuring that the function is included as part of the global strategic process. Some organizations establish global watch lists that focus continuous scanning on certain geographical regions or specific business drivers such as World Bank loans, loans by other supranational lenders, or industry-specific R&D breakthroughs.

Location

Some large organizations have centralized programs at the corporate level; however, day-to-day knowledge of customers and competitors is found in the far reaches of the organization. Although each situation is different, I do not recommend the development of a single large data base. It is better to tap many smaller sources closer to the battle lines.

METHODOLOGY

Global screening (mapping) is the continuous and systematic gathering, recording, and analyzing of data about problems relating to the manufacture and marketing of goods and services in the international competitive setting. It is the process of supplying information for strategic and tactical business decisions, and those decisions can be about planning, problem solving, or performance control. It can be a one-time response to a particular question, but it is most often an incremental, systematic, and methodical collection of all relevant information in an attempt to create a holistic, future picture of the firm in the global setting. In Japan this is a major organizational function in all banks and major companies.

In the context of mapping time-future, intelligence should be correlated to but not restrained by, the results of stages 1 and 2. In other words, data collection should be targeted toward the scenarios developed in strategic workshops and the ultimate corporate strategies, but not limited such that significant opportunities or potential disasters not foreseen by management are not brought to light. Bad news must be presented along with the good news.

Mapping is a systematized method of analysis and assessment that permits management to identify and prioritize a number of desirable markets by eliminating those judged to be less attractive. You should think of this as a building process wherein the researcher starts with a problem and ends with a presentation of the findings to top management. The methods have been perfected in modern business, and the risk of not doing research is loss of profits and time. This does not mean that all intelligence begins with a cold deck. Actually the process should be ongoing, with periodic pauses for summation. Classically, the approach to intelligence collection and analysis has seven steps.

1. Define the problem.
2. Develop a research plan.
3. Identify data sources.
4. Collect the data.
5. Analyze the data.
6. Interpret the data.
7. Present the results for application (decision making).

| *Strategic Intelligence Needs* | Mapping is the essential element of building a global strategy because it is the basis for educated forecasts, scenario building, and informed decision making. It also provides early warning of dangers ahead. A strong intelligence base allows you to specifically define the firm's environment instead of referring to it in generalities. |

But information is of no value if you cannot appreciate what it means. Understanding data is vital; in fact, an analyst cannot even know what to collect unless he or she understands the underlying issues.

Figure 9–1 shows the nine-step screening process explained in Chapters 10–18. The global strategist must sort through volumes of information in these nine vital mapping areas. This method provides a systematic way to understand the data and provides for competent mapping.

SOURCES

Many industrialized countries such as the United States are information rich. Government information is a major source in democratic nations. But how else can citizens remain informed? Less-developed nations suffer from a lack of funds to build this necessary ingredient for business success. Nevertheless, there are many ways to gather that which is needed.

Primary Data

Human intelligence is the richest source of solid intelligence. The firm's marketing department usually has a broad network of employees who can scan the marketplace on a regular basis for customer as well as competitor changes. Salespersons should be trained to assist your intelligence program.

Remember that the intelligence process is not just a collection process. It must be seen as a two-way street wherein the intelligence function feeds back to operators who are often the best source. To do this, many firms have established a computer network using electronic mail software that permits easy access and the ability to share internal documents. One such system is the Business Information Exchange™ which is a menu-driven, full-text data base operating within ALL-IN-1™ electronic mail. It uses Synchrony™ software from Henco Software, Inc. for synthesis of full-text information.

Your intelligence will be focused on your firm's specific needs. You will want to know what people think about your product, prices, and promotion. Primary data are gathered directly from the people who know—the customers.

GFOT

Another important way to gather primary data is through your own GFOT. Everyone in the firm should be encouraged to be on the lookout for and collect intelligence about their segment of the business.

Market Research

Formal market research programs using specially designed instruments are also necessary. These should be carefully designed because people in different countries react differently and have varying views about responding to data collection. In some countries responses are driven by culture where a polite answer is given no matter what a person's real feelings might be. In other countries the suspicion of government is very high, yet in others illiteracy is the significant barrier.

Secondary Data

Most research begins with secondary data, that is publications, journals, periodicals, official government documents, and so on. In advanced countries there is a wealth of material, but for most world markets there is a serious shortage of secondary data. Nations with low per capita income have commensurately smaller government budgets to collect and analyze statistical data. For example, some countries have never taken a census. Others have few publications which deal in the kind of information you might need.

FIGURE 9–1
Nine-Step, Global, Time-Future
Intelligence Screening Process

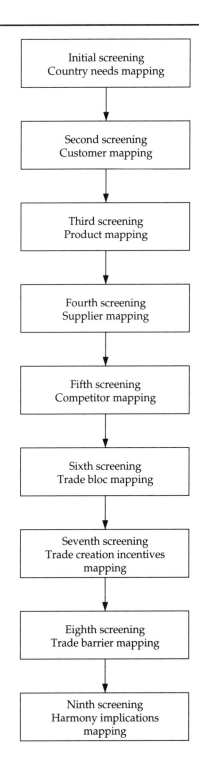

Libraries

Libraries—public, private, and university—are the source of most intelligence. A strong understanding of how to use a library and a good relationship with the staff pays dividends in terms of time. Most data are not in automated data bases. Many data are published in newspapers, magazines, technical journals, annual reports, and government reports and records, all of which can be found in libraries.

Data Bases   Automated data bases are growing worldwide. More information is found in computers linked by communications networks. Careful selection of key words will save you money and time.

Language   In lieu of readily available information, researchers may have to design data-collection instruments. The sequence for this effort is to design, translate, test, redesign, retest, conduct the study, then finally translate back to the parent language. Needless to say communications and primary data collection are compounded when a country has several languages.

Communications   Probably the most frustrating condition for the international intelligence-gatherer is the lack of modern communications. In some countries customers do not have telephones and the mail systems are unreliable. Data then have to be developed from street questionnaires or interviews gathered in popular metropolitan areas. Then the data must be extrapolated for the country as a whole.

Service Companies   Many small firms do not have a corporate-level, intelligence-gathering capability other than that which may have been developed in their domestic marketing department. Even then, most marketing organizations are often no more than a sales effort. Salespeople lack the time or the opportunity to be isolated long enough to take on the kind of research and analysis necessary to bring about thoughtful information for decision making.

Many firms are well advised to contract with a private service company that specializes in international research. These firms have the experience to not only gather and sift through the magnitude of information, but also to tailor the analysis to the specific needs of the client.

Offline Data Sources   Much of the information needed to forecast global strategic decisions is held in offline data sources by embassies, or in paper media, and in special library collections.

Embassies and Consulates   Most embassies and some consulates have on staff a foreign commercial officer whose job is to assist firms to export goods from that country. Often solicitation of information from these officers results in significant data about businesses and opportunities.

Banks and Trade Ministries.

Bank of Korea	Kotra
Trade Ministry	Jetro
Commerce Ministry	Japanese Keidanren
World Bank	International Bank of Japan
Mexican-American Chamber of Commerce	International Monetary Fund

Special Collection Libraries.

- Harvard's Yenching Collection (Cambridge, Massachusetts) is an important source about China.
- The University of California at San Diego has an excellent collection on Mexico.

To unlock the U.S. government's treasure chest of information, call the office of Business Liaison in Washington, D.C., at (202) 482-3176. Ask for a copy of the *Business Services Directory*.

- The African and Middle Eastern Division of the Library of Congress in Washington, D.C., is very good.
- The American Academy of Asian Studies Library in San Francisco is noteworthy.
- The Latin American Data Bank Library at the University of Florida in Gainesville should be examined.
- The Hudson Institute in Indianapolis and the Brookings Institute in Washington, D.C., are both very good.

You can also contact the following organizations.

- London Business School Information Service. Tel: 011-44-71-724-2300; FAX: 011-44-71-706-1897.
- University of Warwick Business Information Service. Tel: 011-44-203-523-251; FAX: 011-44-203-524-211.
- Manchester Business School Information Service. Tel: 011-44-61-275-6502; FAX: 011-44-61-273-7732.
- The British Library Business Information Service. Tel: 011-44-71-323-7457; FAX: 011-44-71-323-7453.
- British Library Science Reference and Information Service. Tel: 011-44-71-323-7926; FAX: 011-44-71-323-7930.
- The Economist Intelligence Unit (EIU). Tel: 1-800-938-4685; FAX: 1-212-505-1895.

Journals, Periodicals, and News Services.

Daily newspapers	*International Business Week*
Trade publications	*Toyo Keizai*
Government publications	*Business Week*
Conference Board	*Financial Times*
Economist	*Forbes*
Fortune	*Moody's Corporate News-International*
Dun's Market Identifiers	*Citibank World Outlook*
Moody's Investors Manuals	*The Journal of Commerce*
World Construction	*Nilekei*

Overseas Business Reports, Global Surveys, and *Country Market Sectoral Surveys* all available from the U.S. Department of Commerce

The Wall Street Journal (Asian and European editions)

Canadian Business (ranks the leading 500 Canadian firms like *Fortune*)

Extel (a British publication similar to *Moody's Investors*)

The worldwide yellow pages being compiled by International Business Clearinghouse, Western Union, and ITT

BBC's External New Services

Foreign Periodical Services such as the German News Company and Overseas Courier Service

Online Data Sources	There is a growing amount of information in computer banks around the world. Here is a partial list of how to tap those sources.

Infonet. An advanced telecommunications support center established in Brussels will serve global companies that use Notice 400 messaging service and electronic mail software, global public data network, notebook network, private data network, and enterprise-defined hybrid or private network services. This toll-free number is available for European users.

U.S. Data Bases

NEXIS/LEXIS. A full text data base of journals, newspapers, and documents about news and law.

DIALOG. The world's largest bibliographical data base system. DIALOG contains over 320 individual data bases covering nearly every topic in abstract form.

European Community Data Bases

To tap into these data bases, contact the Commission of the European Communities Eurobases 200, Rue de la Loi B-1049 Brussels, Belgium. The telephone number of the Data Base Help Desk in Brussels is 011-32-2 235-00-01

Celex. European Community law including a file on Member States' measures of implementation of community directive; contains full-text abstracts of EC laws, treaties, and preparatory documents.

Scad. References to both official EC documents and articles from over 2000 periodicals; contains 80,000 citations to articles, publications, and documents covering the EC.

Info92. Easy-to-use, menu-driven data base on the completion of internal markets.

Eclas. Bibliographic data base of the Commission library; contains over 90,000 records covering all aspects of the EC, including statistical publications, monographs, documents, and articles from periodicals.

Rapid. Full text of press release material from the EC spokesperson's service; updated daily.

European Community Host Organization (ECHO) Service

To make use of the following data bases, call ECHO Luxembourg at 011-352-488-041.

Brokersguide. Contains references to 800 EC information brokers; includes individuals, companies, and organizations and their areas of specialization.

Dianeguide. Describes more than 650 data bases that hold EC information.

Euristote. Contains 10,000 citations with abstracts on current and completed EC research.

Eurodicautom. Contains 420,000 translations of EC terms and phrases.

Japanese Data Base

The Cosmos2 (Japanese Corporate Information File) is now available in the English language under the name "Teikoku Databank: Japanese Companies" for online access via Dialog.

> *EC Information in the United States*
>
> - American National Standards Institute
>   Tel: 202-639-4090; FAX: 202-434-8240
> - European Community Delegation
>   Tel: 202-862-9500; FAX: 202-429-1766
> - Office of European Community Affairs
>   Single Internal Market: 1992 Information Service (SIMIS)
>   Tel: 202-482-5276; FAX: 202-482-2155
> - U.S. Chamber of Commerce, International Division
>   Tel: 202-463-5460; FAX: 212-463-3114

SUMMARY

Let there be no doubt about the importance of mapping information. Intelligence is no longer a nice thing to have. It is the sixth factor of production; in fact, it may rank higher in priority than capital and technology. Your survival in the global setting depends on it.

CHECKLIST

- Does your intelligence program complement your global strategic management process?
- Do you have an action plan for your intelligence program?
- Is your program an ongoing process of building a base of knowledge from human intelligence sources as well as collecting information from secondary sources?
- Is management supporting the intelligence program by defining issues in time for you to act?
- Have you considered electronic, computer-aided intelligence as a two-way method between operators and intelligence?

Chapter 10

Initial Screening: Country Potential

To maintain a leadership position in any one developed country a business. . . increasingly has to attain and hold leadership positions in all developed countries worldwide. It has to be able to do research, to design, to develop, to engineer, and to manufacture in any part of the developed world, and to export from any developed country to any other. It has to go transnational.

Peter F. Drucker, *Clarke Professor of Social Sciences at the Claremont Graduate School*

The context of global strategic management is the world view. So picture yourself high above the earth looking down on a world of about 200 nation-state markets and an untold number of subcountry markets. Even within a subcountry market there are subsets of customers and competitors. Each market is different, each holds more or less appeal for your company's products. Your intelligence collection will, of course, be company and industry specific.

Today, if you are a U.S. manufacturer your primary market may be North America, but tomorrow it might be Japan, Germany, or even the former Soviet Union. As much as 75 percent of the global market lies beyond the borders of America.

If you are a Middle Eastern manufacturer your major market may be Europe. If you are a Mexican manufacturer, your best future market may be the United States.

INITIAL SCREENING

Approach strategic market mapping in a common-sense way. Where will the best country markets for my products be in the future? What are the trends? You may think the answer is simple and say "my home market." But in the future that may not make the best business sense. It may be a comfortable decision because there are no cultural or currency problems, but it may not keep you in business during the era of global interdependency.

The issues are: Who will have the money, in the future, to buy my product? What product will satisfy their want? Even if there is a need and a market in the home country there may be a better and larger market in another country.

A practical model for the market-mapping process includes the following:

1. What are the implications of a changing world?
2. What will happen to the third world?
3. What are the implications of the haves and have-nots?
4. What about Asia; the Five Tigers and Japan?
5. What are the size and structures of the new world order?
6. What will be predictable about the 21st century?

Figure 10–1 shows this subscreening process.

FIGURE 10–1
Country-Screening Process

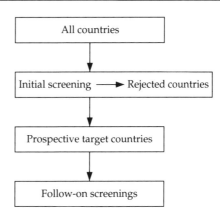

COUNTRY TRENDS

The ad hoc workshop, discussed in Chapter 8, produced several scenarios and country strategies which were the result of in-house knowledge and supplemental opinions. Begin this step of the intelligence-screening process with the information gained from the GFOT workshop. Intelligence mapping must be focused. But don't limit yourself to only the results of the workshop because your research may uncover opportunities others have overlooked.

For purposes of formulating global strategy through the country-mapping process, you will find that not all nations are equal. Similarly, not all cities, communities, and markets are equal. Some countries are wealthy; some are in abject grinding poverty, destitution, and squalor. Your trend analysis should follow a pattern such as this one.

- Climate.
- Geography.
- Topography.
- Natural resources.
- Country classification.
- Per capita income.
- Gross national product.
- Free market development.
- Trade theory.
- Government intervention.
- Entrepreneurship.
- Type of industry.

- Political stability.
- Population.
- Classes.
- Management.
- Education.
- Technology.
- Business maturity.
- Financial structures.
- Inflation.
- Exchange rate.
- Credit availability.
- Global business strategies.

Climate

What are the temperature, humidity, and seasons of your target countries? What are the implications of climate to your product line?

Geography

This refers to both the in-country geography and the country's relation to the rest of the earth. Because most of the developed countries are in the Northern Hemisphere and most of the developing nations are in the Southern Hemisphere, the terms *north* and *south* are often used as identifiers. This may not affect your product line, but it could change your priorities.

Certain aspects of in-country geography may affect your product, such as rivers and ports for delivery. The country's relationship to its neighbors may be a bonus for distribution. You should also be interested in the location of major urban areas.

TABLE 10–1
Country Classification Trends

Global business	Technology	Education	Management	Classes	Population/Unemployment	Political stability	Type of industry	Entrepreneurship	Trade theory	Free markets	Geography	GDP	Per capita income
Mature	High	High	High	3	Low/Low	High	Service/Manufacturing	High	Outward	High	North	Developed	High
Maturing	Medium	Medium	Medium	2 ½	Average/Low	Medium	Manufacturing	Medium	Mixed	Medium		Developing	Middle
Maturing	Low	Low	Low	2	High/High	Low	Agriculture	Low	Inward	Low	South	Under-developed	Low

Topography

Are there mountains or desert? What difference could that make for your products? Is it easy to get from one urban area to another?

Natural Resources

What are the natural resources of the countries that your potential marketing targets? Do the resources complement your products?

Market Research

The position of nations in terms of growth are classified in many ways. No matter how they are labeled, no inference of superiority or inferiority is intended. Table 10–1 shows these groupings as they relate to the various ways to measure a nation's business potential.

Per Capita Income

Of course people have varying amounts of personal wealth. Some countries have three classes: the rich, the middle class, and the poor. In those countries even the size of the classes vary. Others have only two classes: rich and poor. Nations can be classified by per capita income as high income, middle income, or low income. Some believe there are only two groups: the haves and the have-nots. Today, the average annual income of people in countries can be as little as $400 per year to as much as $20,000 per year.

Who are the developed, developing, and underdeveloped?   None of the classifications are accurate. There are no finite divisions. Not only do country groupings blend, but the positions of nations on lists move all the time. Countries graduate to higher rates of growth while others, as a result of competition, natural disasters, or war, are demoted.

Developed nations (high income).   In this category we include nations whose citizens have at least $2,000 per capita income. This includes Canada and the United States, all of Western Europe, Australia, Israel, Japan, New Zealand, and South Africa.

Developing nations (middle income).   This grouping includes those countries where the people have a per capita income greater than $400 but less than $2,000. It includes the Organization of Petroleum Exporting Countries (OPEC) and the Newly Industrialized Countries (NIC) such as Singapore, South Korea, Thailand, Taiwan, and Hong Kong.

Underdeveloped.   This group includes 36 or so of the poorest nations whose people have per capita incomes less than $400. Most are in Africa, but a few like Afghanistan, Bangladesh, Bhuta, India, Laos, and Nepal are in Asia. Haiti is the only country in the Western Hemisphere so classified by the United Nations.

Graduation.   Graduation is the assumption that individual developing countries are capable of assuming greater responsibilities and obligations in the international community. Within GATT, UNCTAD, and the World Bank there are rules for graduation that relate to import restrictions, the Generalized System of Preferences, and low-interest loans. As developing nations advance their standard of living, donor countries may remove the more advanced from these special eligibility programs. The World Bank may also move a graduated country from dependence on concessional grants to nonconcessional loans.

> The peaceful revolution of 1989 saw the beginning of a movement from Marxism toward market theory. But in Central and Eastern Europe *perestroika* is suffering in its attempt to leap forward from state enterprise to private ownership. Because there are few entrepreneurs and little private capital, the immediate mechanism, more likely, adopted by these nations will be a hybrid mixture of Marxist-market which takes the best of the two theories for the good of the economic growth of the regional nations. The ultimate change to privatization could take two or more decades.

Demotion.   Of course the reverse can also happen: A nation can be demoted in terms of need due to a reversal of economic conditions. In such a case the nation may become the recipient of economic assistance from various supranational organizations and developed nations.

Gross National Product (GNP)

The United Nations organizes countries by GNP in terms of developed, developing, or underdeveloped. But what are the implications of the future? Are your target nations on the move? How soon will they graduate to a higher level of economic development? What will be the major sources of future income?

Free Market Development

Typically the people of developed nations have money, so you should logically expect those nations to have the greatest market potential. Developing countries might have average or low market potential. The major consumer markets of the world coincide with the most developed nations, which coincides with a leverage toward free markets. Europe, North America, and Japan dominate because they are highly industrialized, and the people there have funds to spend.

Markets are created by entrepreneurs—the miracle workers of the world—the heros of international trade. By making something and selling it all over the world they create jobs. And people with jobs are consumers—they have money. The entrepreneur's motive is *profit*. It is a good word and worn as a badge on all employees of any private firm. It is a proud motive because it creates jobs and is the major contributor to global welfare. Because private sector job creation plays such a major part in your global strategy, your firm will be linked to the growth development process.

The period from 1945 until the beginning of the new century has been cited as the most revolutionary period in world history. During that time the United States rose to economic eminence espousing a laissez-faire economic policy. Simultaneously there were major changes in Asian country growth patterns. Europe's international trade grew at phenomenal rates. Trading blocs began to form, and the world witnessed the significant and sometimes chaotic changes in central and Eastern Europe.

Two Worlds from Three

The year 1989 was one of the most significant years of the 20th century. It was the year the Berlin Wall crumbled signifying the peaceful revolution of central European nations retreating from nonmarket economics. Even more significant was 1991. It was the year the Soviet Union splintered into its individual parts. It was the year the world sifted into two worlds.

Figure 10–2 shows and describes the new nation-markets. Figure 10–3 is a pictorial of the western, free market countries organized by per capita income alongside those of the nonmarket nations.

FIGURE 10-2
New Nation Markets

Central Europe

Poland. Aggressive; stores full of people with no money; racing to export; big debt; be creative.

Czechoslovakia. Healthiest; political turmoil caused split into two countries; most industrial before World War II; has a capitalistic memory; aggressive; wants western goods; will import; privatizing over 3,000 large enterprises; welcomes all kinds of investment.

Hungary. Aggressive; big debt; racing for western markets; will import; has currency in foreign banks.

Rumania. Cheap wages ($15/month); western goods are scarce; making progress.

Yugoslavia. Civil war; turmoil; bank ranking slipping fast.

Bulgaria. High debt load; still has Communist potential.

Albania. Least opportunity.

Eastern Europe

Estonia. Per capita GNP approximately $6,240; reform oriented; business minded; industrial; infrastructure; entrepôt of high-tech services and industry.

Latvia. Per capita GNP approximately $6,740; corridor for former Soviet Union; enthusiasm for western things; moving to privatize; attracting foreign investors for full ownership and repatriation of profits.

Lithuania. Per capita GNP approximately $5,880; moving toward Scandinavian-style economy; limited comprehension of market economy; some privatization.

Byelorussia. Per capita GNP approximately $5,960; railroad center for linking many industrial cities; investors attracted to timber.

Ukraine. Per capita GNP approximately $4,700; second most powerful new nation.

Georgia. Per capita GNP approximately $4,410; rapid privatization with focus on Black Sea access and steel.

Maldavia. Per capita GNP approximately $3,830; moving toward privatization

Russia. Per capita GNP approximately $5,810; most politically powerful; sweeping economic reforms; broad privatization; shortages; many joint venture opportunities; investors may buy hard currency and repatriate profits and dividends; foreign trade activity authorized; 280 million people on a land mass three times greater than the United States.

Azerbaijan. Per capita GNP approximately $3,750; population 7 million; large oil producer; grows cotton, grapes, and silk.

Kazakhstan. Per capita GNP approximately $3,720; population 16.6 million; large oil and coal producer; grew one third of former Soviet Union's wheat.

Kirghizia. Per capita GNP approximately $3,030; population 4.3 million; mines coal and mercury ore; produces cotton.

Tadzhakistan. Per capita GNP approximately $2,340; population 5.1 million; produced 11 percent of the former Soviet Union's cotton.

Turkmenistan. Per capita GNP approximately $3,370; population 3.5 million; largest sulfur deposits in the world; largest cotton producer in the world.

Uzbekistan. Per capita GNP approximately $2,750; population 19.9 million; grows 67 percent of the former Soviet Union's cotton.

TRADE THEORIES

Another measure of economic growth may be attributed to the adoption of one international trade theory over another. Those nations that adopted Adam Smith's free market theory and outward orientation have developed at faster rates than those that adopted Marxism and inward trade orientation.

Inward Orientation

Some have-nots argue that inward orientation is the cause of underdevelopment. That is a strategy which biases government incentives in favor of domestic strategy and against global business. Those against this strategy believe that it tends to turn people, businesses, and governments inward causing them to become absorbed in getting through the day, paying the bills, and meeting immediate obligations. Inward theories involve overt, high protectionism and are often

FIGURE 10–3
Global Economic System

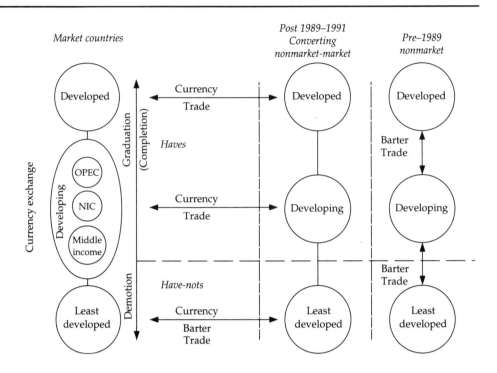

associated with high inflation and extensive bureaucracies. These government strategies gradually cause businesses and nations to become isolated and self-absorbed. Their intellectual and emotional horizons shrink, and they lose contact with the world outside themselves becoming myopic to their larger meanings and roles.

Outward Orientation

An outward strategy is characterized as being neutral between productivity in the domestic and export market. The haves argue that outward orientation brings growth. Because international trade is encouraged, outward orientation is often, though sometimes misleadingly, referred to as an export promotion strategy.

Import Substitution

Import substitution is a strategic attempt by a nation to reduce imports (and hence foreign exchange expenditures) by encouraging the development of domestic industries. These government strategies are extremely protectionist because they restrict imports of consumer goods. Local manufacturers are encouraged to replace the imports. This is known as adopting the theory of import substitution. Because there is less competition, this theory tends to build high-cost industries that eventually become a drag on the economy and bring high prices to consumers. An additional pitfall is that, over time, products without competition become nonexportable because they have lost world-class quality.

*Infant Industry
Argument (Peril Point)*

Infant industry argument is the view that temporary protection for a new industry or firm in a particular country through tariff and nontariff barriers to imports can help it become established and eventually competitive in world markets. Peril point is a hypothetical limit beyond which a reduction in tariff protection would cause injury to a domestic industry.

Grappling with a global economy and an emerging democracy, Mexico, under President Salinas, is attempting to move rapidly from nearly eight years of crisis marked by stagnation and inflation toward an outward orientation. By dropping barriers and eliminating protections for the country's domestic producers, the nation's policies now encourage an export strategy and an open invitation for foreign investment which could make Mexico a world-class trading partner, create jobs, and raise the standard of living for its citizens.

The counterargument is that industries which have been established and operated with heavy dependence on direct or indirect government subsidies or similar protection have found it difficult to relinquish that support. It is better that uncompetitive businesses decline naturally and government support be thrown to new competitive industries.

Government Intervention Governments attempt to artificially steer and guide the development of nations. Political motives vary, but in general the intent is to ensure that whatever wealth accrues within the borders is distributed according to the needs and preferences of the people of the sovereign lands. In practice the people's preferences vary greatly.

Markets are artificially stimulated through a process known as growth or economic development. This is a comprehensive term which includes the many improvements to a nation such as infrastructure, education, and capital formation. But the major element of economic development is business development. Economic development is measured in terms of growth because the intent of most governments is for nations to have a continuing rise of per capita income through improved techniques of production and marketing.

Growth or economic development has different meanings for different people. For the international economist it typically means the improvement of growth for what are conventionally called the least developed countries. For the local politician it may simply mean creating jobs for his or her constituency—they may not even know the process has a name. For still others economic development means land reform and the redistribution of agribusiness.

It is not unusual that nations formulate development strategies. Therefore international trade is extremely regulated by interstate (national) controls and is intimately linked to economic development.

Country market mapping keys business strategy to the economic condition of nations. Therefore understanding the theories and beliefs that drive interstate controls is essential. In fact, all global business strategy should begin with: What does the country want?

Some country markets are freer than others and regulation of international trade varies. Few, if any, adhere to pure laissez-faire trade policies. Most manipulate the market in major ways.

Many of your strategic and tactical business decisions will be based on economic development schemes presented by governments. The primary influence of country strategy is a combination of theory and whatever works for a given nation.

Your firm was founded and headquartered in a country that adopted both a general and international trade theory. Until you began to think global, you may not have had to consider other strategies, but now you will be operating your business all over the world.

Figure 10–4 shows the primary spectrum of general economic theories as they relate to control by governments. Your strategic plan must include a discussion of your markets and competitors. For the global business a major segment must include strategies about which countries your firm will do business in, and how to deal with the interstate controls of these nations.

Extrapolating Business Strategy

By closely monitoring and analyzing changing theoretical concepts, the modern global business strategist can proactively anticipate government strategy changes, identify profitable ventures, and satisfy owner expectations. In the case of a global business, as it expands its international reach, the strategic decision to enter a country requires an examination of the laws and regulations and the underlying theories generally professed by the strategy and policymakers. By extrapolation, the company can decide whether to do business in a given country at all, and if so, to design business tactics that accommodate those strategies. In other words, business managers monitor for changes in the political thinking of the rulers of nations, then tailor business strategy country by country.

Too many global managers focus only on their own business, its competitors, and its industrial environment. They roll with the punches of governments, accepting political strategies and interstate controls as they are. Because international trade is so regulated, however, it is incumbent upon today's managers of small as well as large companies to be proactive instead of reactive by imparting their ideas to elected officials who often have little or no understanding of the realities of private sector business.

Entrepreneurship

On the overall, nations which place greater emphasis and reward on entrepreneurship have achieved higher growth rates.

Type of Industry

Nothing is discussed more among social scientists and economists than the changing environment of growing nations. Some suggest that nations begin their growth as agricultural based, move through an industrial stage, then arrive at a postindustrial stage where the industry is more service oriented than manufacturing.

Political Risk

A high degree of political stability is generally recognized as a prerequisite of growth. Countries that have frequent coups and revolutions tend to be less developed than those that change peacefully through democratic processes.

Political risk (other synonymous terms are *country* risk, *sovereign* risk, and *noneconomic* or *nonbusiness* risks) mostly conveys a negative connotation related to major political events such as coups and wars. In recent times analysts have attached the term to the barriers and incentives given and taken away by government actions. Appendix E shows one such political risk forecast chart.

The haves say the economic conditions of the have-nots are brought about by not having political stability. There is a long list of methodologies the haves use to analyze political risk. They use either quantitative, hard, and objective data; qualitative, soft, and subjective data; or mixed data to assess, forecast, and manage the risk of doing business in certain countries. Typically these studies focus on government actions. Soft data are based on the expert advice of the GFOT. Hard data, dominated by the banking industry, are the result of quantifying data in indices, ranking countries, econometric models, computer models, and statistical appraisals.

In reality political risk is about the relationship of politics to the economy. It is a company-specific risk that managers face.

Obviously for the global business, political risk is a major element to mapping a given country. Things to look for include the following:

FIGURE 10–4
Government Economic Control

Least control	Capitalism
	Socialism
	Sociocapitalistic
Most control	Marxism

1. Creditworthiness and the ability to obtain hard currency.
2. Government actions related to your business.
3. Political and societal changes which significantly alter the rules of the game.

Population

Much of the literature about population points to an inverse relationship between population growth and economic development. Nations experiencing low or no population growth have less unemployment and are better off than those with high population growth rates.

Classes

Economies tend to do better when a nation has a strong middle class. Yet there are still some countries that have been unable to cast off religious or colonial roots that brought only two classes, the rich and the poor.

Management

Included in the definition of management is the concept of knowing how to handle day-to-day problems, and having the know-how of finance, production, and strategic planning. These skills are typically found in the higher classifications of economic growth.

Education

Defining what is meant by education is often difficult. Do we mean trainable, quantity, quality, or methods? For purposes of economic development we mean education throughout the population spectrum not just the elite class. Educated people are capable of responding to an increasingly complex scientific, social, and technical life.

Technology

Those nations that place high value on human capital leading to education, inventiveness, and technology have higher growth than those that don't.

Business Maturity

With the expansion of global businesses, I suggest there is a new classification with only two descriptions of nations: matured business countries and maturing business countries. Closely related to entrepreneurship, this classification focuses on the success a nation has had in developing outward-oriented businesses capable of taking products to global markets.

Financial Structures

This part of the mapping process includes an analysis of the trends related to the banking industry, stock markets, and the growth of equity financing structures that are available to support global ventures.

Inflation

To what extent are your target country markets experiencing inflation and what is the trend? What would be the implications of those trends for your organization?

Exchange Rates

Stability of exchange rates is the foundation of international trade. Therefore of major importance are issues of convertibility and fluctuations as they relate to your organization's strategy.

Credit Availability

Nations have credit ratings just as people and businesses do. Therefore when targeting country markets, consider an assessment of credit availability.

Adopting Global Business

The concept of adopting cross-border industries or global businesses is spreading rapidly. The extent countries are encouraging this strategy for certain businesses implies a receptiveness to foreign entry.

Rank Among Other Potential Markets

This screening step should be finalized with a list of potential country markets organized and ranked as they relate to your organization.

SUMMARY

Country market mapping is the first of nine intelligence screening elements to support time-future formulation. It should be approached in a systematic way. The trend checklist offered in this chapter provides such a method. The strategist should not be limited to investigate only the results of the GFOT workshop, but should consider additional opportunities which may have been overlooked.

Of particular importance to country intelligence screening is government intervention. All nations have strategies which in turn drive market development. Understanding the historical theories upon which governments have been built provides the foundation for time-present and insight into the future.

CHECKLIST

When reviewing intelligence about prospective countries for business expansion you will seek the answers to several questions that will assist you in your go, no/go recommendations.

- What are the classification trends of the target nations?
- Who will have money?
- Who are the haves?
- Who are today's have-nots?
- Who are tomorrow's haves
- What is the theoretical basis of today's government?
- What is the country trying to achieve?
- What are the implications of the future based on a given nation's historical past?
- What is the trend in relation to the major bodies of political theory?
- What does the country want to buy?
- What does it want to sell?
- What is its economic development strategy?
- What are the implications of a changing world on the future of that country?

Chapter 11

Second Screening: Customer Mapping

Why do some companies based in some nations innovate more than others? Why do some nations provide an environment that enables companies to improve and innovate faster than foreign rivals?

Michael Porter, *professor, Harvard Business School*

In the past, most intelligence, or market research, has been focused on studying what customers like among available products. The most important question for today's organization, however, is what products and services will be required in the future. Today's companies must then work toward satisfying those needs. The analyst is looking for the paradigm shift that will satisfy both consumers and industrial customers in the future.

Now that you have researched potential world markets and come up with a short list of countries your company might be interested in, the next step is to focus on the second screening phase of strategy formulation. Customer market mapping is about the relationship of business strategy to the people and businesses that buy your products and what they want tomorrow. This chapter is about understanding the behavior of global customers. In other words, who cares, what they care about, who has money to buy a product, and what the trends are. The discussion explains the tools necessary to understand customer needs in terms of strategy formulation.

The Global Customer

Few companies have a true global customer, that is, a description by age, income, need, or other indicators that are homogeneous throughout the world. There are some global customers such as cola drinkers, chocolate candy eaters, and those who enjoy McDonald's hamburgers; but most customers are like beer drinkers, they differ from country to country. Tastes, spendable income, and cultural preferences vary; therefore, customer mapping is an important part of the strategic formulation process.

Market Mapping

Mapping the trends of buyers, with money to spend to satisfy their wants and needs, represents a major element of your strategy. There is also a mapping opportunity for the industrial product market which includes durable goods for the manufacturing process as well as the growing production-sharing process; that is, competitively priced labor, technology, or capital that stimulates production and assembly. The major elements of customer mapping are

- Total sales volume.
- Potential for globalization.
- Degree of localization.
- Cultures and values.

- Historic growth trends.
- Identificaton of the decision-makers.
- Segmentation by product type: Which segments are growing? Why? Which segments are declining? Why?
- Technology.
- Customer type: consumer or industrial.
- Key customers.
- Distribution channels.
- Price.
- Other discriminators.

Total Sales Volume

Even before an analysis of customers can begin, total sales volume in a target country must be potentially available. There is strong evidence that customers' spendable income, that is, the ability to pay, is the major variable. For example, even though the population of the People's Republic of China is a delicious target, the segment of the population that can afford your product may be quite small. Your total sales volume may be more in a less-populated but richer country.

Potential for Globalization

As a result of improved communications and the impact of television, movies, and travel, customer tastes and requirements are converging. More products of global businesses are considered for standardization to meet the blending needs of local customers who may not be satisfactied in terms of quality, culture, or tastes, with home-market producers. The potential for economies of scale increases dramatically if the global customer phenomenon can be identified by your firm. Nevertheless, most of the world's customers remain local in culture, and local adaptation of your product is necessary.

Degree of Localization: Regional Tastes

Economies of scale remain a potential even if there is not a global customer. Often there is a blending of cultures in a region. For example, the customers in Egypt are essentially the same in terms of tastes and needs as Saudi Arabian and other Gulf States customers.

Cultures and Values

Regardless of the trend toward global customer blending, the fact is, customers in different countries have different cultures. These cultures often dictate buying attitudes, values, and tastes.

Culture is a set of meanings or orientations for a given society or social setting. It's a complex concept because there are often many cultures within a given nation. For you, the global business strategist, the definition is more difficult because a country's business culture is often different than its general culture. Thus international business is composed of vastly different languages, religions, values, attitudes, law, education, politics, technology, and social organizations.

Culture gives you a set of codes to deal with phenomena in a social environment. It sets priorities among the codes, and it justifies the need for the culture, usually by means of an associated religion. Whatever a nation's culture is, it works for them. In order to function within it, the firm's strategy must accommodate it.

The Japanese do this very well. They learn how to penetrate international markets by sending their managers to live and study in the other person's shoes. The Japanese don't try to change the way of life in the other country, they just learn about it. When they go home they are specialists in marketing and production in the country they researched.

It's a country's culture that regulates such things as sexuality, child rearing, acquisition of food and clothing, and the incentives that motivate people to work and buy products. All of these things are, of course, major factors in customer market mapping. In order to understand the customer, there must be an appreciation of the impact on buying attitudes of language, religion, values, laws, the legal system, education, technology, and social organization.

Language

Language is the thing that sets humans off from other forms of life. It is the way you tell others about your history and your intentions for the future. Language is the means of communicating within a culture. For the global strategist, consideration of language is vital because it defines socialization—a critical element of international marketing.

Religion

Religion plays a major part in the cultural similarities and differences of nations. Religion is often the dominant influence for consumers. Such things as religious holidays determine buying and consumption patterns. Knowing what is forbidden and what a society expects as a result of its various religions affects market strategy.

Values and Attitudes

A society's values determine its attitudes toward wealth, consumption, achievement, technology, and change. You must evaluate your product or service in terms of the host culture. Researching attitudes about openness and the receptivity to new technology are the essentials of marketing America's changing products.

Laws and Legal Environment

The laws of a society are the rules established by authority and society. Most of the world's legal systems can be classified under three major bodies: code law (for example, France), common law (for example, England), and Shari'a (for example, Saudi Arabia). About half of the nations of the world are under a form of either code (based on constitutional law) or common law (based on case law), but the other half are under Shari'a which is based on the Koran.

The laws and legal environment of a given nation are important because there is no international law per se. There is only a set of agreements, treaties, and conventions among two or more nations that dampen legal differences. The strategist is not only interested in contract law, but also liability and environmental issues.

Education

The biggest difference among cultures is the educational attainment of the populous. The next biggest difference is the educational mix. It is not unusual to find only the elite of some nations educated to the levels Americans assume for all people. Therefore, the impact of education is profound for customer market mapping, because good communications is often based on relative educational capacities and standards.

Technology

Customer needs vary in relation to technological growth. Not every culture is ready for the bells and whistles of high technology. Even if customers would like the higher technological product, their national infrastructure may not support it. For example, electricity may not be available to support modern microwave ovens, and garages may not support the repair of new automobile safety equipment. Nevertheless, customer technological wants should be mapped from available data with the intent to find the niche for a growing future opportunity.

The most recent technological change is our growing control over energy and information. The word *technology* begets concepts such as science, development, invention, and innovation. Some older languages don't even have words to express these concepts.

Understanding the technological gap among nations is an essential element to exporting products across borders. Wide gaps still exist between the most advanced nations and those that are traditional societies. The implications for you are that such things as training needs for technology transfer, and the impact of that transfer on social environments, must be considered. You should always look at technology from the importing country's point of view.

Social Organization

International trade cannot be conducted without involvement in foreign social relationships. In order to develop market segmentation and target markets, the social organizations of a country must be studied.

Social stratification is the hierarchy of classes within a society—the relative power, social priorities, privilege, and income of those classes. Each class within a system has distinct tastes, political views, and consumption patterns. Many countries have a socioreligious ideology that allows rank to be intrinsic and inherited biologically. This implies that different categories of humans are culturally defined as if consisting of different worth and potential for performance. Regardless of how you react to such noncompetitive socialization, such ideas are predictable in some countries. Faced with such a system of socioreligious rank, it is essential that you learn how to deal with it—not attempt to change it. Insensitivity to the customs of the customer will not only result in misinformed decisions but could also precipitate resentment and, in some cases, recrimination.

Historic Growth Trends

Historic growth trends of a specific customer group will show a potential even before the total sales volume is in place. Some firms lead the swell by taking a position in the country in advance of the trend. A clear example of that is McDonald's opening a reataurant in Moscow in the mid-1980s.

Identification of Decision-Makers

Some businesses believe there is only one kind of customer—the one who can say yes to the purchasing decision. In reality there are also those who influence the purchase. Therefore, decision-making units must be segmented in several ways. For instance, in some countries only the women of the families do the buying, while in others, for certain products, the young people decide for themselves what they will buy. In some firms, buyers will only deal with their own national representatives, in other firms decisions are made by committee, and in others only the president makes the decision. For some products, customers' buying decisions are almost totally driven by certain influential organizations or people. As an example, in the medical field, without the approval of a key certification organization, sales might not only be impossible but also illegal.

Segmentation

There is a trend in marketing to generalize customers by calling them "the market." What is needed is a serious analysis of what makes up the segments of a market—customer type by product, who actually makes the decision, and who influences the decision.

Segmentation requires a two-tiered approach. First, at a macro level, potential customers should be mapped by broad characteristics such as geography, demographics, development level, income, cultural characteristics, and behavior. Second, the mapping should analyze at the micro level, such as pinpointing actual decision-makers and decision-influencers.

From this analysis should come an idea of which segments are growing and which are declining and why. Go, no/go decisions are based on growing segments.

Technology

Technology levels in a country are of major interest in customer market mapping. Some countries are just not ready for your product. Consider, as an example, the introduction of microwave ovens in a less-developed nation. In the first place the average home in the nation may not yet have electricity. More important, the homemakers may not be ready to give up their gas or wood-burning ovens for this relatively new equipment.

Customer Type

Customers vary according to product needs. Obviously consumer products lend themselves to reaching the general population while industrial products have a totally different focus. Consumer needs include agricultural, household, automobile, and the vast array of daily consumed products worldwide. Industrial products include those in the manufacturing process as well as the growing production-sharing process—competitively priced value-added labor, technology, or management that stimulates business.

Key Customers

Key customers are those who represent the major market share in a given segment for your product. Their importance in terms of size will vary from segment to segment. Yet their share of purchases will be controlling in terms of your success. Key customers offer several ingredients for your firm: They serve as an intelligence source regarding changing needs and their perception of existing suppliers. Of major importance to you is providing the service needs for key customers, constantly finding out their changing demands, and responding to them.

Distribution Channels

Key customers are often the distribution channels that can reach your ultimate customer. Channels vary from culture to culture. Of vital importance to a successful strategy is the adoption to the channels which are culturally comfortable to a nation's customers.

Price

Another key element in the strategic decision process is the price customers are willing to pay. Sometimes re-engineering is required to bring costs in line with customers' ability to pay.

Other Discriminators

In some cultures, key customers respond to discriminators other than price and quality. Such things as who you know or a national industrial policy might influence their buying patterns.

SUMMARY

It is not necessary to have a global customer to be a global business. But the customers' need remains the most important element in your strategy formulation. Needs will vary according to culture and many other discriminators, and your sensitivity to these discriminators will be the key to future needs.

Your analysis of customers leads to one of the major elements in the strategy formulation. It need not be a go or a no/go, but in some cases a weighted evaluation to be considered against the potential customers of other national markets.

CHECKLIST

- What will customers need in the future? When will they need it?
- Is there a global customer for any of your company's products?
- Do any of your products have potential as a global product?

- What are the cultural implications for your products?
- How can cultural differences be accommodated in your company's products?
- What are the technological implications?
- Are the country's customers changing?
- What is the effect of the trends on your products in the future?
- Who are your key customers?
- How do they discriminate?

Chapter 12

Third Screening: Product Mapping

You must carry out consumer research, look toward the future, and produce goods that will have a market years from now—and stay in business.

W. Edwards Deming to the Japanese

Global strategizing requires a new viewpoint for the development and introduction of product. Many companies work hard at preparing for the future, but all too many firms remain passive and reactive, waiting for the telephone to ring.

This chapter has two parts: technology and product. The necessity to analyze the trends of need, differentiation, culture, and technology will be discussed. Also, understanding the impact of government regulations on the product in the global setting of the 21st century will be explored.

TECHNOLOGY

A whole new range of terms are related to the notion of technology, and those terms take on special significance when considering strategy. One of the early elements of global product mapping is defining a firm's core technology. From that comes the ability to see product linkages in other cultures and the international economic system as a whole, and that becomes a major element of global strategic formulation. Thus, we ask: From our technology what products can we produce to satisfy our global customers' future needs? In the international arena, one company's use of a technology can drive firms in another country to either adopt new innovations or be driven out of business.

Core Technology

Kyocera has been making things from potter's clay. Thus, ceramics is Kyocera's core technology. It has improved during more than 30 years, and now it has many innovative uses. Kyocera makes ceramic products that are used as nose cones for space rockets, solar panels, integrated circuit packages, modems, computers, and laser printers.

The theory of the technology *S* curve, as shown in Figure 12–1, holds that each technology has a limit, or point of diminishing returns, and that there are common danger signals of when the limit is being approached. As a result of this kind of thinking, many firms give up on their core technology, thinking the world has progressed beyond its usefulness. Others just don't know what their core technology is. If Kyocera had followed this theory, it would have given up at the pottery stage of development.

Much of the problem is understanding the difference between science, technology, and technology innovation. According to the dictionary, science is the state or fact of knowledge, technology is applied science, and innovation is the act or process of introducing something new, such as a new method, custom, or device.

Science, inventions, and discoveries are the source of technology, but technology is meaningless if it sits idly in the library or the garage of the inventor. Technology is knowledge (skills and techniques) used in the production of goods and services. It is the how-to of making something.

FIGURE 12–1
Technology S Curve

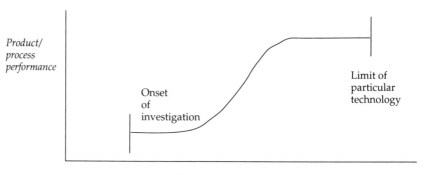

Technology must be applied to production to become innovation. It is technology innovation that brings new products. Technology innovations serve customers in two ways: first, in the making of wholly new products (not imitations), and second, in new, economic ways to serve and produce old products. Figure 12–2 shows the hierarchy from basic science to products.

Technology, then, is the systematic application of scientific or other organized knowledge to practical purposes. It includes new ideas, inventions, technologies, and materials. Technology innovations are the line of products and processes related to the core technology.

Kyocera uses the *science* of mixing minerals, the *technology* of shaping and heating minerals into useful objects, and the *innovation* of continuous new products for new uses.

Defining the core technology of the firm may be one of the most difficult processes of strategy formulation. IBM has only recently realized that its core technology is office machinery applications, not computers or typewriters.

Technology Development

Technology development is the activities involving the design, creation, and improvement of methods and activities in the value chain, not just in the manufacturing process. This requires a stock of know-how in terms of human resources that understand the firm and have the entrepreneurial instincts to innovate. The level of these human resources often determine whether the firm becomes a leader in its field, a niche player, or a follower.

Technology Forecasting

Technology forecasting is a quasi art that attempts to estimate technology advancement and grasp its impact on the firm's operations. There are several methods in use today. Reading scientific journals, trade publications, and on-site plant inspections; word of mouth; and hiring away knowledgeable employees from other firms are all ways of staying current. Brainstorming and variations of the Delphi method are also used. In brainstorming, a firm attempts to map its technological future by bringing technology experts together for some unrestricted creative thinking. The Delphi methods attempt to achieve the same results by gaining a consensus among a group of experts. Typically the Delphi method is a three-step process. First, there is a survey of the anonymous opinions of the experts. Second, each expert gets the other panelists' answers and anonymously evaluates them. Third, another round of forecasting begins for several iterations of survey and evaluation until a convergence of opinion is achieved.

FIGURE 12–2
Hierarchy of Technology

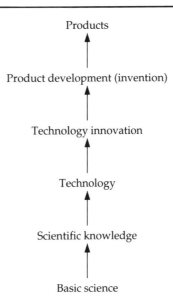

Products

↑

Product development (invention)

↑

Technology innovation

↑

Technology

↑

Scientific knowledge

↑

Basic science

PRODUCTS

Like technology, the concept of product conjures a long list of related terms which have importance in the global product mapping process. These include options such as standardizing the global product, product differentiation versus globalization, world-class versus domestic, and global versus local positioning. All of these are linked to where the product is in its life cycle.

Product Life Cycle

Products can be at one stage of the life cycle in one country and be at another stage in a different market. By life cycle I mean a product's change in marketability and profitability over time. As shown in Figure 12–3, the cycle has six general stages: development, growth, shakedown, maturity, saturation, and decline.

Understanding the product's place in the cycle, country by country, is essential to decisions about globalization. Products in the saturation or declining stages in an industrialized nation often continue as a viable product in a less-developed country. Similarly, those in the early-to-market stage have potential for standardization.

The Global Product

A global product is one that has a single brand and marketing approach and serves a common set of customer requirements in multiple countries. More firms are seeking to globalize one or more products such that they are perceived as acultural and anational.

Much of the movement toward global products is driven by the high cost of research and commercial investment. The other cost-driver is the amortization of fixed costs, such as advertising, across multiple world markets. High-technology products such as computers, automobiles, pharmaceuticals, and airplanes are good candidates for globalization. A product that is first to market has the best opportunity to establish global characteristics.

Differentiation versus Globalization

Differentiating products and marketing programs for individual countries, or globalizing them, is based on multiple criteria. Each decision should be analyzed carefully.

- Where is the product in the life cycle?
- Is there market share potential? Is it for a differentiated product or will globalization work?

FIGURE 12–3
Product Life Cycle

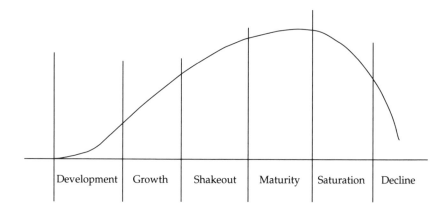

- Do customer and market differences justify the loss of globalization?
- What are the cultural issues?
- What are the hard, cold profitability factors? Cost-revenue analysis will reveal this truth.
- Are there economies of production?
- What are the logistics and maintenance issues?
- What is the impact on product management? Is it improved and less complicated or does it matter?

World Class

This is the quality issue wherein many products that satisfy the local market are not in the class that stands up against global competition or under the critical eye of global customers. Whether attacking or being attacked in a given country modern firms must be increasingly aware of the requirements of the world-class product. Quality looms high in the development of a world-class product for several reasons. The global customer is more discriminating; however, quality increases durability and reduces the logistics support chain. Better products need fewer repairs, smaller inventories of spare parts, and reduced transportation and inventory costs.

Designing for the Customer

Analyzing consumer needs leads to marketing opportunities, but sometimes the analysis reveals huge gaps which lead to product innovation opportunities. When this analysis results in the same gap in multiple countries, the result may be a new global product. Differentiating by customer segments adds to cost, but should not be discarded because, often, only slight modifications can make a quantum jump in sales.

Designing for Globalism

Many firms are building the global concept into product development from the design stage forward. Research and development issues are a part of global business strategy decisions.

Impact of Technology

Some countries are technologically ready for some products while others are not. Technology changes have happened at incredible rates during the 20th century, and the rate of change is predicted to increase in the new century. National infrastructure and cultural changes often lag these introductions. For example, some nations are not ready for the microwave oven. A country's electrical system must support the equipment for a modern kitchen.

EC Quality Code

A new quality assurance code adopted by the European Community to weigh the merits of products will impact imports. The EC is moving toward requiring all goods and services imported into member states to be certified by registrars under the new code. Your purchaser could ask if your product meets International Standards Organization (ISO) 9000 standards.

ISO 9000 is a series of standards used to document, implement, and demonstrate quality assurance systems used by companies that supply goods and services internationally.

For up-to-date information about registrars who are certified to give approval, contact your local department of commerce.

Changing Strategic Boundaries

To achieve globalization, strategic boundaries become a major consideration. What you do and what others do for you are integral to quality, price, delivery, and reliability of the global product. Global marketing in itself is *forward integration*; that is, going on the offensive to achieve increased sales volume. This might lead to strategic decisions to open retail stores or to begin a direct mail marketing operation. On the other hand, standardization decisions may lead to *backward integration* to reduce costs and attain economies of scale. Offshore production or joint venturing with national partners are possible ways to backwardly integrate.

Cultural Considerations

Culture has an impact on customer needs and buying decisions, but it is also important from a global product point of view. Such things as product name, brand name, packaging colors, and language are all driven by an understanding of culture and its impact on the global customer. As an example, an American might believe that red, white, and blue are the favorite colors worldwide. When one analyzes the colors of national flags, however, it becomes readily apparent that green, blue, and yellow are the dominant colors. Similarly, English might be a common language in some regions, but Spanish is the only way to sell in Latin America.

Product Positioning

How the firm positions products in the global market is also a complex matter. Positioning is defined by market share country by country. Is it increasing or decreasing? What about prices? Customer buying decisions, technology implications, and the products place in its life cycle all affect product positioning.

Distribution

Distribution networks and methods vary from country to country. Although there are many national distribution networks to accommodate the growth of high technology in global transportation networks, there are many culturally driven distribution systems remaining. An example is the Japanese fractionalized retail network that Americans find obsolete. It remains in place despite its inefficiency—because it is the Japanese way.

Logistics

The farther away the country market is from the manufacturing site, the more logistics support becomes a factor. Inventory carries a high cost which not only shows up on financial reports, but also shows in terms of value. From the beginning, logistics issues must be included in global strategic decisions because they are intertwined with designing for world quality.

Laws, Regulations, and Standards

Product market mapping must include implications of government regulations on the product in the global setting. Even though GATT has made great gains in the harmonization of standards, national laws and regulations will continue to vary in their impact on product marketing and production. In cases where the impact is minimal, exporting may be the correct tactic. In severe cases, however, you may be driven to take an insider position in order to compete.

SUMMARY

No aspect of global mapping accentuates the complexity of global strategy more than product mapping. The entire company team must become tuned to the firm's global objectives. Technology, logistics, product development, and marketing must be mapped country by country before knowledgeable strategic decisions can be made.

Product market mapping is a major factor of your strategic decision making. Obviously, some countries will have strong market appeal, yet have weaknesses related to government regulation, or distribution networks. In order to make your decisions, develop a weighted matrix of the variables discussed in this chapter.

CHECKLIST

- What is your company's core technology?
- What is the forecasted advancement of your technology?
- What is your customers' forecasted level of technology?
- What do customers want?
- Do your firm's products satisfy customers?
- What do you have to do to products to satisfy customers?
- Where are products in their life cycle?
- Are the products global?
- Are they world class?
- What are the implications of culture on your firm's products?
- What are the logistical implications?

Chapter 13

Fourth Screening: Supplier Mapping

We need to learn how to spend our time and effort working on the future, instead of continually rearranging the past.

Philip Crosby

During the 20-year period from about 1965 to 1985, international firms introduced a growing lineup of improved products. Today the list of world-class competitors includes quality manufacturers on every continent. The window for buying decisions has never been wider.

During the global strategic formulation process vertical integration will be one of the issues that will surface. Questions will be asked: What do we make ourselves? What do we buy from suppliers? These will be important issues to face in every country where you consider expansion, because suppliers account for most of the income statement (cost of sales and other vendors) and much of the balance sheet (inventory, property, plant and equipment, and most of the current liabilities).

There are many reasons why you may want suppliers to become part of your globalization process. There are equally sound reasons for the firm to integrate backwards and retain control of the supplier function. This creates more complex sourcing decisions which affect the manufacturing process.

Worldwide purchasing has become a big player requiring new approaches and redefinition of business boundaries. A firm no longer has the luxury of limiting make-or-buy decisions only to its domestic country, because good, unemotional business sense requires consideration of international alternatives.

This chapter contributes to your understanding of global sourcing. It offers a description of the tools necessary to understand the trends and to make the best strategic decisions possible for your firm.

Phenomenon of Content

Whether it be consumer or capital goods, today's purchasers are discriminating and fickle. The phenomenon of content is the declaration by people all over the world who care little about where the product is made, only that it have good quality, the right price, and stable production. To compete in the global marketplace with world-quality products, small manufacturing firms will, sooner than later, be required to consider a mix of foreign and domestic content.

Tariffs. To meet country-of-origin requirements for lower tariffs, local content may be a requirement to conduct business profitably.

Production sharing. Lower labor costs are the primary reason for examining the production-sharing alternative.

Multiple sources. Suppliers represent a valuable addition to the context of team play, yet they also can hold up the firm in their demands. Multiple suppliers offer the ability to negotiate without the pressure of having to shut down essential production.

Best source. Quality is on the tip of tongues everywhere in the world. The best quality may not be in the home country, and competition may include products or components from many parts of the world.

Just-in-Time (JIT)

Modern businesses attempt to avoid large inventories and their associated warehousing costs. High inventories represent lost revenue because they are assets not earning even the lowest of market interest rates. Of course, some inventory must be carried, but most companies limit that to no more on the shelf than the minimum required to meet predetermined statistical fill levels.

Most manufacturers have instructed their purchasing department managers to move toward a method called just-in-time (JIT). The term means just what it says—components and materials needed in the production process arrive precisely at the time they needed, thus limiting the required inventories and reducing the concomitant costs of production. Underlying the JIT philosophy is the elimination of waste, with waste being defined as anything which adds only cost to a product and not value.

The Decision

The decision to enter the world of global sourcing holds two major obstacles for top management. The first is attitudinal; that is, management must commit to give it a go. This requires a cultural adjustment and an understanding that foreigners will now be in the purchasing loop. The second decision barrier is the issue of whether to source directly (do-it-yourself) or indirectly (use an intermediary). The wise company considers a mix of these methods.

Value Analysis (VA)

Value analysis is a major part of the JIT process. By definition, only an activity that physically changes a product adds value. Thus, machining, plating, and assembly add value. Activities such as moving something to and fro, counting, or storing adds only cost, not value. The JIT process demonstrates that value-adding operations comprise only a miniscule portion of the entire operation—some have calculated to less than 1 percent.

It must be noted that JIT has its own set of problems, such as quality control, reliability of sources, and cash-flow performance. These are significant barriers to overcome for the domestic buyer and can seem insurmountable when sourcing internationally. Nevertheless, many firms have established sound relationships and integrated manufacturing systems with overseas firms, often at significant cost savings. The complexities of today's modern manufacturing system require a point of view that seeks relationships with companies, foreign and domestic, so as to work as a team to optimize the JIT concept.

Strategic Sourcing

To achieve the optimum integrated system, many firms have established an office, often with a single person whose task is to step away from the day-to-day rat race of purchasing and look at the total procurement picture. The title commonly used for this position is world-wide purchasing manager (WWPM).

By virtue of his or her separation from the typical headaches of day-to-day buying, the WWPM can take a proactive approach to sourcing. This same person can include JIT and VA philosophies as part of this new approach to sourcing, and he or she can even be included at the product-design stage. Those who have taken this step have learned one thing: It pays off handsomely in savings through the reduction of primary cost-drivers.

In the past, most purchasers have used the traditional, simplistic buying criteria of price, quality, delivery, and service for all items and have only searched the domestic market. Strategic sourcing is the technique of starting with the current situation for the firm's product. It consists of investigating JIT, VA, pricing, supply assurance, adequacy of quality, and a host of services as these criteria relate to the total cost of the product; isolating the significant cost-drivers; then searching the world for the right suppliers of those cost-drivers.

Cost-Drivers

In the production process of capital equipment, as well as highly differentiated consumer products, parts can generally be separated into two categories. The first, typically called the trivial many (not categorized this way to downgrade their importance but rather to expose their costs), are those parts which often account for only about 20 percent of the total product cost. The second category is often referred to as the vital few because they are the primary cost-drivers of the final product. They often only amount to 20 percent of the total items yet can account for as much as 80 percent of the cost. Identified as the significant cost-drivers, it is the vital few that receive the concentrated effort through a multifunctional commodity management approach.

The Commodity Management Approach

The strategist does not focus on the trivial many but rather on the vital few. When using this sourcing technique, it is important to remember to establish market-driven target costs on a landed basis so as to be able to compare apples to apples. This is vital when comparing foreign sources with domestic sources. What may seem a good deal from an overseas supplier may prove to be too expensive when transportation, tariffs, and coordination headaches are included in the calculation of landed cost.

Commodity Management Team (CMT)

To analyze the vital few, the WWPM typically forms and chairs a commodity management team (CMT) made up of key players from design, quality assurance, manufacturing, finance, marketing, and any others needed to satisfy product requirements. Through a facilitation process, the CMT develops marketing, technical, quality, and commercial objectives for every major cost-driver in the production process in terms of cost, state-of-the art requirements, quality, supply assurance, product development, financial, managerial, and stability criteria. The outcome of CMT meetings is the development of a market-driven target cost (landed) with well-developed criteria for each of the vital few.

The strategic team then assists in prioritizing the vital few so that the WWPM can state purchasing objectives in such a way as to derive a strategic master purchasing plan. The purpose of this plan is to reduce costs yet maximize the macro business decision; that is, in some instances purchasing must subordinate its goals to achieve what is best for the company.

The analytical method used by the CMT for the sorting, choosing, and prioritization is one that forces the CMT to make rather simple decisions of must have and want. These techniques force line managers to assign priorities (usually on a scale of 1–10) to the vital few, component by component, in such a way that a ranking can be determined. This kind of decision analysis should not be avoided under the false perception that it requires sophisticated computers. It can be done by fairly simple manual number manipulations.

The Request for Proposal

The traditional steps of purchasing are: (1) issue the invitation for bid or request for proposal which defines specifications; (2) wait for responses; (3) analyze and then accept the lowest price of responsible bidders.

Now, using the CMT method, the approach is reversed. Members of the purchasing organization make individual invitations for bid or requests for proposal releases against the master plan. This plan defines for the bidders precisely what the target price of each vital few component must be in order for bidders to compete. In other words, the buyer tells the source what the price must be and explains the objectives that must be met for that price.

Advantages

Lower ultimate costs is the most obvious advantage to using the CMT method. More important, however, are the increased efficiency, reduction of suppliers, synchronous flow, and improved transportation costs

Disadvantages

The worldwide purchasing approach requires a continual internal dialog of the overall business concept and how specific commodities can best contribute to business objectives. As a result, there is a time cost due to the need for increased and continuous training of purchasing and manufacturing personnel.

Search Capability

Don't be misled. It is not just the vital few that are sourced worldwide. The trivial many have excellent potential for international sources, but these are generally left to the operational buyer. This means, just as it did for international marketing, that the prerequisite for international sourcing success is intelligence. Modern firms must invest in research, either by their own personnel or with the assistance of a firm that specializes in the collection of international data. Purchasing personnel need information in order to satisfy the JIT requirements of providing the required amount, at the required time, at the lowest ultimate cost, and at the highest quality.

To meet this critical need, many large firms have organized special divisions dedicated to supporting purchasing's needs for such information as worldwide labor costs, raw materials, floating exchange rate information, and tax and tariff implications of overseas sourcing. Small firms rely on a cooperative approach where information gathered by overseas marketing personnel is shared.

Problems

One of the major problems faced in the supplier market mapping process is convertible foreign exchange to pay for parts. Another is reliability of suppliers to meet schedules and quality. Each problem requires research in advance of committing resources.

SUMMARY

Global businesses can be both suppliers and receivers. Today's customer is less concerned with labels than with quality and price. Therefore considerations of vertical integration become important to your strategy formulation. High inventory costs and value analysis drive the modern firm to consider strategic sourcing and integrated manufacturing techniques.

CHECKLIST

- What are the implications of the phenomenon of content in your company's target markets?
- What are the barriers for suppliers?
- Are there multiple sources?
- Do suppliers fit with your value analysis?
- Can your firm participate in integrated manufacturing?
- What about the trends of strategic sourcing?
- Is the company's intelligence providing sufficient search capability?

Chapter 14

Fifth Screening: Competitor Mapping

You can and should shape your own future; because if you don't, somebody else surely will!

J. Barker

Businesses spend too much time worrying about who will "capture the hill." In the global market your primary focus should be toward your customer, although competitors do play a major factor in the strategic formulation process.

Some liken business to a game where the idea is to outwit and outperform competitors. This chapter reviews the important elements of competitor market mapping which determine not only the go, no/go of strategic decision, but also the tactic best suited to attack a new country market.

The Players (Competitor-type)

As interdependence grows into the next century, each country will find increasing competition between the global firm and the home-market firm. Nationalism will be a continuing issue; therefore, the relationship of the home competitor to its in-country market will be one of the driving factors in determining whether or not there is a need to have an internal country position. Competition for the global business will not just be from local firms producing and marketing like products. When competing in Germany the competition will, of course, be German, but also French, British, Japanese, Brazilian, Mexican, and many more.

Another approach to competitors is to consider them as direct, indirect (substitute products), or even potential entrants. This requires complex intelligence and analysis to provide the highest degree of attention and monitoring.

Size

Market share of each competitor, whether global or home market, should be assessed. In one country your firm could be a niche player, while in another a major shareholder.

Product Range

Each competitor approaches the customer in different ways with different products. A country-by-country survey of the product range of each competitor equips your firm to compete in several ways. It sheds light on the needs of customers. Why reinvent the wheel? This survey also provides valuable information concerning where the product gaps are for a given country customer. In each country make sure your analysis includes using your competitor's products and discussing the products with your key customers.

Technologies	What is the key technology of your competitors? Are they at the cutting edge of production capability and are they keeping up with the latest technology for the industry? Are they reverse engineering your product? How much should you be concerned about intellectual property protection? How are competitors organized for R&D?
Geographic Scope	Are your competitors strictly local? Are they regional or global?
Main Strategies	By main strategies I mean competitors' approaches to reaching key customers. What are their methods? How do they advertise? How do they get to the decision-making units?
Production/Distribution/ Marketing	Competitors vary in their channels. Some are vertically integrated while others are horizontally integrated. How does your firm match up with the production/distribution/marketing channels in the countries you are considering?
Key Financials	Some competitors are hanging on by their teeth while others are getting fat. Some have a lot of firepower behind them while others are not well financed or supported by shareholders and applicable technology.
	Remember, in the burgeoning global competitive climate of the 21st century, there will be no cash cows for very long. Understanding your competitors internal financial position provides some of the information needed to determine you strategic decision. Market share, sales, costs, and earnings are important comparative yardsticks.
Quantitative Goals	Some of the information about a company's quantitative goals can be found in financial and annual reports which show profitability, growth, leverage, and market share. Prospectus and stock exchange reports are other sources. For privately held companies and small, closely held firms, however, this kind of information may only be gotten from insiders who are hired away or who otherwise make the data available.
Qualitative Goals	Qualitative goals refer to such things as customer loyalty, ethics, employee satisfaction, image, and stockholder stability. This information can be found in articles written about the firm or in annual reports. More likely the best information is opinion surveys of industry sources.
CEO Watching	Not every CEO has the leadership qualities the title implies, but companies do tend to mirror the philosophy, values, and style of top executives. Some CEOs are take-charge people, others are more collaborative in their approach. Intelligence about top executives should include qualitative information like: aggressive or conservative; risk-oriented or risk-averse; authoritarian or people-oriented; stubborn or flexible; and lazy or tireless.
	Keep a personal profile on the people who are running the game. Know who the key people are—those who have authority, influence, and power.
Competitor Wargaming	Some firms have adopted the military wargaming process to business activities. Using intelligence, competitor wargaming pits teams representing competitors against each other in a paper exercise that helps anticipate and deal with competitors' strategies.

SUMMARY

Competitive analysis ranks high among many strategists, but it is not as important as the customer. Nevertheless, there is a valid concern for investing significant resources into competitor intelligence. The process is complex, particularly in the global marketplace where competitors are both local and global. To accomplish this important segment of the formulation process, it is essential to frequently use your competitors' products, to educate your entire GFOT to contribute information, and to look closely at competitor organizational structures and style as well as their products or services.

Competitors are usually a relative factor in the strategic process. The absence of competition suggests that maybe customers don't care about the product. The go, no/go decision in the case of competitors is most often a weighted decision.

Besides your competitors' financial position, other strengths and weaknesses such as management, key personnel, technical know-how, and market share are essential factors. Competitive analysis involves a business-by-business assessment of each local and global competitor vis-à-vis your own company. Search for the answers to these questions.

CHECKLIST

- Who are the players?
- What is its size?
- What is its product range?
- What are its technologies?
- Does the firm have a brand image?
- Is brand image strong?
- Is brand image local or international?
- Does it have a training program?
- Who gives the training? Staff or outsiders?
- Who are the outside trainers?
- How important are its service and sales managers?
- Who makes spending decisions?
- What is its style of management?
- How is the company organized?
- Are there unique features or packaging?
- How effective are its themes and messages in its promotions?
- What is the target of its advertising and promotions?
- Do you understand your competitor's sales compensation schemes and selling costs?
- Do you understand its executive compensation formula?
- How does your competitor measure customer service?
- What were the career paths of the top ten executives?
- How does your company stack up against your top two competitors? Against any potential new arrivals?
- Are your competitors reverse engineering your products?
- Are you routinely using the competitors' products?

Chapter 15

Sixth Screening: Trade Bloc Mapping

The move toward a regional headquarters in North America (to take advantage of the U.S.–Canada–[Mexico] Free Trade Agreement) is fast becoming an essential part of almost every successful company's transition to global competitor status.

Kenichi Ohmae, *head of McKensey & Company's Tokyo office*

Business in Germany is German business; business in Japan is Japanese business; business in the EC is EC business. The study of global strategy is the study of how to do business despite political and economic borders. Country markets can no longer be mapped in isolation. Strategists must also consider the economic linkages that nations form with each other. By mapping changes of negotiated economic integration within regions and blocs, the global strategist better understands the trends that will impact target markets. He or she can then match company strategy to bloc strategies. The purpose of this chapter is to provide you with the tools to map markets in terms of national economic integration.

ECONOMIC INTEGRATION

The economic integration of nations to stimulate regional exchange of business is not a new concept. The United States was one of the earliest integrationists when, in 1776, visionary leadership established free movement within the original 13 states.

There is strong evidence that total trade increases within an agreed area or union of trading nations due to the reduction and harmonization of interstate controls. Businesses are thus stimulated to expand their operations into other markets within the union. Economic integration tends to have an overall positive effect on trade by providing increased understanding among trading blocs and more cooperation among nations. Consideration of interstate trading unions therefore becomes a major implication of business strategy.

FORMS OF COOPERATION

Forms of cooperation between nations to improve trade range from the least complex—a very simple bilateral agreement—to the highest level of cooperation, the formation of an economic union. *Unions of trading nations* is a commonly used term. Other labels include: *bloc forming, regional integration, free zone, free trade agreement, free trade association, customs union, common market, economic union*, and *political union*. These terms must be used carefully because each implies more or less control and/or loss of sovereignty. All forms of integration require very careful, point-by-point interstate negotiations.

Free Trade Zones

Free trade zones (FTZ) were the earliest form of economic cooperation among nations. These were areas of property: a warehouse, a fenced-in field, or a regional land area designated within the customs territory of a nation. Here goods might be stored without paying tariff until the articles were entered into the customs territory. No tariff was paid until the goods were re-exported. These were typically fenced warehouses or even areas surrounding factories which were under the enforcement of the customs service. Goods brought to the zone may be manipulated or otherwise changed prior to re-export or entry into the customs territory. Figure 15–1 shows the underlying theory of the FTZ physically within a customs territory. Figure 15–2 shows the sharing of an FTZ by two nations.

Free Trade Agreement (FTA)

Free trade agreements (FTAs) are between two or more countries and may be bilaterally or multilaterally negotiated. The contents of the agreement include many conditions that range from customs procedures, to rules of origin, to the products included (such as, industrial or agricultural ones).

Typically the nations involved agree to reduce or abolish mutual import duties and other restrictions, often defining a time period during which duties are gradually changed. Negotiations could include some nontariff barriers. A common internal tariff and quota system tends to improve the uniformity and transparency of existing interstate controls.

Free trade agreements do not go so far as to harmonize the economic policies of the negotiating nations. Nor is there a negotiated common external tariff and quota. Each member country retains its own tariff and quota system on trade with third countries. As a result, outside exporters sometimes scheme to send their goods by way of the country with the least tariff for their particular good or service. Therefore, these agreements can be defective unless rules of origin are carefully enforced. This leads to complaints from exporters and shippers of having to go back to the grave for information on parts or for an ingredient's origin. Major examples of these agreements include: European Free Trade Association (EFTA), North American Free Trade Agreement (NAFTA), Latin American Free Trade Association (LAFTA), Australian, New Zealand Free Trade Area (ANZAC), and Caribbean Free Trade Area (CARIFTA). Figure 15–3 shows a free trade agreement composed of four nations.

Customs Union

A customs union abolishes all protectionism inside the union and sets up a common external tariff system with regard to third countries. It includes common nontariffs as well. A union is a sophisticated level of economic integration, but it does not go so far as to harmonize the economic policy within the negotiated region. Examples of customs unions include: Belgium, Netherlands, and Luxembourg (BENELUX); Economic Community of West African States (ECOWAS); and Central African Customs Economic Union (UDEAC). Figure 15–4 shows a customs union with its common external tariff.

Common Market

While having the same trade policy as a customs union, a common market also allows the free transfer of the factor endowments and intelligence as well as products. Under certain crisis situations, such as massive unemployment or foreign exchange shortages, an individual nation may temporarily erect barriers to the free flow between itself and the other members. Major examples of common markets are: European Community (EC), Central American Common Market (CACM), West African Economic Community (CEAO), Association of South East Asian Nations (ASEAN), and Andean Common Market (ANCOM).

Economic Union

This is an even greater degree of economic integration than the common market, because of the effects of harmonization of national economic policies. The major characteristic of this stage of economic integration is the surrendering of sovereignty beyond the common internal and external tariffs and quotas of the

FIGURE 15–1
Free Trade Zone (FTZ)

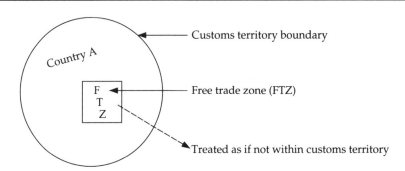

FIGURE 15–2
Joint Free Trade Zone

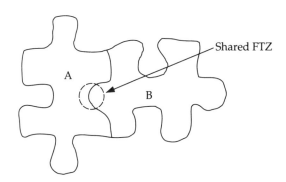

customs union to allow a supranational government to be responsible for economic policy. As in the United States, the economic union has a single monetary system, central bank, and a common industrial/economic policy. This is a difficult stage to attain. Unlike the United States, which essentially achieved this stage from its birth, blocs such as the EC must attempt to harmonize national laws and rules that have been in place for centuries.

Political Union

The ultimate form of multinational integration is only achieved after a supranational body is promoted to unite the political environment of an earlier stage of economic integration. It requires the subordination of national entity to that of the union's entity.

The former Union of Soviet Socialist Republics (USSR) had been, since its founding in 1922, the world's largest integration in the form of economic and political union. The Council of Mutual Economic Assistance which included the USSR, Bulgaria, Czechoslovakia, East Germany, Hungary, Mongolia, Poland, Rumania, Cuba, and Vietnam was formed in 1949. This Moscow-based Eastern bloc organization was an example of a coordinating group to facilitate trade among the Communist nations. In early 1991, with the disintegration of the bloc, the group changed its name to the Organization for International Economic Cooperation.

The election of a European Parliament within the EC was the first step toward forming a European political union which will become a reality with the ratification by all 12-member states of the Maastricht Treaty.

Figure 15–5 shows the hierachy of economic integration. Table 15–1 summarizes these cooperative forms and shows the escalation of these integrative forms with the concomitant loss of sovereignty. Table 15–2 shows a summary of the forms of economic integration in place in the early 1990s.

FIGURE 15–3
*Free Trade Agreement
with Four Nations*

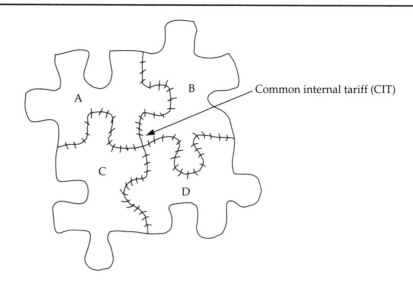

Common internal tariff (CIT)

FIGURE 15–4
Customs Union

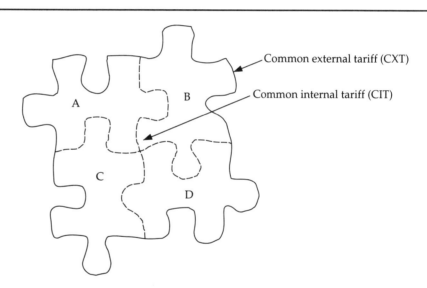

Common external tariff (CXT)

Common internal tariff (CIT)

THE ISSUES

Economic integration requires harmonization of interstate controls and brings with it political as well as welfare issues. Some of these issues, discussed below, can affect your strategy.

*Sovereignty versus
Integration*

Nations in regions all over the world are considering economic integration. The success of these unions is predicated on the extent the people will allow the political managers of their government to transfer sovereignty to those unions. Nationalism plays a large part in the success of economic integration.

Borders

Borders are also under attack in every corner of the modern world. In fact, borders may be the last barrier of globalism. Governments have increasingly recognized that their role is to smooth the way for free enterprise, not stand in its way. Those who argue for elimination of borders acknowledge it is doubtful there will be rapid change; however, when it happens, be certain that it will be the global

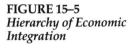

FIGURE 15–5
Hierarchy of Economic
Integration

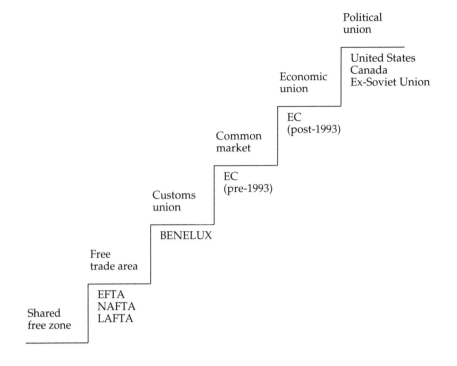

businesses that will lead the way. They will at least reduce the impact of sovereignty on the well-being of free enterprise and humanity.

At this juncture, those against elimination of borders dominate global thinking. They argue that the free movement of people, capital, and goods would be disruptive. They say people would migrate to specific locations leaving the planet with full pockets of wealth and empty pockets of poverty. Those who support border elimination argue that Adam Smith's "invisible hand" would soon turn the pockets of poverty into pools of wealth never conceived possible.

Insider

A major issue for the global business is the importance of taking an insider position within the trading bloc. In order to find an export outlet for goods within, many manufacturers believe the best positioning is to own or co-own a plant inside. This way they can take advantage of the beneficial rules of origin.

Inward free trade. Blocs tend to expand markets for companies within by lowering barriers and encouraging intratrade.

Outward isolation. The focus on trade within the bloc tends to drain efforts to extend markets across the trade region's border.

Trade diversion. Trading unions tend to shift from low-cost producers outside the union to high-cost producers inside the union.

Trade creation. This induces a shift from high-cost producers within to low-cost producers within the union.

Unequal results. Nations with relatively equal economic strength tend to gain equal value from integration. Weaker nations tend to gain more from the collective reduction of barriers and the resultant increase in trade.

TABLE 15–1
*Summary of
Economic Integration*

Stage of integration	CIT	CXT	CNT	Surrender sovereign?	Common economic policies	Free move of capital, technology, or labor
Free zones	No	No	No	No	No	No
Free trade agreement	Yes	No	Could	Some	No	No
Customs union	Yes	Yes	Could	More	No	No
Common market	Yes	Yes	Yes	Same	No	Yes
Economic union	Yes	Yes	Yes	Much	Harmony	Yes
Political union	Yes	Yes	Yes	Most	Yes	Yes

TABLE 15–2
*Forms of
Economic Integration*

Free trade area	Customs union	Common market	Economic union	Political union
EFTA	BENELUX	EEC	CPCM	Ex-Soviet Union
NAFTA				United States
LAFTA	ECOWAS	CACM	EC	Canada
ANZAC	UDEAC	CEAO	AEU	
CARIFTA		ASEAN		
		ANCOM		

MAJOR TRADE BLOCS

In his book *The Borderless World*, Kenichi Ohmae calls the major trade blocs "The Triad." What he refers to is the development of three trading blocs consisting of the industrialized nations which some believe will dominate world trade into the next century.

The Triad includes the 12 nations of the EC plus any others of that region which may be approved to integrate; the North American Trading Area including Canada, United States, Mexico, and a growing number of South American nations; and Japan and the ASEAN group which originally included Brunei, Indonesia, Malaysia, Singapore, Philippines, and Thailand, but may include South Korea, Taiwan, and Hong Kong. Tables 15–3 and 15–4 show Triad statistics.

European Community (EC)

The EC is a modern evolution of a customs union (formed a CXT system about 1968) expanding to a common market then to an economic union and now possibly a political union. The level of difficulty to form such a union has been far greater for the EC than for the United States in that the original 12 EC members have well-established ways. Although in 1776 the leaders of the American states did debate states' rights, the nation had not sufficiently matured compared to the problems confronting Europe in the 1980s and 1990s.

The struggle to develop a common economic bloc in Europe is not new. It began in 1952 when the Coal and Steel Community was formed between Belgium, France, the Federal German Republic, Italy, Luxembourg, and Holland.

TABLE 15–3
Major World Trading Blocs

Trading blocs	Number of countries	Population (millions)	National income (billion U.S. dollars)	National income per head (U.S. dollars)
Western Europe	18	356	4,565	12,940
North America	15*	409	4,601	11,260
Pacific Rim	14	1,653	3,081	1,864

*Excludes countries with populations under 1 million.

TABLE 15–4
Major Trading Blocs: Share of World Trade

Trading bloc	Share of imports	Share of exports
Europe	51%	52%
Asia/Pacific	20	23
United States/Canada/ Mexico	19	15
Central America	3	4
Africa	3	3
Middle East	4	3
Total	100%	100%
Value $ billion	2,980 cif	2,880 fob

In 1957, the European Economic Community (ECC) was formed when the members of the Coal and Steel Community signed the Treaty of Rome.

European Free Trade Association (EFTA)

Standing in the wings to join the EC are many nations that see benefits to the economic integration. The EFTA members as well as nations of central Europe are candidates. Formed in 1959, the EFTA includes the United Kingdom, the Scandinavian countries, Austria, Switzerland, and Portugal. Table 15–5 shows the potential of the European bloc.

North American Free Trade Agreement (NAFTA)

The first step of this integration was an agreement in 1989 between Canada and the United States to harmonize their interstate controls and achieve a common internal tariff over a 10-year period. In 1991, the NAFTA began negotiations to include Mexico. Other nations edging toward joining the North American integration include: Chile, and the Southern Cone countries of Argentina, Brazil, Paraguay, and Uruguay. Table 15–6 shows the potential of the American bloc.

Japan, ASEAN, and APEC

Japan stands alone as the major trading nation of Asia; however, the Association of South East Asian Nations (ASEAN), formed in 1975 and including Brunei, Indonesia, Malasia, the Philippines, Singapore, and Thailand, has considered expanding. Possibly called the Asian-Pacific Economic Cooperation (APEC), it could include South Korea, Hong Kong, Taiwan, China, Australia, and New Zealand.

TABLE 15–5
European Trading Bloc

Country	Population (millions)	National income (billion U.S. dollars)	National income per head (U.S. dollars)
European Community (EC)			
Germany	61.2	1,059.4	17,310
France	55.9	773.5	13,837
United Kingdom	57.1	730.0	12,785
Italy	57.4	687.1	11,970
Spain	38.8	246.6	6,356
Netherlands	14.8	203.3	13,716
Belgium/Luxembourg	9.9	128.9	13,020
Denmark	5.1	88.2	17,294
Greece	10.0	42.4	4,243
Portugal	10.4	33.2	3,192
Ireland	3.5	23.6	6,743
Total	324.1	4,015.9	Average = 11,123
European Free Trade Association (EFTA)			
Switzerland	6.5	161.3	24,815
Sweden	8.4	137.5	16,369
Austria	7.6	102.4	13,474
Finland	5.0	74.3	14,860
Norway	4.2	70.2	16,714
Iceland	0.25	3.3	13,200
Total	32.0	549.0	Average = 16,572

Total Average Europe: 12,940

TABLE 15–6
American Trade Bloc

Country	Population (millions)	National income (billion U.S. dollars)	National income per head (U.S. dollars)
Canada	26.5	575	21,527
United States	250	5,514	22,055
Mexico	88	214	2,490
South America	278.9	529	1,895

Compiled from 1991 data from *World Development Report*, Washington, D.C., 1992.

FIGURE 15–6
Government Economic Control

The ASEAN Nations

Should these countries join, the East Asian bloc would become the largest of the Triad with a total population of about 1.6 billion compared to the EC with about 350 million and the NAFTA with about 400 million.

This East Asian bloc is weakened by its geography and economic gaps. Made up mainly of islands strung north and south, the idea of a single bloc is difficult to grasp. The economic gap is even more formidable. For instance, Indonesia's per capita GDP is about $500 while Singapore's is about $10,000. Figure 15–6 shows the potential and dispersion of the ASEAN group.

MINOR TRADE BLOCS

Over the past 50 or so years nations have been integrating economically by forming blocs. In terms of trade volume the minor trade blocs are as follows.

Latin America Free Trade Agreement (LAFTA)

The Treaty of Montevideo, negotiated in 1960, initiated the LAFTA which includes Argentina, Bolivia, Brazil, Chile, Peru, Uruguay, Mexico, Paraguay, Colombia, and Ecuador. Intended as a free trade area to liberalize trade among the participants, it turned out to be weak because the reduction of barriers had many loopholes. In 1981, LAFTA was superseded by the Latin American Integration Association (LAIA) which changed the purpose to become an area of preferences instead of a free trade area.

Central American Common Market (CACM)

In 1962, the CACM was formed. It includes Guatemala, Nicaragua, Honduras, Costa Rica, and El Salvador.

Southern Cone Countries

In 1991, the Southern Cone countries of South America began negotiations to frame an agreement for a regional trading bloc. Argentina, Brazil, Paraguay, and Uruguay are included in the agreement.

East Africa Economic Community

East Africa formed its Economic Community in 1967. It includes Kenya, Uganda, and Tanzania.

Economic Community of West African States (ECOWAS)

The ECOWAS consists of Nigeria, Ghana, Liberia, Ivory Coast, Senegal, Togo, Benin, Upper Volta, Gabon, Cameroon, Mali, and Gambia.

Caribbean Free Trade Association (CFTA)

In 1968, the CFTA came together. It includes Antigua, Barbados, Guyana, and Trinidad.

Andean Common Market (ACM)

Following on the footsteps of the CFTA, the ACM was formed in 1969. It includes Peru, Chile, Colombia, Ecuador, Bolivia, and Venezuela.

Gulf Cooperation Council (GCC)

On the African continent, six Arab Gulf states—Bahrain, Oman, Qatar, Saudi Arabia, and United Arab Emirites—formed the GCC in 1981. The main objective was regional economic integration, but it also wanted to develop cooperation in the fields of economics, politics, communications, and social and cultural customs.

Arab Economic Union (AEU)

The AEU, was formed in the late 1980s also for purposes of regional cooperation. It consists of Libya, Tunisia, Mauritania, and Morocco.

Arab Cooperation Council (A.C.C.)

One of the most recent attempts at integration is the A.C.C. Formed in 1989, it includes Egypt, Jordan, Iraq, and Yemen.

Benelux

Benelux, made up of the first letters of each of the member country's names, Belgium, Netherlands, and Luxembourg, is an economic union first formed as a customs union in 1948 with a single (common) external tariff. By 1956, more than 95 percent of trade among the nations was free of all interstate controls. It was not until 1958 that the Benelux Treaty established the economic union, which, when it came into effect in 1960, established the world's first completely free labor market. The Benelux nations eventually created a common foreign trade policy which permitted the free movement of goods, workers, services, and capital.

SUMMARY

Nations' strategies include every conceivable method to induce or maximize factors of endowment in order to stimulate growth. The global strategist must take these stimuli into account. An analysis of opportunities among potential markets will result in gaps which may be filled by a given firm in its quest to expand markets internationally.

Empirical observations show that total trade within an economic union increases. The reduction of interstate controls offer a series of benefits which outweigh any negative effects.

- *Market extension*: The elimination of barriers increases market opportunities.
- *Economies of scale*: The integration of marketing allows amortization of costs over a larger market base.
- *Competition increases*: Consumers benefit from the introduction of newer and less expensive products.
- *Innovation increases*: Particularly for firms that produce differentiated products.
- *Capital investment is stimulated*: Trade creation possibilities lead businesses to invest in production and marketing facilities within the region in order to get behind any tariff and nontariff walls.

The negative implications of reducing interstate controls include the following:

- The preference effect of members over nonmembers tends to require nonmembers to seek an insider position.
- Nations of like development make relatively equal gains while developing nations tend to make greater gains than their developed nation-partners.

In addition to its overall positive effects on trade, economic integration offers excellent prospects for improved global welfare. It opens prospects for increased harmonization, and it becomes a building block for cooperation in other areas such as social and political processes.

CHECKLIST

- To what trade blocs do your target countries belong?
- What are the trade bloc rules?
- What are the implications of belonging to the bloc?
- Should the firm continue its outsider position?
- Should the firm take an insider position?
- What are the rules-of-origin implications?
- What are the market implications for your firm's product(s) vis-à-vis the bloc?
- What are the trends toward economic integration?

Chapter 16

Seventh Screening: Trade Creative Incentives

Plan for the future because that's where you are going to spend the rest of your life.

Mark Twain

Government's place is to steer and guide the nation, thus ensuring that what-ever welfare accrues is distributed according to the needs and preferences of the people of the sovereign lands. In practice people's preferences vary greatly. Therefore, governmental policymakers constantly search for what works. As noted in Chapter 2, nations have strategies to artificially stimulate the growth of their economies. Even small sectors such as provinces and communities have schemes to advance local output.

For the global strategist, job growth equates to market development. This chapter introduces another step of the intelligence screening process; it explains how modern governments go about stimulating economic development. This framework provides a systematic method of examining trends.

ARTIFICIAL COMPARATIVE ADVANTAGE

Since World War II, the newly industrialized countries (NICs), particularly Japan and the Four Tigers of Asia (Hong Kong, South Korea, Taiwan, and Singapore), have made dramatic economic gains. Their success has proven to be so effective that most low income nations as well as central and Eastern European countries are adopting the NICs' strategies.

After World War II Japan and the Four Tigers developed an operational paradigm that established new methods by which nations could grow economically. As small islands or insular properties, with low per capita incomes and commensurately small domestic markets, and without significant natural resources, they discovered a way to make incredible growth changes. It is the tigers model that provides the empirical evidence for what has and can happen as the world moves toward a global economy. But what is it that worked for the tigers?

It is the new model—artificial comparative advantage. ACA encapsulates into one complex paradigm a concept that incorporates directed and indicative planning, industrial policy, and an outward oriented world focus. It is a proven model because empirical evidence shows that the NICs have significantly changed their economic lot using it and many other nations have adopted it.

The theory of ACA has evolved over the past 25 years as the fastest-growing nations have taken advantage of the fact that the factors of production are fully mobile. The theory establishes that international trade is inseparably linked to economic development through interstate controls. The framework provides a systematic method to search for trends that represent strategic opportunities.

Lesson

The lesson for the global business strategist is that modern governments no longer take a hands-off, laissez-faire approach. Today's government strategies are much like the old mercantilism theory but convertible foreign exchange is the prize instead of gold. The basis of the new paradigm includes the following:

- There are no dissimilar factor endowments because those that are not provincial (natural) to a country can be artificially induced.
- There is a great deal of technology transfer.
- Factors of production differ among countries but are transferable.

Underlying this model is the notion that a nation's international strategy drives its domestic strategy and therefore its economic growth. Export industries create new labor skills and employment and stimulate the general economy.

International trade is not only sufficient for economic development, it is linked to it. Global trade has become the primary stimulus for nations without sufficient domestic markets to create production demand.

Nontraditional products and entrepreneurship are the keys to the success of ACA, and every sector seeks exports, not just traditional commodities markets. Global business managers increasingly find that governments look and act like businesses. They gather intelligence, assess their domestic position against long-range objectives, and develop strategic plans that drive industrial policy and strategic industries. Figure 16–1 show the elements of this paradigm.

MAPPING TRADE CREATION

All governments have schemes to induce the engines of trade. Supranational organizations such as the World Bank also offer schemes and even explain how to take advantage of their offerings. Opportunities that come in the form of economic development incentives to induce capital, technology, and know-how are available in almost every part of the world.

This part of the chapter is about mapping the process used by nations to stimulate growth; that is, the incentives offered by the supranationals, blocs, countries, states, and provinces that want to stimulate their markets. Three major engines of growth are examined: financial capital, human capital, and technology transfer.

FINANCIAL CAPITAL

Financial capital is the term used to describe money in its various forms. It is the major stimulant of free enterprise business. But financial capital begets two other kinds of capital: real capital which is the equipment, buildings, and instruments of production; and social capital which is the infrastructure—roads, transportation, communications, and education—that makes growth possible.

Capital is a major stimulant of international trade. In its various forms capital is a major factor of production and growth. All forms of capital contribute to increasing business productivity and, therefore, the competitiveness of a nation's products. Without capital, firms and nations are without a major source of growth. With it they are able to move toward an outward orientation and world competition.

At the risk of sounding elementary, recall that the availability of financial capital depends on return versus risk, and it comes in two forms: debt (bank loans, etc.) and equity (ownership). Although not limitless, for the right return there is actually a great deal of capital available. The cost of capital is the going market lending interest rate from a nation's best banks. Savers are not an extinct breed. Much of the world's wealth is still held in the hands of ordinary people who have lead frugal lives and saved a portion of their wages for a rainy day.

People and organizations who have excess financial capital want to do better than the cost of capital. If the bank, which is a very conservative place to invest, is offering a 7-percent return, many would risk a portion of their savings for a 10-percent or 12-percent return even though the investment carried more risk. Therefore, for the right project, financial capital is very available. Even gifts and grants are available.

FIGURE 16–1
*Artificial Comparative
Advantage*

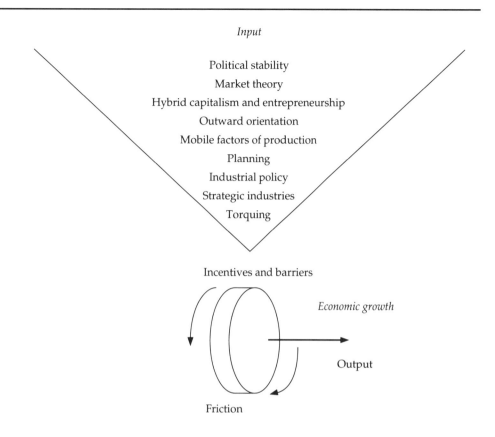

Input

Political stability

Market theory

Hybrid capitalism and entrepreneurship

Outward orientation

Mobile factors of production

Planning

Industrial policy

Strategic industries

Torquing

Incentives and barriers

Economic growth

Output

Friction

*Sources and Mobility of
Financial Capital*

At one time organizations were limited to local lenders and other money markets, but today, financial markets all over the world are convenient. Capital is fully mobile and moves to the beat of the drum of global interest rates and return on investment. A business leader in Bangkok, Thailand, can pick up the telephone and tap into global financial capital markets wherever it makes best business sense. The major sources of financial capital, discussed in the following sections, are: other global businesses, stock markets, venture capitalists, international lending banks, supranational lending banks, and foreign aid.

Global Businesses

Global businesses dominate the means and efficiency of capital investment. Much capital is raised from internal sources, but the search for external sources is an ongoing necessity. Today's global strategist looks to its home sources, but other countries and supranational sources are often tactically necessary, because some nations tie loans and grants to specific projects in specific countries.

    Learning about capital sources has become a science in itself. Because of the mobility of world capital, and the ability to tap these sources, global businesses allocate staff to track changing sourcing opportunities. Similarly, investment opportunities matching the firm's growth needs are equally important. Nations offer a seemingly inexhaustible list of schemes to entice capital investment, some of which are: low-interest rates, repatriation of profits, tax holidays, guaranteed political stability, and techniques which reduce risk (exposure) of capital investment.

Stock Markets

Stock markets are now worldwide. Financial markets are no longer just in London and New York. Stock markets that are open 24 hours a day all over the world include: Tokyo, Hong Kong, Singapore, Paris, London, New York, and San Francisco. Taiwan is moving in the direction of becoming a major financial capital.

Sirs:
The Indian who sold Manhattan for $24 was a sharp salesman. If he had put his $24 away at 6 percent compounded semiannually, it would now be $9.5 billion and could buy most of the improved land back.
                                                                                S. Branch Walker
                                                                                Stamford, CT

                                                                        From *Life*, August 31, 1959.

Venture Capitalists (VCs) These are the organizations that build a pool of funds from those who are willing to take big risks for major returns. The funders are those who generally have excess financial capital, enough that a loss might not put them in the poorhouse. VCs are now operating in almost every country and they are looking for projects that have high potential. VCs often work hand-in-hand with governments to focus capital into those projects which have high national priority and in some way have a measure of government protection.

International Lending Banks It is no secret that the Japanese banks are the largest in the world. International banking and lending organizations are not limited to local funds. They have offices around the world which tap local as well as international investors. Then those funds are made available to borrowers all over the world.

Supranational Lending Banks The World Bank Group is the most prominent supranational source of long-term lending and policy advice for developing countries. It promotes economic development and works to raise living standards by investing in productive projects and promoting the adoption of sustainable economic policies. It consists of four institutions: the International Bank for Reconstruction and Development (IBRD or World Bank), the International Development Association (IDA), the International Finance Corporation (IFC), and the Multilateral Investment Guarantee Agency (MIGA).

The World Bank makes hard loans, that is, at market-rate interest for up to 35 years. These loans must be guaranteed by the borrowing government and repaid in convertible currency. To obtain its funds, the IBRD sells bonds on the international capital markets and sells its loan portfolios to private investors. Loans are principally used for social capital purposes, that is, for infrastructure: agriculture, roads, electric power, water supply, transportation, communications, and education. The article in Figure 16–2 discusses an example of opportunity available to the global business that keeps tuned to the publication of information related to the availability of capital.

The IDA is the soft loan agency for the many developing countries that cannot qualify for World Bank loans. IDA extends credit for periods up to 50 years, repayable in easy terms after a 10-year grace period, and, except for a modest service charge, with no interest. Unlike the World Bank, the IDA does not generate its own capital. It is dependent on member countries for replenishment.

The IFC participates in private sector industrial projects. It does not make loans to governments, but rather is a lender or an investor in equity along with private investors. The IFC gains its funds from member country subscriptions to its capital stock, from sale of its own investment portfolio to private investors, and from its right to borrow from the World Bank up to four times its own unimpaired capital and surplus.

FIGURE 16–2
IMF Approves Loan
for Poland

IMF Approves
Loan for Poland

WASHINGTON – The
International Monetary Fund
Thursday approved a $2.5 billion
financial package for Poland, as
IMF officials predicted improving
Eastern European economic
prospects in 1992.

The IMF loan to Poland, most of
it to be disbursed over three years,
brings to $8.4 billion the total loans
the IMF has committed to five
Eastern European countries since
Jan. 1.

Hungary has been allocated $2.5
billion, Czechoslovakia $1.8 billion,
Romania $1 billion and Bulgaria
$634 million.

Disbursements from these
commitments will total $5 billion
this year, nearly one-third of the
total aid Eastern Europe is expected
to receive in 1991 from international
agencies and Western creditor
nations, IMF officials said.

Most of the commitments are to
help the East European
governments carry out such
economic reforms as price
decontrol, relaxing import
restrictions, tighter fiscal and
monetary management and the
privatization of state-owned
enterprises.

Source: "IMF Approves Loan for Poland," *The Journal of Commerce,*
April 19, 1991.

The MIGA insures private international investment in developing countries
against noncommercial risks as expropriation, civil strife, and inconvertibility. It
began operation in June 1988.

Other Lending
Institutions

The United Nations Development Program (UNDP) assists in the identification,
investigation, and presentation to financial agencies, those projects in developing
nations that make good investment sense.

Membership in the Inter-American Development Bank (IDB) is made up of
the United States and all Latin American countries except Cuba. The IDB offers
three categories of funds: hard loans or ordinary capital at market rates; soft-
currency window loans at easy terms; and a Social Program Trust Fund to
finance low-income housing and other social projects.

The Asian Development Bank (ADB) has 19 Asian members and 11 European
members, plus the United States and Canada. It was established in 1966.

The African Development Bank (AFDB) is limited to a membership of only
independent African countries. It authorizes financial capital for real or social
capital needs.

The European Economic Community (EEC) has formed a new supranational
institution named the European Bank for Reconstruction and Development

> The Inter-American Development Bank approved a record $3.8 billion in lending for Latin America and the Caribbean in 1990, exceeding the previous year's lending by $1.2 billion. That lending included $300 million each for Mexico, Colombia, and Venezuela. About half of the bank's 1990 lending went to transportation and communications, energy, agriculture, and social infrastructure.

(EBRD). This multinational organization promotes democracy, pluralism, and the rule of law to assist the changing central and Eastern European nations who divorced themselves from Marxism during the peaceful revolution of 1989. Its charter will require at least 60 percent of its resources be devoted to private sector projects. Thirty of the 39 member nations sent their presidents to inaugurate its birth in April 1991. According to its first president, Jacques Attali, EBRD's goal is to reunite "the two halves of Europe." To be headquartered in London, the bank will promote business training, advise governments on shifting to market economies, help rebuild infrastructures, take part in creating a banking system and capital markets, assist in privatizing state-owned companies, encourage small business, and help restore the environment.

Foreign Aid

Many industrialized nations have foreign-aid policies and dispense funds to less-developed countries through special agencies. The United States Agency for International Development (USAID) was chartered in 1961 to administer economic and technical programs through grants and loans for private and public sector development projects. In recent times most U.S. capital-dispensing assistance funds have emphasized privatization and the stimulation of industrial programs. Other nations, including Japan, South Korea, Taiwan, and Germany, have increased their foreign assistance programs.

Financial Capital Problems

Capital flows and investment are not without problems. Expanding global business into the international marketplace depends on several factors.

Ability to repay. This is the major contributor to the survivability of the firm. Cash flows must be available and predictable to support debt capital. Sales that contribute to return on investment must support equity capital.

Political risk. Discussed in Chapter 10, the various forms of political risk must be taken seriously when selecting investments. Even the aura of mistrust caused by potential political problems poses major obstacles to the global investor.

Exchange rates and/or inconvertibility. Gains and losses caused by the relative values of currencies are also a major factor.

Exchange rate restrictions. Some nations ration foreign currencies and protect their currency from market forces by restricting rates of exchange.

Inflation. Nothing diffuses the results of a good capital investment faster and should receive your attention more than inflation considerations.

Access to local capital. Just as some nations protect their currencies from the market, others attempt to ration local currency, opting for infusions from global businesses.

Limits on ownership.   Nationalistic thinking often overcomes the need to stimulate growth. Some nations, still harboring fears of foreign business domination reminiscent of MNC days, limit ownership of investments.

Taxation.   The implications of taxes on capital returns remains a major consideration in investment decisions.

Repatriation of profits.   In some ways this may be unimportant, that is, in cases where local expansion is the strategy. But when the use of profits is to stimulate growth of the firm and to offset losses in other business units, restrictions on repatriation of profits is a major investment consideration.

Summary of Financial Capital Considerations

The formulation of global strategy will expose the reality of having or not having sufficient financial capital. The search for the good deals or trade incentives will include an analysis of capital opportunities as a major element of your strategic research.

Along with human capital, financial capital is the most dynamic factor endowment, and the availability of financial capital has never been greater. Its modern mobility offers businesses from all reaches of the world to grow and compete on a global basis. Its availability, however, varies directly to risk versus return.

Risk can be defined in many ways, including payment of debts and currency restrictions; but political instability causing mistrust of government remains the most significant risk.

Human, as well as social and real capital, are by-products of the effective use of financial capital. Private sector global businesses have proven to be the most efficient allocators of those resources.

HUMAN CAPITAL

Human capital is the know-how of the people who make the whole thing work. The development of human capital, more than any other factor, accounts for the differences among nations. It is the reason nations like South Korea, Japan, and Taiwan expend huge sums on the education of their youth. These nations know, in the long run, it is human capital that separates second-class nations from those that compete on a global basis.

Government strategies include the growing use of added-value industries. Throughout the world human capital is thought of as a product. In the past, the concept conjured images of slaves (women and children working on-the-cheap) adding labor content to the assembly process. Today educated, trainable labor is more marketable.

Production Sharing

Production sharing is a form of adding value. Nations and regions develop schemes to promote the factor endowment which they have in greatest abundance. The exportation of added-value labor as a factor of production has become a major scheme among those nations with large populations. On the other hand, in nations such as the United States, Japan, and many European countries, the added-value of financial capital, technology, and know-how are just as exportable for production sharing.

Mexico's scheme to export added-value labor as a component of product content is called the Maquiladora Program. Because of its proximity to the U.S. market, the program is by far the fastest growing and has the largest share of the world's production-sharing industry. India, Singapore, Hong Kong, and many European nations, however, are competing.

TECHNOLOGY

Technology stands alongside financial and human capital as an engine of growth. Everyone wants technology because it affects a nation's production factors, the mobility of those factors, and the training and education of human capital. Technology also increases productivity. In fact, innovations in transportation and communications are among the most important factors that have caused the explosion of global trade. Technology's importance has grown as improved communications have brought to the have-nots the reality of those who have. Therefore, consideration of the following technology factors is a major element of global strategy formulation.

Technology Levels

In today's vernacular, high technology is that which produces aerospace, electronics, bio-chemistry, and replacement goods (nylon for silk, plastic for rubber and steel). Low technology includes mechanical products, labor-intensive products, and those that are at the end of their life cycle.

Need to Transfer Technology

There are wide gaps in basic technology development as well as in innovations that create entirely new products and industries. These gaps are caused by a range of problems in less-developed countries and developed countries alike. Because firms in all nations are competing in the global marketplace, the need for transfer is increasing. The major factors controlling its development and transfer are the following.

Education levels. Education is not a prerequisite, because there are inventors all over the world discovering things. Many of those innovators have little more than a high school education. As the level of technology rises, however, so does the need for higher education. Those nations with weak educational programs often suffer in competition with those which require universal training and have a large output of scientists.

Research and development. The function of R&D in the organization of a firm is generally well understood among the business community; however, it is often the first to go in budget crunches. Strategies which do not include this function are doomed to wither from the inability to respond to future customer and country market demands.

Brain drain. Higher education often brings higher personal expectations on the part of young mathematicians and scientists. Some nations have experienced the flight of their best brains to other countries. Brainpower can be viewed as a product, and its market is just as active as it is for other products. Therefore those who yearn to be better off can be lured by a range of offerings such as better living conditions, bigger titles suitable to their perceived importance, and more salary.

Basic science. The university usually promotes basic science. Great universities court great scientists and place high value on their work. Yet not all basic science is developed in the university. Institutes have been formed in many nations which are publicly and privately funded to attract bright people to produce basic science. These organizations also serve as magnets in an attempt to reduce brain drain.

Demand creation. The marketplace itself is demanding creation and technology innovation. As more firms switch from competitor orientation to customer orientation, marketers are bringing back to the company ideas that drive the R&D function. Companies such as 3M thrive on demand creation and offer high incentives to employees who bring new ideas for research and possible production.

R&D mechanisms. The high cost of R&D is another factor in the search for technology. Many companies and nations cannot afford R&D as an internal function. To meet the demands of the marketplace, R&D is becoming an industry of cooperatives wherein firms take an equity interest in the cooperative giving them some say in the direction of research.

Capital conversion of ideas to product. Entrepreneurs are the first to argue that it is not easy to bring ideas to the market. Yet in every country there are incentives and organizations to assist you in doing just that. In the private sector, VCs await the well-thought-out project that has high expectations for profit. The public sector of most nations has schemes to stimulate the conversion of ideas as well. Often these take the form of low-interest loans or guarantees.

Technology as an industry. Today, global businesses are competing with firms in the same industry from all over the world. The development of technology has become a major industrial sector in its own right. This change is mostly manifested in quality. As firms begin competing across borders, the reality of quality differences among products pushes the global company to assess its production capability and often search for new technology.

Search capability. Central to formulating the technology implications of your strategy is the search for new technology or opportunities to transfer proven technology as a business tactic.

Entrepreneurship. Entrepreneurs bring much of the world's technology to the market. Big business places high premium on the development of the entrepreneur within the firm. Yet it is the independent person in the small firm who seems to create the most magic. Because of that, most incentive programs focus on the entrepreneurial spirit.

How Technology Is Transferred

Contrary to general opinion, opportunities to obtain technology abound for the global market.

Public domain. Much of basic science is published in journals and technical publications by the professors and scientists of universities. Research and conversion from these public domain sources is a continuing process in all nations. In short, much of the world's technology is already in libraries waiting the entrepreneur's innovation or imitation.

Joint venture. The alliance or partnering of producers with those that have needed technology is a two-way street. The tactic is most beneficial to those with minimum financial capital.

Subsidiary. The subsidiary within another national market is another technology transfer alternative. Obviously this method increases exposure for the firm but carries with it increased control.

Licensing agreements. Licensing of technology to a firm in another country market is often the fastest and least expensive way to enter. Depending on variables, such as distribution networks already in place and market readiness for the product, the transferee can expect early streams of income using this method.

Management contracts. Contracts to manage the introduction of technology are a growing method of transfer and go hand-in-hand with licensing across borders.

Official technical assistance programs. Many governments have established technology banks and other assistance programs to connect available technology to private sector development. Strategies to take advantage of these programs should be on the agenda of all global businesses.

United Nations Industrial Development Organization. UNIDO was established by the United Nations General Assembly in 1966 to promote and accelerate the industrialization of developing countries and to coordinate the industrial-development activities of the United Nations system. UNIDO has a technology program to promote the transfer of technology to developing countries. The findings of research projects and colloquia conducted under UNIDO auspices offer opportunities to developing countries to adapt to technological change in such fields as microelectronics and genetic engineering. It continues to be a first-look organization by any private sector firm seeking opportunities to convert technology.

Industrial and Technical Bank (INTIB). In 1979 INTIB was created as a special department of UNIDO. Through its Technology Information Exchange System, it maintains data on technical processes, and patents and licensing agreements for the expansion of private sector firms in developing countries.

World Intellectual Property Organization. WIPO's Permanent Committee for Development Cooperation encourages the transfer of technology from the highly industrialized nations to the developing countries. Its Technical Exchange and Joint Patents program also fosters inventive and innovative activity in developing countries. Global businesses in qualified countries should include this program in their strategies.

Issues of Technology Transfer as a Strategy

Certainly the inclusion of technology transfer as a strategy is important. The process, however, is not without problems. Some of the issues are discussed in the next sections.

Management skills. Notwithstanding the urgent need for technology, some nations do not have the developed management skills to support the innovation.

Bargaining power. The transfer of technology involves negotiations between the host business and the technology owner. Both make valuable contributions to the introduction of the innovation into the marketplace. Perceptions of who has the greater bargaining power cause difficulties in negotiations even when doing business is the given intent.

Risk. There are risks on both sides of the transfer equation. The business which owns the technology risks diffusion and loss of competitive advantage. The buyer, on the other hand, risks that returns will not support the high cost of transfer.

High cost. Typically transfer of technology includes up-front fees, royalties, and the financial capitalization of new equipment to support its introduction into the market.

Cultural. Careful assessment of cultural readiness or interest is also a major implication. This is particularly true when the technology is new and/or considered complex to a society.

Government intervention. It is not unusual that governments cause delays when screening transfers of technology. The intent of this central control in some nations is to avoid duplication.

Worker training. Levels of trainable workers vary from nation to nation depending on education, technical schools, and experience. Often the transfer must include worker training as a condition of the contract.

Dependency. The argument of less-developed nations depending on developed nations raises political issues far beyond the intent of the private sector businesses involved.

Military technology. The use of technology for military purposes is controlled by most nations. Care should be given to potential conflicts with authorities should the transfer be construed to have military implications.

Protection of intellectual property. The transfer of technology must include considerations on the part of the host nation for the protection of the intellectual property rights. Registration of intellectual property is not enough. If the laws of a nation do not succeed in prosecuting counterfeiters, for example, businesses will be reluctant to license transferral.

SCHEMES

In addition to production sharing, all nations offer incentive schemes to promote international trade to achieve their growth development ends. A search of various good deals offered growing global businesses includes the following.

Cheap loans. Usually in conjunction with investment projects or production sharing, these loans may be offered at 2-percent or 3-percent interest rates. They may also have extended payoff periods.

Subsidies. These include subsidies for factory construction as well as for training the laborers needed to produce the goods. Generous depreciation allowances, rent-free land, investment tax credits, double deductions for export promotion expenses, and reduced tax liability (tax holidays) are included in this category.

Duty-free imports. To encourage added-value assembly projects, foreign materials needed in the product are often entered duty-free.

Ownership of export-oriented enterprises. Many nations exclude foreigners from owning land. To promote export-only enterprises, exceptions are often made for 100-percent ownership.

Free remittance of profits and dividends after taxes. Global businesses want control over their profits. Consequently, they often go only where control is permitted.

Personal tax exemptions. Many nations forgo taxes on foreign employees involved in export-oriented projects. This induces transfer of technology and know-how.

Export market development. Some nations offer special program incentives such as product development assistance, trade consultancy services, venture capital schemes, and skills training grants. These go beyond subsidies and tax schemes.

R&D.   In addition to investment and depreciation allowances, some countries offer several other incentive schemes to stimulate quality industries and to promote R&D. Included are double deductions for R&D expenditures, extension of allowances on R&D-oriented buildings, and tax exemptions on income used for R&D purposes.

For you, the global business manager, the identification of incentives as they relate to your product and firm is a key factor in developing your global business strategy. To discover these influences and where they exist, you must search for the *good deals* country by country.

SUMMARY

The intent of the country market mapping process is to gain sufficient intelligence to forecast and make strategic decisions related to government strategies. The concept of artificial comparative advantage has been developing for more than 25 years. ACA links economic development to international trade. Nations offer, through indicative planning, various incentives to stimulate job expansion. The primary trade creation incentives are capital—financial, human, and technological. Nations use an assortment of schemes to induce growth. The global business strategist must monitor these inducements and include them in the global strategic management process.

CHECKLIST

- What is the trend of national strategy?
- Can your firm do business from the outside?
- When must your company become an insider?
- What schemes apply as a result of national strategies?
- How does a given nation's schemes affect your company's strategy?
- How should you adjust your firm's strategy to accommodate a country-by-country strategic mapping?
- What are the opportunities presented by national scheming?
- What kinds of capital are offered? Financial? Human? Technological?
- How strong is your organization's human capital?
- What kinds of capital does your firm need? What does it have?
- What is the availability of financial capital and by whom? Stock markets? VC? International lending? Supranational lenders?
- What are the technological implications of your products?
- What are the government schemes? Capital? Loans? Subsidies?

Chapter 17

Eighth Screening: Trade Barrier Mapping

The only limits, as always, are those of vision.

James Broughton

Suppose your firm has been operating in a country that stresses a free market, free enterprise, capitalistic environment. When it comes time to push through the door of another nation's markets you soon learn Adam Smith's invisible hand of the free market can be crushed with the sledgehammerlike blows of trade barriers.

INTRODUCTION

A distortion is a significant bias in product sales for the businesses of one country over another that are not the result of the free market competitive process. An example might be the permissible entry of goods into North America, but the refusal of similar entry into South America. In real terms, distortions to free trade add cost to your product and, in some cases, keep you out of the market altogether. Thus barriers become another major influence to strategy formulation. In some instances an organization would bypass a given nation for another with more favorable market terms. Also, the method of entry and positioning in a market are dependent on the dominant barriers relative to a given product.

Governments attempt to steer their economy by applying a torquelike combination of barriers and incentives to improve general welfare. As a minimum a global business would like to play by a set of fair trade rules: to do business so long as the rules are transparent and do not cause excessive market distortions. The game plan is to learn where and what the barriers are and to adjust strategy and policies country by country.

Free trade is a goal. It is often blocked by politicians and other lawmakers who either do not adhere to the same general commercial or international trade theories, or who are driven by the self-interest and economic developmental needs of their sovereign nation.

Fair trade, on the other hand, means several things. It can mean operating under the same set of rules, or it can be used to justify protectionism by imposing reciprocal rules on businesses from another nation in retaliation for not negotiating an agreeable rule; thus the term *level playing field.*

Global strategists can do business so long as they know the rules. But many of the nontariff distortions to trade are hidden, that is, only the locals know about them and frequently they only know because of word-of-mouth. Transparency is good for global business, because it means a company from Yemen can compete on favorable terms in the United States and a French firm can be confident that the Japanese rules are forthright. What more could a global manager ask?

> In 1891 the United States collected $216 million in import duties, which was 55 percent of the national revenue. In 1985 the United States collected $13 billion, but that was only 1.8 percent of the national revenue for that year.

This chapter deals with trade barriers. The major elements discussed are: tariff barriers (visibles), nontariff barriers (invisibles), other barriers, trade as a political weapon, international debt, and industrial policy.

TARIFF BARRIERS (VISIBLES)

Every country surrounds itself with a boundary called the customs territory. This line on a map is often synchronous with the nation's frontier geography. It is made operable at each port of entry (air, land, or sea) by persons who decide not only what goods will enter but also what sum of money should be collected prior to entry. Those who circumvent the ports of entry to bring goods into the country are called smugglers.

Impact on Strategy

Tariff barriers distort trade depending on the duty applied to the merchandise. The effect on strategy may range from negligible to a total halt in product trade. Because tariffs cannot be considered prima facie or self-evident unfair, they are, under the rules of the General Agreement on Tariffs and Trade (GATT), permitted. Thus, tariffs are an accepted method of protection under GATT. A very high tariff may not violate international rules unless a country has made a bound commitment not to exceed a specific rate. On the other hand, where measures are inconsistent with international rules, they are actionable under U.S. trade law and through GATT.

- Does the target country have tariffs related to your products?
- Are there quantitative restrictions?
- Are the restrictions absolute or tariff-rate?
- What are the rules of origin?

Tariffs are, by definition, a tax at the border collected on an ad valorem (percentage) of the transaction price as shown on the invoice at the time of crossing. In the vast majority of cases, a tariff is collected on incoming goods (imports), but theoretically they may be collected on outgoing goods (exports) as well.

Some countries use the tariff money as income to operate their central government. For instance, the United States enacted the U.S. Tariff Act of July 4, 1789, as an 8.5 percent duty in order to finance the newly created government. Later, in the early 1900s, the nation shifted to an income tax as its primary means of federal government support.

Developing countries have historically used customs duties to provide a major share of government revenues. For some, duties provide as much as 60 percent of national revenue, and, for most, the range is between 20 percent and 50 percent. Typically extremely high tariff charges have been encountered on products not produced or unlikely to be produced in the developing nation.

More often tariffs are collected as a deterrent to competition in order to shield home industries. In most countries, tariffs serve both purposes and are a preferential method under the GATT because they are more visible and apt to be more fair than other barriers. Some countries go so far as to specify certain duties as *protection* or *revenue*.

In as much as all countries use a border tariff the method has become very transparent; that is, each nation has adopted a method, usually a book, which shows its schedule of duties. Most countries have even joined in the effort by the Customs Cooperation Council (CCC) to standardize the nomenclature and numbering structure making it even easier to do business across borders.

For decades, the international trading community was confronted with problems caused by different classification and numbering systems covering the movement of goods. In 1970, with the assistance of 48 countries and more than a dozen private and public organizations, the CCC began a 13-year process to develop a system capable of meeting the principal requirements of customs authorities, statisticians, carriers, and producers. The result was the adoption of a Harmonized Commodity Description and Coding System by most of the nations of the world. Thus, beginning in 1983, tariffs have become even more transparent.

Historically there have been conditions when average worldwide tariffs exceeded 50 percent. The U.S. law, the Smoot-Hawley Act of 1930, stipulated duties was 50 percent, and tariffs imposed by Western nations on goods from Communist countries are often 40 percent or more.

Tariffs vary from product to product depending on the international trade theory adopted by each nation. Prior to the Uruguay Round of GATT, Table 17-1 shows a selected group of nations and their tariff rates.

Quantitative Restrictions

Quantitative restrictions or quotas are another transparent means of controlling product entry, because they are also listed in the Harmonized System. Quotas include limitations and complete bans on the import or export of specific commodities. Typically, quanitative restrictions are divided into two types: absolute and tariff-rate.

Absolute. Absolute quotas limit the quantity of goods that enter during a specific period. Some are global while others are allocated to certain countries.

Typically, because absolute quotas are filled at or shortly after beginning the quota period, they are usually opened at a specific time on the first workday of the quota so all importers have the same opportunity for simultaneous presentation of their entries. If a quantity of quota merchandise offered at entry exceeds the quota, the commodity is released on a pro rata basis; that is, the ratio between the quota quantity and the total quantity offered for entry. If not filled at the opening, quotas are filled on a first-come, first-served basis. Imports in excess of the quotas are usually warehoused for entry during the next quota period.

Tariff-rate quotas. Tariff-rate quotas permit a specified quantity of imported merchandise to enter at a reduced rate of customs duty during the quota period. There is no limitation on the amount of product that may enter at any time, but quantities entered during the period in excess of the quota for that period are subject to higher duty rates.

Rules of Origin

Countries require imported articles produced abroad to be conspicuously legible, indelible, and permanently marked with the country of origin. There are three purposes for these markings:

1. To provide transparency to the ultimate user, the name and country of manufacture and/or modification. The user is the consumer or the last person to receive the product in its form.
2. To substantiate tariff requirements.
3. To prevent exporters from circumventing bloc borders.

TABLE 17–1
Tariff Rates of
Selected Countries

Nation	Tariff rate
Argentina	0–38%; 55% on autos and 10–90% on infomatics
Australia	Average 15%
Brazil	Average 45%; sometimes over 200%
Canada	Average 9–10%; for the United States will reduce to 0% over the next 10 years
Chile	Average 50%
China	Average 9.2%
Columbia	Average 51.6%
European Community	Variable levies (VLs) designed to raise import prices to EC prices
Finland	Average 1.5–4.1%
India	Average 137.6%
Indonesia	0% on needed raw materials; as high as 100% on luxuries
South Korea	Average 20%; agriculture 30–50%
Malaysia	Average 15%
Mexico	20–30%
New Zealand	25% on many goods, but 40–85% on goods competing with domestic products
Pakistan	Average 67%
Philippines	Average 29.17%
Taiwan	Average 20%; up to 57.5%
Thailand	Average 23.5%; 40% on consumer goods
Venezuela	Average 45%; up to 70%
United States and Organization of Economic Cooperation and Development (OECD) members	Average less than 5%

NONTARIFF BARRIERS (INVISIBLES)

At least tariffs and quotas are visible. You can see them and determine their impact on your profits and business plans. But it is the nontariffs or invisibles that can keep you from doing business altogether. They affect not only goods but also services, investments, and property rights. The United States classifies the nontariffs into 10 categories.

1. Are import licenses required?
2. Are there customs barriers other than tariffs and quotas?
3. What are the standards requirements, such as testing, labeling, and certification?
4. What are the government procurement rules?
5. Are there export subsidies?
6. Does the target country have intellectual property protection?
7. Does the target country require countertrade and offsets?
8. Are there services barriers?
9. Are there investment barriers?
10. Are there other barriers?

Import Licenses

Import licensing is the process of requiring a permit or documentation other than that required for customs purposes as a prior condition for importing goods. Licenses are used by governments to keep track of the nature and quantity of imports and to administer restrictions such as quotas. Developing countries often use licenses to monitor and control the use of convertible currency.

TABLE 17–2
Examples of Quotas

Commodity	Absolute	Tariff-rate
Textiles	Cottons, silk blends, fibers of cotton, wool, synthetic products, and vegetables	
Steel	Stainless steel bar and tungsten	
Food	Ale, stout, beer, chocolate, sugars, peanuts, candy, apple and pear juice, and white wines	Tuna fish
Dairy products	Butter, cheese, animal feeds, milk, cream, and ice cream	
Other consumables	Watches and watch movements	Whisk brooms

Such licensing may have acceptable uses, but trade is frequently made more difficult by many countries as a result of inappropriate use. For example, applications for licenses are often ambiguous, complicated, and require documents which are completely unrelated to the function of the license. Sometimes documents must be submitted in multiple copies which serve to tie up administrative employees in unnecessary paperwork, resulting in needless delays. In addition, licensing officials sometimes cannot be located, or they require submission of documents at certain hours or particular days before the vessel carrying the goods is due to depart, causing carrier scheduling problems.

Prior to the Tokyo Round of the GATT, trade restrictive measures such as embargoes and quotas were covered by rules, but most aspects of import licensing were not. The GATT Licensing Code effective since January 1, 1980, sets forth general provisions on procedures in terms of automatic and nonautomatic import licensing.

Automatic. In the context of the GATT, automatic import licensing means that government approval of a license application will be freely granted. These usually are methods employed to collect statistical data or other information regarding imports when no other appropriate procedure is available. The intent of the code is only to prevent trade-restrictive effects and to encourage their discontinuance as soon as their underlying purpose can be achieved in another way.

Nonautomatic. Nonautomatic licenses refers to import licensing used in the administration of quotas and other import restrictions. The aim of the code is to eliminate any trade restrictive effects those licenses may have which are incidental to the imposition of the restrictions. This is principally done through the code which requires transparency and distribution of information well in advance of the opening and closing dates of quotas.

Customs Barriers

The valuation of goods as they pass through customs has been inconsistent among nations. Prior to the Tokyo Round of GATT, the most common method was the Brussels Convention on Valuation (or Brussels Definition of Value/BDV), drawn up by the CCC in 1950. Several nations, including the United States, maintained their own independent valuation system which was considered by trading partners as a trade barrier.

Tokyo Round negotiators developed a uniform customs valuation called the Customs Valuation Code. Its goals are to: ensure fairness and simplicity; conform to commercial reality; outlaw arbitrary or fictitious customs values; and give importers and exporters predictability in assessing the amount of duty owed on imported goods.

Standards, Testing, Labeling, and Certification

A standard is a technical specification approved by a recognized standards body which sets out a product's characteristics in terms of dimensions, safety requirements, or performance. The standard can also specify testing requirements and methods, labeling, and the procedures for administering the specifications.

Needless to say, many government regulations in this category are legitimate. They protect plant, animal, and human life and prevent consumer fraud. But trade can be distorted when the standards become disguised discriminatory trade restrictions.

The importance of the differences between nations' standards, testing, and approval procedures had long been talked about, but little had been done about their impact on international trade until the Tokyo Round of the Multilateral Trade Negotiations (MTN). On January 1, 1980, a Standards Code, negotiated and accepted by GATT, was entered into force. The code is composed of four different types of provisions: general principles, open procedures, information and assistance, and dispute-settlement procedures.

The code's most important aim was to eliminate unnecessary trade barriers by encouraging the use of appropriate international standards and of standards based on performance instead of design criteria. It obligates countries to treat imported products no less favorably than domestic products.

Signatories are required to use open (transparent) procedures when developing new or amended standards and rules of certification systems. The code requires access through an inquiry point, the purpose of which is to provide information to other signatories regarding technical regulations, standards, and certification systems. This section of the code makes provision for special and differential treatment for developing countries, since they may need specific advice on establishing national standardization bodies and certification institutes.

A primary intent of the code was, for the first time, to establish international rules between governments' regulating procedures by which standards and certification systems are prepared, adopted, and applied, and by which products are tested for conformity with standards. Finally, the code establishes a Committee on Technical Barriers to Trade which meets periodically to oversee implementation and administration of the agreement, as well as to discuss any new issues or problems which should arise.

Government Procurement

With the increase of privatization, less of the world's manufacturing is done under the auspices of a government; however, the buying of goods is another thing. Governments remain among the world's largest purchasers of goods. By discriminating against global businesses, buy-national policies obviously constitute a significant distortion to international trade and constitute a considerable nontariff barrier

Prior to the Tokyo Round, where the Agreement on Government Procurement was developed, GATT rules requiring national treatment (that is, prohibiting discrimination against imports), did not apply to "procurement by government agencies of products purchased for government purposes" (GATT 1969). Under the agreement, signatories undertake not to discriminate against or among the products of other signatories in purchases of goods by government entities (such as ministries and departments) listed in an annex to the agreement. In 1987 the

On October 23, 1990, the government of Mexico gave two weeks' notice of new labeling requirements for textiles imported into that country. Under one provision of the procedures, labels must name both the American exporter and the Mexican importer, a requirement most traders find almost impossible to meet since most shipments go to a number of different importers. U.S. exporters charged that the new requirements were an ill-concealed attempt to stop a surge in imports from the United States after Mexico lowered textile tariffs and eased licensing rules the previous year.

code covered contracts for product purchases above the level of 150,000 Special Drawing Rights—an amount equal to $171,000.

The agreement includes the following:

- Detailed requirements for open and fair government purchasing procedures.
- Strong dispute-settlement procedures.
- Exchange of data on purchases covered by the agreement.
- Provisions for special and differential treatment for developing countries.
- Regular meetings of the signatories to discuss the operation of the agreement.
- Expansion of the coverage, including service contracts, within three years.

The agreement does not cover national security items, state and local government purchases, or federally funded grant programs. Services such as construction contracts are covered only to the extent incidental to procurement of goods.

Export Subsidies

In general terms, a subsidy is a bounty or grant, usually provided by a government, that confers a financial benefit on the production, manufacturing, or distribution of a good or service. An export subsidy is a direct government payment or other economic benefit contingent upon export.

All governments maintain subsidy programs of one form or another. Some of the typical forms are: direct cash grants, credits against taxes, concessionary loans, or infrastructure services. Some subsidies are granted to foster the elimination of regional economic disparities, called domestic or internal subsidies, but most have the objective to stimulate exports of goods or services. Thus the subsidy affords a competitive advantage to nationally produced products in one country over the unsubsidized production of another. The result is a distortion to international trade.

Recognizing that subsidies can cause or threaten real economic injury to competing industries in other countries, the defense used by many countries is to impose what is called "countervailing duties" at the border. The international Subsidies Agreement negotiated and accepted during the Tokyo Round acts as the basic set of rules governing both subsidies and countervailing measures. The code flatly prohibits subsidies on industrial and mineral products, regulates the use of export subsidies on agriculture products and primary fishery and forest products, and sets out broad guidelines for the use of domestic subsidies.

Countervailing duties can be imposed in any amount no greater than the net subsidy borne by a product and then only where subsidized imports cause or threaten material injury to an industry in the importing country. The code provides for dispute settlement and special retaliatory countermeasures against the trade of the country that has broken the rules.

Intellectual Property Protection

Intellectual property are innovations and creations. The protection of intellectual property fosters creativity, development of technology, and expertise, and encourages investment in research as well as new facilities to exploit the results of successful research. The forms of intellectual property protection include: patents, copyrights, trademarks, trade dress, trade secrets, and semiconductor mask works.

In practical terms, the underlying purpose of protection is to encourage inventors (through payment of royalties, etc.) to bring their creations out of the garage or back rooms so the rest of the world can benefit. Piracy and counterfeiting occur, however, because copying is far less expensive and risky than developing and building a market for a new product.

Many countries do not have laws that enable authors, inventors, or trademark owners to acquire, exercise, or effectively enforce rights to prevent others from pirating their creative works. Even in those countries where there are adequate laws, effective enforcement may not occur. Inadequate penalties or lack of governmental commitment to enforce laws encourages pirates and counterfeiters to take advantage of resources without sharing the developmental costs.

Countertrade and Offsets

The availability of convertible currency in some countries continues to be a trade barrier. As a result, a variety of commercial compensation arrangements have been developed which are intended to reduce or offset the need for money. Some of these are mandated by governments for budgetary and balance of payments reasons while others are just creative methods of doing business. Regardless of their origin, the objectives of countertrade practices are to:

- Reduce or offset the budgetary or balance-of-payment effect of major import transactions.
- Create employment.
- Stimulate exports.
- Stimulate technology transfer.
- Accomplish creative marketing.
- Deal with controlled (nonmarket) economies.

Actually *countertrade* is the umbrella term for a variety of these unconventional reciprocal trading arrangements. It includes the following:
- *Counterpurchases* obligate the supplier to purchase from the buyer goods and services unrelated to those sold.
- *Reverse countertrade* contracts require the importer to export goods equivalent in value to a specified percentage of the value of the imported goods. This obligation can be sold to an exporter in a third country.
- *Buy-back arrangements* obligate the foreign supplier of plant, machinery, or technology to buy from the importer a portion of the resultant production during a 5–25 year period.
- *Clearing agreements* are between two countries that agree to purchase specific amounts of each other's products over a long-term specific period, using a designated clearing currency or barter in the transactions.
- *Switch arrangements* permit the sale of an unpaid balance of a clearing account to be sold to a third party, usually at a discount, that may be used for producing goods in the country holding the balance.
- *Swaps* are schemes through which products from different locations are traded to save transportation costs.
- *Barter* directly exchanges goods between two parties deemed to be of approximately equivalent value without any flow of money taking place.
- *Offsets* are generally used for long-term sales to help recover the hard currency drain resulting from the purchase. These can be directly or indirectly related to the product in question. For direct transactions, local producers joint

venture with the vendor. Indirect offsets involve the vendor buying unrelated goods or investing in an unrelated business.

- *Combinations* of all of the above are among the bag of tricks a creative global business can use when all else seems improbable.

Theoretically, international trade in an environment of countertrade could approximate the free market; however, it is more likely distortions and increased costs would be introduced. In addition, despite the long list of arrangements available, the need to do business in lieu of using currency causes many small firms, without the necessary experience, to avoid doing global business altogether.

Services Barriers

The service industries of many countries far outpace manufacturing industries in terms of employment and sales volume. Yet many barriers exist that limit the ability of such businesses to go global. These nontariff obstacles have become increasingly distortive to international commerce. In recent years trade barriers against the globalization of such services as banking, insurance, telecommunications, transportation, data processing, construction, and engineering have received great attention in the international business community.

Investment Barriers

Some governments refuse to grant investment by global businesses on the same basis as domestic investment. When this happens the trade effects are distorted compared to those effects created by quantitative restrictions. By denying investment, host-country producers and consumers lose the benefits of additional production as well as product and service exports.

On the other hand, incentives which link the attraction of investment to performance in terms of product content can also distort trade by artificially increasing the supply of the affected products in world markets and by displacing more efficient home-market production and exports. Similarly local content requirements displace home- or third-country imports and have the same effect as quotas.

Other Barriers

In addition to those barriers generally included under the tariff and nontariff barrier labels, other barriers have emerged which deserve consideration when screening intelligence for strategy formulation purposes. These include the following:

- Structural impediments.
- Trade only through state trading companies.
- Violation of antitrust.
- False advertisement.
- Uncompetitive pricing and/or dumping.
- Public health.
- Excise taxes.

Structural barriers. The list of nontariff barriers must include problems considered routine by the home country, but significant to the global competitive process. These structural impediments include a number of government measures and, in some cases, historical ways of doing business which are so inconsistent with modern management that they contribute to significant cross-border distortions. One Japanese businessman observed, "You Americans perceive our retail and wholesale layering is intended to keep you out of our market. But it is the way we have done business for hundreds of years."

Nevertheless, layering of archaic distribution systems and other trade organizations, such as preshipment inspection firms, only add to the inefficiency of the market. According to the U.S. Department of Commerce, preshipment firms operate in 25 countries in Africa, Asia, Latin America, and Central America. These firms are under contract to the government and essentially act as the country's customs service by standing between the companies involved to manage scarce foreign exchange and eliminate customs fraud and capital flight.

Global businesses see these types of structures as inefficient methods propped up by trade associations and governments to sustain employment or protect balance-of-payment problems at the expense of modernization. Artificial distribution systems are nontransparent barriers to market access, add to the cost of all products not just imports, and have a direct impact on the consumer pocketbook.

Trade only through state trading companies.   Bureaucracies are not always a barrier to trade. Many serve as business filters ensuring strong competitive processes. But, in the case of state trading companies, used extensively in non-market countries, bureaucracies are, for market-oriented global businesses, like a wall. Time is money and these kinds of organizations are corruptive of not only time but efficiency.

TRADE AS A POLITICAL WEAPON

Rightly or wrongly the disruption of international trade is among the bag of tricks one nation can use against another to win the political chess game. From least disruptive to most disruptive to trade, these tactics include the following:

- Threats.
- Orderly market agreements (OMA).
- Extended negotiations.
- Foreign exchange controls (FEC).
- Cancellation of licenses.
- Boycott.
- Embargo.
- Expulsion.
- Coup d'etat.
- Revolution.
- Expropriation.
- Terrorism.
- Blockade.
- War.

Although not on the list, the threat of or the actual carrying out of a strike by private sector unions can have the same devastating effects on international trade.

Threats

Least disruptive of general international trade between two nations, yet very effective in terms of the product in question, are threats. An example might be an industrial nation threatening to cut off general systems of preferences of a less-developed nation if certain perceived unfair trade practices are not stopped.

Orderly Market Arrangements

Alternately called voluntary restraint agreements, these arrangements act as political pressure to protect a nation's industry without resorting to a tariff barrier.

Extended Negotiations

This is among the least disruptive to general business and is usually focused on one company or industry. It can come about as a result of a lawsuit or even an ethical disagreement. Extended negotiations essentially act as an embargo for the goods of the firm involved and sometimes require government intercession on behalf of the global business.

Foreign Exchange Controls

These controls stem from a shortage of foreign exchange held by a country. They are a form of rationing in which a company earning freely convertible foreign exchange through exporting must sell this exchange to the control agency, usually a central bank. Except for state trading companies, exchange controls are the most complete method of regulating international trade. In practice, exchange control amounts to a government monopoly of all dealings related to foreign currency. That also means the exchange is in scarce supply.

A company wishing to import goods must buy exchange from the control agency rather than in a free market. The government only rations its currency for those supplies that it favors for the good of its economy. Generally currency is released for needed raw materials or capital equipment, and expenditures for luxuries are avoided.

Cancellation of Import/Export Licenses

In those countries that require licenses, these are controlled goods. They can be used as weapons against the global business. For example, a nation could use them to stimulate or protect certain industries from foreign competition.

Boycott

Boycott is the refusal to do business with or have other contact with a person, corporation, or country. International economic boycotts are used by one country against the trade of another. Such is the case of the Arab boycott of Israeli goods.

Embargo

An order to stop the movement of persons or property is an embargo. There are several types of embargoes. A hostile embargo is one which a government uses in times of peace to exert pressure on another government for political or economic reasons. It may include the seizing of goods or detaining of persons in or out of ports of entry. This type of embargo is usually a prelude to war. If war breaks out, the property is seized as a prize. If peace prevails, the property is usually returned to its rightful owner. Hostile embargoes were condemned by the 1907 Hague Convention.

Civil embargoes are those used by a country to internally restrain its own people and property. The intent of this type of embargo is to keep needed supplies in a country or to prevent vital supplies from being shipped to a warring country.

Freight embargoes are internal constraints used as emergency measures because of bad weather, strikes, or unusual traffic conditions. These embargoes are sometimes issued by transportation companies or regulatory agencies. Control of military arms is another form of embargo.

Expulsion

For the global business, expulsion would be the ultimate economic sanction brought about by a sovereign nation. This act could be caused by unethical or immoral behavior or could accompany expropriation.

Coup d'Etat

The violent overthrow or alteration of a government by a small group is defined as a coup d'etat. Its effect on international trade varies, depending on the nature or causes for change. The causes very often are based in economics; therefore, the coup d'etat can change the nation's entire approach to international trade.

Revolution

The internal strife caused by a revolution typically sets a nation's international trade efforts backwards. The result is a reversal of any economic development progress it may have gained during peaceful times.

Expropriation

Expropriation is the act of the state taking or modifying the property rights of an individual in the exercise of its sovereignty. A global business might experience expropriation following a revolution or coup d'etat.

Terrorism

In the 1970s and 1980s the world was exposed to a series of terrorist acts which amounted to political actions by groups without portfolios. These acts had a pronounced effect on world trade. People were concerned about travel and their personal safety as well as the implications when the terrorist acts were against production and assembly plants of selected firms.

Blockade

Like the embargo, there can be hostile or pacific blockades. The hostile blockade can only be declared by a nation that has the power to enforce it; that is, a naval force so large that it can guard a given port in such a manner that a merchant ship cannot run the blockade. International case law requires that countries formally declare a blockade and must notify neutral nations. A pacific blockade, like the one President John F. Kennedy ordered in 1962 to halt shipments of missiles to Cuba, applies only to ships of the nation being blockaded.

War

War is the ultimate political action and it causes the greatest setback to international trade. Routine business stops while the nations involved concentrate on war-making. It is not unusual that a nation's economic development and international trade are so reversed and upset that generations will suffer long after the war has ended to regain prewar economic and trade levels.

INTERNATIONAL DEBT

Every nation keeps a set of books using a double entry accounting system which classifies and aggregates all the international trade and economic transactions. The data are collected by requiring each cross-transaction to be recorded on special forms and then entered into a central computer. This summary of all transactions between residents of one country and the residents of another country, which usually covers a period of one year, is kept in three accounts: (1) current account, (2) capital account, and (3) official reserves account. Residence of businesses is generally determined by the country in which they are incorporated.

The balance of payments of a country then, is really the summary of three balances: the balance of the current account (BOCuA), the balance of the capital account (BOCaA), and the balance of the official reserves account (BOORA). These accounts are the records of imports and exports of merchandise and services, cash payments, gold flows, gifts, loans and investments, and other transactions. The accounts provide an overall view of a nation's international economic position. They are particularly valuable in the formulation of governmental as well as business strategy.

The BOCuA is composed of two subaccounts: balance of merchandise trade (BOMT) and balance of goods and services (BOGS). The BOCaA records the net changes in capital imports and exports, and the BOORA shows the net foreign transactions of the nation's central bank.

Balance of Merchandise Trade

BOMT is a component of the balance of payments. It is the surplus or deficit that results from comparing a country's expenditures on merchandise imports and its receipts derived from its merchandise exports. Simply put, the BMOT equals exports minus imports.

Balance of Goods and Services

BOGS is the BOMT plus or minus net services. These include sales and purchases of such things as transportation, insurance, travel, and return on investment (interest, dividends, profits, royalties, speculation on currency, etc.). Simply put, the BOGS equals BMOT plus or minus net services.

Balance of Payments

To summarize then, the balance of payments consists of:

1. BOMT = merchandise imports – merchandise exports
2. BOGS = BOMT ± net services, which include ROI
3. BOCA = BOGS – unilateral transfers
4. BOCaA
5. BOORA

Strategy Effects

How does the balance of payments affect global strategy? Typically when a nation's balance of payments goes into a deficit position, it is a signal to global business strategists that government policymakers of that country will begin to consider means to return the balances to a neutral or stable condition. This can be accomplished by several methods: (1) curtailing imports and emphasizing exports in hopes that a surplus of foreign currency will be introduced to bolster the balance; (2) deflating the domestic economy by adjusting monetary and/or fiscal instruments; (3) devaluing the exchange rate; or (4) imposing exchange controls over international transactions. All of these methods become barriers to international trade.

The story is not pleasant for many third-world nations. Flushed with petrodollars to lend in the mid-1970s, the major banks of the industrial nations got into economic development in a big way. They saw that most third-world nations were desperate for development capital; therefore, they were prime candidates for loans. The result was bankers pushed the money to third-world borrowers. The problem was third-world countries didn't make and sell enough product in global markets to generate the convertible currency cash flow to even pay the interest on the debts. To service even a partial amount, these nations began capturing foreign currency at the borders from exporters and rationing it only to importers of national priority goods.

Blocked Funds. The capture and control of foreign convertible currency is called blocked funds. The controls are designed to repay loans. Global business managers are caught in the middle because, in the name of economic development, competition has been stifled and the consumer shortchanged.

INDUSTRIAL POLICY

Some nations guide their national economy through planning and industrial policy. The underlying assumption of these governmental policies is that they believe market forces alone do not create the desired effect; therefore, these governments establish five-year plans and announce industrial policies which identify strategic industries, protect domestic industries, provide for incentives to achieve their goals, emphasize exports, and promote business cooperation instead of competition. Whether by directed or indicative planning methods, governments then give administrative guidance which amounts to managing international trade.

The issue then is whether these plan-driven policies are a barrier to free trade. To the extent the planning is transparent and global business is permitted to participate, the effects are minimal. When interstate controls used to achieve the planning goals curtail business goals, however, the planning and/or industrial policy can have a distortion effect on your company's success and that will certainly affect your strategy.

SUMMARY

One could construe that the road to global success is strewn with the rocks and pebbles of trade barriers such that a comprehensive strategy is unattainable. Certainly tariff and nontariff barriers pose gamesmanship problems; however, the overall effect on international trade is probably not more than 10–15 percent. Most of your global strategy will be driven by the vast opportunities found in a constantly changing world.

CHECKLIST

- What are the visible barriers to your product in a given country?
- What are the invisible barriers?
- Are the barriers insurmountable and too costly, thus forcing your strategy toward an insider position?
- What political weapons are being used?
- What is the balance-of-payments position of the target country?
- Does the country have debt problems?
- If so, what are the debt implications to your products?
- Does the country have an industrial policy?
- What are the barrier implications?

Chapter 18

Ninth Screening: Harmony Implications

If trade could be encouraged, then our destinies would be bound together. We could not afford to go to war with each other.

Henry Kissinger

International trade is highly regulated for two reasons. First, in business there are always an unscrupulous few who attempt to take advantage of the ethical many. Unlawful actions often lead to increased regulation. Second, global trade is inseparably linked to growth economics, and governments of every nation attempt to manage growth, particularly as it relates to job creation. As a result, every nation has a constantly changing number of barriers and innovative schemes that cause distortions to international markets.

This chapter is about screening the growing number of globally harmonized rules (commercial code) as they relate to your company and products. Global businesses can operate in the highly regulated world of international business, but they must understand and monitor the impact of supranational rules on strategic decisions.

WHAT IS HARMONIZATION?

All nations have interstate controls; however, these laws, regulations, procedures, and practices vary among the states making it difficult for businesses to operate on a cross-border basis. Harmonization is the process of defining, then peacefully negotiating, a common set of rules (fair trade) and procedures so that international trade can progress. To the extent they create major distortions and restrain free trade, interstate controls cause conflict. This leads to protectionism, depression, and war. Therefore, there is a need for harmonization.

Many people believe the key to peace is contented people—they don't fight. Therefore, the concept of supranational organizations offers opportunities for harmonization. As an example, there have been attempts, over time, particularly by intellectuals, to establish strong global supranational organizations to administer the harmonization of global social and political processes in addition to international trade. Some, like the League of Nations, have failed. Others, such as the United Nations, still exist under the hope that sovereign nations might see fit to make them work.

FLUCTUATING CURRENCY VALUES

Money is the lubricant that allows the economic machine to move, but money can also be a barrier to trade. It is one of those influences that causes some small companies to avoid the international marketplace because it is just too much of a pain. You should, however, treat money like any other kind of barrier and design your global strategy to take it into account.

Barrier versus Commercial Disputes

This chapter is not about the resolution of international commercial transaction disputes. These are matters of everyday business which do require resolution; however, they are handled in the courts or through arbitration. There are three primary bodies of international commercial law: common, code, and Islamic (Shari'a). There are also many subordinate bodies of law practiced in small states. A clause which specifies which body of law and in which country a commercial dispute would be adjudicated should always be clearly delineated in a commercial contract. Most international businesspersons believe it is even better to specify an arbitration body such as the International Chamber of Commerce. Seeking settlement through arbitration is less expensive than the courts.

Each nation has its own national banking system, creates its own money, and manipulates that currency according to its general internal welfare needs. That means every currency has a relative price to every other currency—so many dollars equal so many yen, and so many pounds equal so many marks. That wouldn't be so bad except that the relative prices are almost continuously in movement. Some currencies are not even convertible to another.

All other things being equal, you as a global strategist would like worldwide currency conditions to be as if you were doing business in your own country—no fuss, no bother. There might be a windfall gain if, in the short run, your own currency was weaker than that of another country, thus making your products a bit more salable. But in the long run, more total business is done globally if the relationship of one currency to another is stable. When that happens business is conducted in terms of the commercial factors that everyone understands: quality, price, service, and so on.

Historically, business has been done across borders despite instability. Also, global business managers have recommended to government leaders and the best of the world's economic advisors that they needed to improve the system so more business could take place. Today there are three mechanisms working to ensure monetary stability: (1) the International Monetary system, (2) the European Monetary system, and (3) manipulations by the G–7 (fully explained later in this chapter). Each must be monitored by the global business strategist.

International Monetary System

After World War II, leaders from 44 nations met to establish the International Monetary system (IMS). These wise people wanted a system that would prevent countries from changing exchange rates for competitive advantage. They wanted stable currencies so business managers could trade with confidence. Included in the articles of agreement were provisions to: (1) promote international monetary cooperation; (2) facilitate the growth of trade; (3) promote exchange rate stability; (4) establish a system of multilateral payments; and (5) create a reserve base for deficit countries.

The U.S. dollar became the equivalent of a universally accepted currency, freely convertible to gold with all other currencies fixed within 1 percent to the dollar. The problem with the system was that the United States essentially became the world's banker, and that spelled eventual doom for an otherwise reasonable solution. Eventually the perception that the United States was gaining a windfall profit (called *seigniorage*) as well as political power by this unofficial banker role caused first France and then other nations to convert their dollar holdings into gold. Unfortunately for global business, a system that had worked for more than 25 years came unraveled.

The dollar lost its stability against gold, and erratic movements, then sharp declines caused the largest 10 countries (called the Group of Ten or G–10) to meet and recommend that the U.S. dollar be devalued to $38 per ounce of gold, and that all other currencies develop parity against the dollar. This recommendation came in August 1971 and became known as the Smithsonian Agreement.

Several methods were adopted to keep currencies within a stable range so global companies could do business. Central banks intervened to buy or sell their own currency using the official rule that has become known as the tunnel; that is, no greater than 2-1/4 percent on either side of the dollar, or a total band vis-à-vis the dollar of 4-1/2 percent. The stronger ECC countries elected to keep their range narrower, in a range of no more than 1-1/8 percent either side, or a total band of 2-1/2 percent. That has become known as the snake. Some nations within the EEC went even farther to maintain their range of difference at less than 1-1/8 percent, and they called that the worm. Finally, some nations intervened to peg their currency so that it moved exactly with the dollar. The peg within the worm within the snake within the tunnel became the world's monetary system. Gold was officially demonetized, and floating exchange rates were approved at the Jamaica meeting of the G–10 in 1976. Figure 18–1 shows this in graphic terms.

1979 European Monetary System (EMS)

With central banks now intervening to manage their own floats, the European common market countries, less Great Britain, decided to create a new form of currency to be used for settlements. The European Currency Unit (ECU) and called *ecu* for an ancient coin used during the Middle Ages in France, is actually an equivalency of six European currencies. Participating countries must maintain exchange rates within 2-1/4 percent on either side of ecu par. Thus, for practical purposes, the world has two monetary systems: The European Monetary system became a monetary system within the IMS.

Group of Seven (G–7)

In September 1985 the Group of Five or G–5 (United States, France, Great Britain, Japan, and West Germany), agreed to an informal system of managed float. This meant *intervention* (buying and selling) by central banks in foreign exchange markets, but in coordination with the other members of the major industrial nations (now the G–7 with the addition of Canada and Italy). Further, the group would hold periodic economic summits to coordinate economic policy.

At the 1986 Tokyo Economic Declaration, finance ministers were asked to "review their individual economic objectives and forecasts collectively at least once a year." As a follow-up, a formal commitment was reached among the G–7 nations at the Louvre Accord in February 1987 to formulate a mechanism of agreed-upon parameters (target zones) for exchange rates. Using these indicators, finance ministers began reviewing their economic objectives and sharing their ideas. This was the beginning of world economic coordination. Figure 18–2 shows the road to currency stabilization, from gold to coordinated intervention.

Hedging

As a global business manager you do not want money to be a barrier. Take away the risk and uncertainty. Resolve unpredictable movement. Invisible product costs caused by instability only inhibit world trade.

There is a way around instability, but it adds cost, not value, to the product and can be a factor in your firm's noncompetitiveness. That method is called hedging against the unspeakable chance that the relative value of a currency might change against your favor during a transaction. By using the forward markets, a specified relative value of one currency to another can be locked in for a future date. It is done at a daily rate of as much as $50 billion. Most major international banks can handle this kind of contract for you. Figure 18–3 is a clipping from the *Journal of Commerce* that shows the forward rates in 30-, 60-, and 90-day

FIGURE 18–1
1972 Floating Exchange Rates   U.S. $ < Tunnel ± $2^1/_2$%   < Snake ± $1^1/_8$%   < Worm ± $1^1/_8$%   < Peg

FIGURE 18–2
Road to Currency
Stabilization

1900 >_____	1940 >_____	1944 >_____	1971 >_____	1985 >_____
Gold	Guns/butter	Gold/$/ intervention	Float (market)	Coordinated intervention

intervals. By matching a forward contract with a payable denominated in a foreign currency you can eliminate any future instability.

HARMONIZING INTERSTATE CONTROLS

There are several methods by which nations negotiate to harmonize trade of products and services. Each should be monitored as they relate to your firm's products and international business strategy.

Bilateral Negotiations

A commercial treaty called friendship, commerce, and navigation (FCN) is one way to establish trade relations and negotiate harmony in cases where there are trade distortions between two nations. Specific intestate problems such as joint cooperation over a waterway or a special tariff arrangement. There are many treaties in effect, and the procedure is still commonly used for specific interstate problems.

Multilateral Trade Negotiations (MTN)

Following World War II the leaders of the victorious nations realized that cooperation was essential to maintain peace. But before harmony could be achieved more effective ways than bilateral negotiations would have to be established. The bilateral method just took too long. By negotiating item by item, minor points became the subject of protracted argument, which gave manufacturers' lobbyists more time to pressure negotiators.

Multilateral trade negotiations (MTN) are an improvement over bilateral negotiations in that a large number of countries can simultaneously agree to a set of rules for the liberalization of trade. This method, however, requires nations to surrender some sovereignty and subject themselves to international procedures.

The alternate method of MTN is most-favored nation treatment (MFN) or nondiscriminatory tariff treatment. Instead of negotiating country by country, the benefit of any bilateral tariff reduction is extended to all most-favored countries. This principal simply means that one nation treats a second nation as favorably as it treats any third nation.

General Agreement on Tariff and Trade (GATT)

The most important trade negotiation process to be monitored by the global strategist is the General Agreement on Tariff and Trade. GATT came into being in 1947. Its original purpose was simply to keep the records of various tariff negotiations. Like an accounting system, it was needed so that one concession was not undercut by another. Today the organization has 101 contracting parties representing over four fifths of world trade.

GATT was never intended to become the International Trade Organization (ITO) or even a supranational organization; however, it became a de facto supranational organization. In many ways it has been more effective than others so constituted. GATT has become the major harmonizing institution for international trade. It is the keeper of the rules and a forum to argue and settle disputes.

FOREIGN EXCHANGE

The New York foreign exchange rates below, provided by EAB New York, are selling rates among trading banks of $1 million and more as quoted at 3 p.m. Eastern time. Retail transactions provide fewer units of foreign currency per dollar. Foreign currency values are expressed in terms of currency units per dollar unless otherwise noted. To obtain the comparable dollar value, for those rates not quoted in dollars, divide into one. For example, when one U.S. dollar buys 6.9075 French francs, one dollar divided by 6.9075 francs equals $.1448 or 14.48 U.S. cents per franc.

Tuesday, May 25, 1993

	Tues.	Mon.
*U.K. (Pound)	1.5430	1.5360
30 days	1.5392	1.5321
60 days	1.5368	1.5288
90 days	1.5327	1.5254
CANADA (Dollar)	1.2600	1.2607
30 days	1.2618	1.2622
60 days	1.2632	1.2637
90 days	1.2649	1.2657
NETHERLANDS		
(Guilder)	1.8247	1.8305
30 days	1.8312	1.8373
60 days	1.8364	1.8324
90 days	1.8412	1.8474
SWITZERLAND (Franc)	1.4575	1.4685
30 days	1.4600	1.4734
60 days	1.4626	1.4756
90 days	1.4644	1.4798
GERMANY (Mark)	1.6295	1.6348
30 days	1.6363	1.6417
60 days	1.6470	1.6468
90 days	1.6566	1.6522
FRANCE (Franc)	5.4855	5.5035
30 days	5.5087	5.5274
60 days	5.5262	5.5434
90 days	5.5440	5.5613
JAPAN (Yen)	109.37	110.50
30 days	109.38	110.51
60 days	109.38	110.51
90 days	109.37	110.50

	Tues.	Mon.
ITALY (Lira)	1480.00	1486.00
NORWAY (Krone)	6.8890	6.9044
PORTUGAL (Escudo)	153.95	154.80
SPAIN (Peseta)	124.52	124.74
SWEDEN (Krona)	7.3300	7.3303

ASIAN AND OTHER COUNTRIES

	Tues.	Mon.
*AUSTRALIA (Dollar)	.6997	.6945
HONG KONG (Dollar)	7.7270	7.7280
*INDIA (Rupee)	.031925	.031935
INDONESIAN (Rupiah)	2085.00	2085.00
ISREAL (Shekel)	2.6839	2.6731
*KUWAIT (Dinar)	.30160	.30111
LEBANON (Pound)	1735	1735
MALAYSIA (Ringgit)	2.5647	2.5668
*N. ZEALAND (Dollar)	.5480	.5445
PAKISTAN (Rupee)	26.8331	26.8331
PHILIPPINES (Peso)	27.000	27.000
SAUDI ARABIA (Riyal)	3.7504	3.7504
SINGAPORE (Dollar)	1.6115	1.6160
S. AFRICA (Rand)	3.1865	3.1965
S. KOREA (Won)	801.40	801.30
TAIWAN (Dollar)	26.08	26.06
TURKEY (Lira)	10260.00	10258.00

LATIN AMERICA

	Tues.	Mon.
ARGENTINA	1.0000	1.0000
BRAZIL (Cruzeiro)	39667.00	39186.0
CHILE (Peso)	418.70	419.00
COLOMBIA (Peso)	663.00	663.00
MEXICO (N Peso)	3.1280	3.1175
PERU (New Sol)	1.9640	1.9580
VENEZUELA (Bolivar)	87.49	87.60

GOLD

Price per oz.	Mon.	Tues.
LONDON, 2nd fixing	379.75	374.50

*These currencies are expressed in dollar price per unit.

OTHER EUROPEAN

	Tues.	Mon.
AUSTRIA (Shilling)	11.4685	11.5100
BELGIUM (Franc)	33.504	33.624
DENMARK (Krone)	6.2377	6.2592
FINLAND (Markka)	5.5211	5.5303
GREECE (Drachma)	220.80	221.50

CUSTOMS RATES

Federal Reserve Bank of New York certified buying rates for certain foreign currencies to be used for customs purposes or appropriate cases.

Tuesday, May 25, 1993

Country	Rate
*AUSTRALIA (Dollar)	.7001
AUSTRIA (Shilling)	11.4550
BELGIUM (Franc)	33.4700
BRAZIL (Cruzeiro)	N.A.
CANADA (Dollar)	1.2606
CHINA (Yuan)	5.7433
DENMARK (Krone)	6.2280
*EUR. CUR. UNIT (ECU)	1.2025
FINLAND (Markka)	5.4950
FRANCE (Franc)	5.4880
GERMANY (Mark)	1.6290
GREECE (Drachma)	220.55
HONG KONG (Dollar)	7.7280
INDIA (Rupee)	31.600
*IRELAND (Pound)	1.5005
*ISREAL (Shekel)	N.A.
ITALY (Lira)	1478.50
JAPAN (Yen)	109.50
MALAYSIA (Dollar)	2.5670

Country	Rate
NETHERLANDS (Guilder)	1.8242
*NEW ZEALAND (Dollar)	0.5473
NORWAY (Krone)	6.8800
PHILIPPINES (Escudo)	N.A.
PORTUGAL (Escudo)	154.000
SINGAPORE (Dollar)	1.6144
SOUTH AFRICA (Rand)	3.1900
SOUTH KOREA (Won)	804.400
SPAIN (Peseta)	124.370
SRI LANKA (Rupee)	N.A.
SWEDEN (Krona)	7.2800
SWITZERLAND (Franc)	1.4950
TAIWAN (Dollar)	N.A.
THAILAND (Baht)	25.2500
*UNITED KINGDOM (Pound)	1.5420
VENEZUELA (Bolivar)	N.A.

*These currencies are expressed in dollar price per unit.

"Foreign Exchange," *Journal of Commerce and Commercial*, Wednesday May 26, 1993.

Fair trade, which can be viewed in a protectionist sense, can also be viewed in a positive sense as a set of rules and a council of peers, both of which GATT provides. The guiding principles or rules of the game are as follows:

- MFN treatment or reciprocity is the cornerstone.
- The exception to MFN is regional unions which do not have to offer treatment agreed to internally to the whole world.
- Tariffs are not forbidden, but increases of existing tariffs are. Once a tariff is fixed by binding or lowering then binding, it cannot be raised, only lowered.
- Except agriculture, quotas are forbidden.
- Maximum levels of tariffs are fixed.
- Settlements are to be negotiated by consultation and conciliation.
- The organization must meet the needs of developing nations. Essentially this means assisting countries ignite the growth development process.
- Contracting parties must agree to abide by principles of GATT.
- Countries that break the rules are called to order.
- Disputes are brought before a GATT panel.
- Appeals and escape clauses are provided.
- Appeals (a temporary departure) may be made for balance-of-payment problems and in some cases under the Infant Industry Argument.
- Escape clauses (more permanent departure) may be asked for under the following provisions: economic development, balance of payments, national currencies, infant industry arguments, retaliation, technical transfer, and industrial policy.

GATT Rounds

Members of GATT meet in regular annual sessions as well as at periodic tariff conferences. These are called rounds and are extended negotiating sessions to bargain tariff and nontariff barriers. A Council of Representatives deals with matters between sessions and prepares the agenda for each session.

The first seven GATT rounds concentrated on reducing tariff rates using the MFN or reciprocal agreements' method. Table 18–1 shows the results.

Tokyo Round

The outcome of the Tokyo Round was significant tariff cuts, but more important six trade agreements or Codes of Conduct and one special rule on nontariff issues were negotiated.

Subsequently, The Trade Act of 1979 changed U.S. laws to conform to the Tokyo agreements. Seven volumes, in booklet form, that explain the code and its applicability to businesses can be ordered from the U.S. Department of Commerce. They are titled

Volume 1: *Subsidies and Countervailing Measures*
Volume 2: *Government Procurement*
Volume 3: *Trade in Civil Aircraft (Special Rules)*
Volume 4: *Technical Barriers to Trade*
Volume 5: *Antidumping Duties*
Volume 6: *Agreement on Import Licensing Procedures*
Volume 7: *Customs Valuation*

Uruguay Round (1986)

The Uruguay Round, launched in Punta del Este, Uruguay, in September 1986, set the agenda for the most ambitious and complex round of multilateral trade negotiations under GATT auspices. Representatives of 74 countries agreed to continue the work of the seven previous rounds, by taking up the issues left unresolved, by

TABLE 18–1
Multilateral Trade Negotiations Under GATT

Date	Name	Outcome
1947	Geneva	About 45,000 tariff concessions representing half of world trade.
1949	Annacy	Modest tariff reductions.
1950–1951	Torquay	Twenty-five percent tariff reductions in relation to 1948 level.
1955–1956	Geneva	Modest tariff reductions.
1960–1962	Dillion	Modest tariff reductions.
1962–1967	Kennedy	Average tariff reduction of 35 percent for industrial products; only modest reductions for agricultural products. Concentrated on tariffs, but for first time discussed nontariffs.
1973–1979	Tokyo	Average tariff reductions of 34 percent for industrial products.
1986	Uruguay	To be decided in forthcoming negotiations.

Source: *Focus*, GATT Newsletter, No. 44, March 1987, p. 5.

improving rules already implemented, and by extending the rules to aspects of international trade that remain largely outside GATT discipline.

Fifteen additional text subjects (codes of conduct) are being negotiated which will constitute the guidelines for international trade in the following areas: agriculture, intellectual property rights, textiles, safeguards, services, FOGs, dispute settlement, tariffs, nontariffs, tropical products, trade-related investment, MTN agreements and arrangements (Tokyo codes), subsidies and countervailing measures, GATT articles, natural resource-based products, standstill and rollback, and rules of origin.

UNCTAD

The GATT ministerial recognizes its responsibilities to less-developed nations; however, the rapid expansion in the world economy following World War II gave rise, in the 1960s, to the need for a multilateral organization to assist developing countries in their efforts to industrialize and participate in world trade. In 1964 the General Assembly convened in Geneva the United Nations Conference on Trade and Development (UNCTAD-1). It decided later that same year to maintain the conference as one of its permanent organs.

The intent of UNCTAD is to analyze the practices of international trade, to enhance economic development wherever possible, and to formulate international trade policy harmonization through mediation of multilateral trade agreements, and coordination of trade and development policies of governments and regional economic groups. To promote international trade harmony, UNCTAD's 168 members, with its full-time secretariat, have come together at conferences held every four years, with some exception. The sequence has been: 1964, Geneva; 1968, New Delhi; 1972, Santiago; 1976, Nairobi; 1979, Manila; 1983, Belgrade; and 1987, Geneva. The Trade and Development Board holds twice-yearly sessions at Geneva.

The objectives of the board are reflected in its subsidiaries: the Committee on Commodities; the Committee on Manufactures; the Committee on Invisibles and Financing Related to Trade; the Committee on Shipping; the Committee on Preferences; the Committee on Transfer of Technology; and the Committee on Economic Cooperation among Developing Countries.

Commodities

One of the primary responsibilities of UNCTAD is the stabilization of commodity prices by financing global stock operations during periods from acute shortage to surplus. The conference also seeks to stabilize the world economy through promoting the negotiation of commodity agreements for sugar, tin, cocoa, rubber, jute, olive oil, and wheat.

Manufacture

UNCTAD attempts to stabilize exports of manufactured goods through its Generalized System of Preferences, established during its 1968 session in New Delhi. The system is based on the principle that developing nations should not allow developed countries the same degree of market access as the developed should allow the developing.

UNIDO

The United Nations Industrial Development Organization (UNIDO) was established in 1967 by the General Assembly to promote and accelerate the industrialization of developing countries and to coordinate the industrial development of the United Nations system. It became a specialized agency of the United Nations on June 21, 1985.

The principal organ of UNIDO is the Industrial Development Board which is a member of the United Nations or of the intergovernmental agencies associated with the United Nations. The board meets annually to act on the reports of a permanent committee and to formulate principles and policies.

General conferences of UNIDO review the background to international economic problems and look for ways to alleviate obstacles to industrial development. There have been four conferences: 1972, New York; 1975, Lima; 1980, New Delhi; and 1984, Vienna.

The harmonizing functions of UNIDO have been to propose a number of measures aimed at: (1) an end to protectionism through trade liberalization; (2) a balanced approach to external financing of industry through a mixture of investment, commercial bank lending, and official development assistance; and (3) a reversal of the net outflow of capital from the developing world.

HARMONIZING SPECIFIC BARRIERS

In addition to the harmonization of trade matters through GATT and other multilateral approaches, there are several other organizations that can affect the strategist's ability to compete in a specific international industry.

Customs Cooperative Council (CCC)

The Brussels Tariff Nomenclature (BTN) met in December 1950 and signed three conventions: the convention on Nomenclature for the Classification of Goods in Customs Tariffs; the convention on the Valuation of Goods for Customs Purposes; and the convention establishing a Customs Cooperation Council (CCC).

The purpose of the CCC was to implement the two specialized conventions into a single organization and "to secure the highest degree of harmony and uniformity in Customs systems and especially to study the problems inherent in the development and improvement of Customs technique and Customs legislation in connection therewith."

The inaugural session of the Council was held in Brussels on January 26, 1953, under the chairmanship of the Belgian Minister of Trade with 17 member countries. From its limited European origins, the CCC has developed into an influential organization of worldwide scope and influence. Membership now exceeds 100 countries and the CCC administers 15 international conventions and some 50 recommendations dealing with various customs matters.

Usually meeting in Brussels on an annualized basis, the CCC has also met in other locations such as: 1971, Vienna; 1973, Kyoto; 1975, Buenos Aires; 1977,

Nairobi; 1979, Canberra; 1981, Varna; 1984, Seoul; 1987, Ottawa; and 1989, Williamsburg, Virginia.

Significant CCC Accomplishments

The primary accomplishment of the CCC has been the development of the Harmonization Commodity Description and Coding System. This multipurpose nomenclature system has some 5,000 article descriptions organized into 21 sections and 97 chapters.

Beginning in 1970, the Harmonized System Committee made a comprehensive study of the system to meet the needs of four groups of practitioners: customs authorities, statisticians, carriers, and producers. The result of 12 years of work by experts from 60 countries was adopted by the council in 1983 and made effective January 1, 1988.

Forty-six parties initially contracted to what is now called the Harmonized Convention. This convention has subsequently been integrated into GATT framework and adopted as the United Nations economic classification and the Standard International Trade Classification (SITC Revision 3).

Another CCC accomplishment has been the implementation of an agreement between the GATT Secretariat and the Customs Valuation Committee to ensure technical uniformity and interpretation of customs matters. The Permanent Customs Technical Committee (PTC) has produced the Kyoto convention, which is an international convention on the simplification and harmonization of customs procedures including standardization of the ATA Carnet and adoption of ADP information support systems.

Very significant has been the work of the Customs Enforcement Committee. The Nairobi convention provided for the prevention, investigation, and repression of customs offenses. This committee cooperates with the United Nations and several other international organizations. In conjunction with the work of the Enforcement Committee, the Technical Cooperation and Training Committee expressed in its Seoul declaration a program of customs cooperation including annual training programs and seminars.

Registration of Intellectual Property

Over time, nations have developed treaties and foreign conventions for registration of intellectual property. As an example, the Paris Convention guarantees citizens of other countries the same rights in patent and trademark matters as is given its own citizens. Ninety-three countries belong to this convention.

Negotiated in June 1970 and effective since January 24, 1978, with 41 member countries, the Patent Cooperation Treaty has centralized filing procedures and a standard application format. The Madrid Arrangement for international registration of trademarks has 22 members. The European Patent Convention has 16 European-area members while the Community Patent Convention has nine EEC member countries. The World Intellectual Property Organization (WIPO) is a specialized agency of United Nations which administers the Paris Union, otherwise known as the Bern Union, another collective registration organization.

The problem is not registration; it is protection. There has been little, if any, world enforcement of intellectual property rights. Unethical entrepreneurs from all too many countries think nothing of taking the creative work of another and turning it to profit for themselves without providing for the originator. As a result, there has been a slow dissemination of technology—creators hide their work as long as possible and consumers suffer.

Some nations do not have effective protection under national laws, and bilateral negotiations take too long. Trade distortions have been caused due to absence of dispute-settlement mechanisms, particularly about how to deal with imports of products that infringe intellectual property. Therefore, strategists should be keenly aware of progress in both registration and protection of intellectual property.

Orderly Marketing
Agreement (OMA)

Under the Carter administration, orderly marketing agreements (OMAs) were developed whereby importing countries would set up trigger levels to control, by quotas, the volume of goods entering a country. Alternately called voluntary restraint agreements (VRAs), these are self-imposed quotas such as those established for Japanese car exports to the United States.

OMAs tend to restrict international competition by preserving national markets for local manufacturers; however, they are even used within the United States. For example, imports of fruit, vegetables, and nuts, and certain meat products are limited.

Multifiber Arrangement
(MFA)

The Multifiber Arrangement (MFA) is the largest OMA and serves the textile and apparel industry. This labor-intensive, highly market-competitive industry employs mostly women. It is everywhere.

The original treaty called the Long-Term Arrangement Regarding International Trade in Cotton Textiles (LTA) involved 33 countries. It was first negotiated and extended twice under the aegis of GATT in 1962.

By the late 1960s, synthetic fiber textiles had grown so fast that in 1973 representatives of 50 nations, under GATT's aegis, formalized the MFA into a four-year agreement. MFA came into force January 1, 1974, but has been extended in four-year increments. The latest, called MFA IV, extended the treaty eight years through December 1993.

MFA is a framework for regulating international trade in textiles and apparel to obtain orderly marketing and to avoid market disruption in importing countries. MFA includes coverage to include all known fibers including: cotton, wool, and synthetic fibers, and all negotiable fibers and silk blends. It provides a basis for countries to negotiate bilateral agreements or to impose restraints on disruptive imports. It also provides standards for determining market disruptions, minimum levels of restraints, and annual growth of imports.

The Textile Surveillance Body (TSB) supervises the arrangement and examines disputes. The United States, Japan, and the ECC are its permanent members. Although textile issues are discussed apart from other trade issues, MFA signatures retain their GATT rights. The United States, as an example, has negotiated bilateral agreements with 29 signatory countries and 10 nonsignatores. The TSB seeks a broader definition of circumvention to include transshipments and false declaration and has increased cooperation requirements to detect and prove circumvention.

REMEDY SYSTEMS

Neither GATT nor any other of the formal harmonization processes provide for resolution of all trade disputes. At best these methods can only address the major distortions. Interstate controls interfere with global competition opportunities. Therefore, nation-states have developed internal methods by which businesses may bring their trade problems to the attention of government representatives.

The United States has developed a complex method which includes informing the International Trade Administration of the U.S. Department of Commerce, the U.S. Trade Representative (USTR), and the International Trade Commission (ITC) if specific U.S. laws pertain to an industrial dispute. If investigated and found unfair, the offending nation can be placed on what is commonly called the Super 301: Watch List. Many nations have developed similar procedures.

SUMMARY

The harmonization system of trade distortions caused by inevitable competition in the free market economic system is complex. Individual businesses and governments stretch free enterprise for their own self-interest causing a need for regulatory mechanisms. The trading system prior to the peaceful revolution of 1989 had free market-oriented nations interacting through bilateral and multilateral treaties coexisting with GATT codes and UNCTAD's economic development efforts. Now there is increased complexity as the Western market countries attempt to reconcile and include the newly forming market countries of central and Eastern Europe. In order to prepare for future opportunities, global businesses must monitor and factor these changes into their strategic plans.

CHECKLIST

The issues pertaining to harmonization are related to your specific products; however, there are general strategic issues which have importance. For instance, each business should, from a broad perspective, wish to contribute to the codification of the international rules. Long-term global strategy should account for this participation.

- Must your firm deal in foreign currencies?
- Are the currencies stable?
- Should the firm hedge against future fluctuations by purchasing futures contracts?
- What FCNs are applicable to your firm?
- Which nations do you intend to deal with have MFN status?
- What GATT rules impact your business strategy?
- To what extent do the negotiations of UNCTAD impact your firm?
- What will be the impact of harmonization negotiations on the marketing of your products?
- What are the existing rules that influence your business?
- What should your contribution be toward greater international business harmony?
- How can you protect against rule violations?
- What are the implications of harmony negotiations on your global strategy?

T A S K

4

FORMULATE TIME-FUTURE

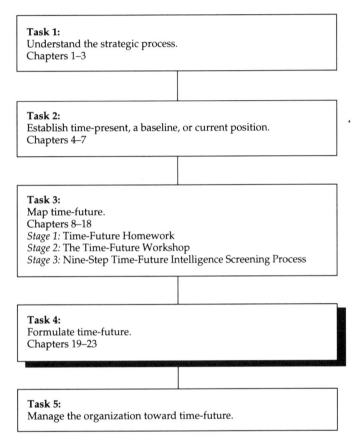

> **Task 1:**
> Understand the strategic process.
> Chapters 1–3

> **Task 2:**
> Establish time-present, a baseline, or current position.
> Chapters 4–7

> **Task 3:**
> Map time-future.
> Chapters 8–18
> *Stage 1:* Time-Future Homework
> *Stage 2:* The Time-Future Workshop
> *Stage 3:* Nine-Step Time-Future Intelligence Screening Process

> **Task 4:**
> Formulate time-future.
> Chapters 19–23

> **Task 5:**
> Manage the organization toward time-future.

The purpose of Task 4 is to develop the final strategic plan. Chapter 19 is a companion to Chapter 8, in that the ad hoc recommendations of that chapter are compared to the findings of the intelligence screening process. This way, future strengths, weaknesses, opportunities, and threats (SWOTs) are identified and a new mission and objectives are decided.

Chapter 20 then develops the strategies to accomplish the objectives. Chapter 21 explains how to match tactics to selected strategies. Chapter 22 shows how to prepare the plan, and Chapter 23 discusses the approval process.

Chapter 19

Future SWOTs and Objectives

*The man of yesterday
has died in that of today,
that of today
dies in that of tomorrow.*

Plutarch

To this point in the global strategic process you have established time-present, that is, the baseline position of the firm. You have also developed some ad hoc strategies and analyzed the nine drivers of global strategy. The purpose of Task 4 is to explain how to pull everything together into a comprehensive strategic plan using the existing company position as a jumping off point.

This chapter provides a framework to guide you in the search for SWOT and strategic objectives based on the data you have collected. Figure 19–1 shows this flow of choices.

PULLING IT TOGETHER

The intent of the strategic management process is to put together a winning strategy that focuses the offensive thrust of the firm into the global future. Without a clear strategy, day-to-day operations take over.

The external process begins with the most complex use of strategy, which has as its goal market expansion in the international setting. The assumption of the approach is this: If the firm is not in some way growing or at least considering expansion into global business, long-term survival is unlikely. A do-nothing strategy is not valid because increasing competition from other global businesses in the organization's home market will most assuredly lead to a defensive strategy. The correct questions to be answered all begin with the global dimension.

- Where is the firm now (time-present)?
- To what degree is the firm already a global business?
- What is the next step in the globalization process?
- What will the world be like in five, 10, and 15 years?
- What will be the impact on your company and its products?
- When can you take the next steps?
- Have you defined your global mission?
- What are your future SWOTs?
- What objectives can your firm accomplish?
- What will be your strategies?
- What is the best match of tactics to strategy?

Second GFOT Workshop

Collaboration continues to be a goal of the global strategic management process. To achieve participation, the GFOT is again called to a two-to-three-day workshop. (Note: If the company's intelligence program is ongoing, this workshop may be combined with the first GFOT workshop.)

FIGURE 19–1
Flow of Choices

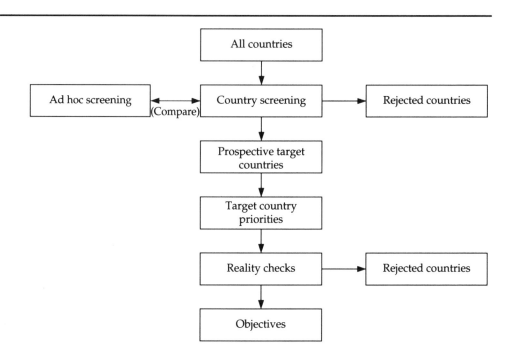

Workshop Stages

Before your vision of the future can be finalized, the GFOT must take several actions.

- Opportunities search.
- Gap analysis.
- Trend analysis.
- Scenario development.
- Focus group review.
- Reality checks.
- Prioritization of the opportunities.
- Link to operations.
- Wrap in the reality of the budget.

In the final analysis the GFOT must answer the questions: What will the world be like in the future? How many of the new opportunities can this firm afford? What are its priorities? Figure 19–2 shows the strategic paradigm as it applies to your organization.

The second GFOT workshop has four stages.

Stage 1: Review the results of the first workshop and the ad hoc visions.

Stage 2: Search for future SWOTs.

Stage 3: Conduct reality checks.

Stage 4: Develop new mission and objectives.

Stage 1: Review the Results of the First Workshop

In Task 2, the firm's GFOT was formed in an I-think, let's-try gestalt setting. That resulted in the GFOT's vision of the company's global strategy. The GFOT may have used one or more forecasting techniques, but its results were based on what the group collectively thought about the future.

Analysts used the GFOT's results as a starting point and went to work, country by country, to map the nine strategic drivers: country needs, customers,

FIGURE 19-2
Strategic Opportunity Paradigm

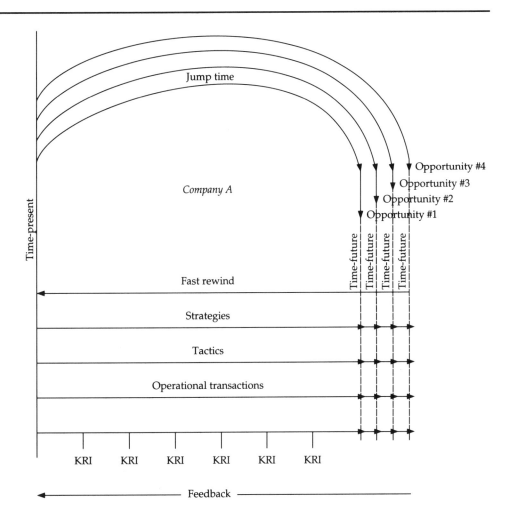

products, suppliers, competitors, blocs, trade incentives, barriers, and the implications of harmonization. From that analysis a priority of recommendations about risks and rewards was made for each country. All of that is now ready to be put back into the hands of the GFOT to formulate coherent objectives with supporting strategies.

Considerable time may have passed since the team first met, but everyone who was present for Task 2 should be recalled for this important task. Much of the formulation process is behavioral and all of the implementation process is behavioral. Great ideas of many excellent executives have died the death of good intentions because they never became imbedded in the culture of the firm. Therefore, substitutes should be minimized for several reasons.

1. Continuity of thought is important when pulling a vision together.
2. There is a learning curve to understanding the strategy formulation process.
3. The team is made up of the key people who will make or break the firm's new strategy; keep in mind that this is a multidisciplinary process.
4. The same team members will be recalled for the next iteration of the process whether that is scheduled on an annual, biannual, or triennial basis.

The team should be brought to a setting other than the workplace, but this time the work is not gestalt. At this meeting the team reviews the results of Task 3. Based on the hard cold facts of the intelligence projections, the team begins the process of converging on the vision of the future.

Stage 2: Search for Future SWOTs

In its quest for a long-term strategy, the global business is attempting to find the opportunities of the future. They will be discovered in terms of the factors of endowment: land, capital, labor, technology, know-how, intelligence, and market opportunities. Figure 19–3 shows the framework for Task 4 beginning with gap analysis and ending with the approval process for the new strategic plan.

Opportunities. Opportunities often become exposed without the need for unusual analysis. For instance, it may be clear from country information that there are only two products like yours in a given country or that entry into a country is particularly easy.

Caution! Remember this process is about strategy—and hence, about future opportunities. That is not to say that something should not be done about an immediate opportunity that is revealed. On the contrary, depending on company resources, action should be taken immediately—so long as it is compatible with the organization's strategy. Do not chase opportunities unrelated to your strategic thrust!

Gap analysis. This is a useful process in formulating global strategy. Because opportunities are a natural fallout of gap analysis, this process has two subelements: formulation gap and performance gap.

A formulation gap is determined by comparing the results of Task 2 against the facts of Task 3. In a few instances there will be no difference or gap. In most instances, analysis will reveal new information. It is important to identify information gaps to determine the correct direction of your strategy. If there are no gaps or very small gaps, then the strategic direction of the firm may involve only incremental adjustment of the current strategy. On the other hand, large gaps represent strategic opportunities and will cause the GFOT to consider major shifts in strategy.

Performance gaps show up when comparing company capabilities against strategic alternatives. The projection of future performance must be compared against current strategy and each alternative strategy. Here are some examples of gaps which may become apparent from analysis.

- There is no competition for your product in Country A.
- Country B needs your technology.
- The price of competitive products is too high in Country C.
- There are excellent distributors in Country D.
- Tariffs are low in Country E.
- Country F is offering an excellent trade creative incentive.
- A nontariff barrier in Country G is a sufficient trade distortion that an insider position is needed.

Scenario development. Visualize scenarios upon which to base your strategy. What are the major issues? Revisit those developed in Task 2. Do they still hold? Do new scenarios come to mind? This is the time to refine scenarios. Think of regional as well as global scenarios. Reexamine Figure 8–3 and look for branching points for your scenarios. For each country list the assumptions on which your scenarios are based.

FIGURE 19–3
Task Four Framework

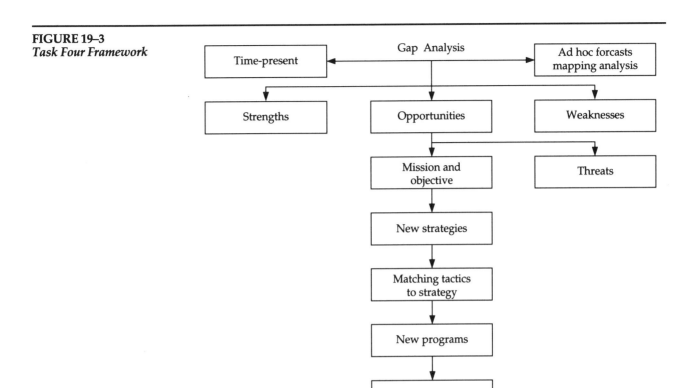

The following items should also be identified in the Task 4 framework.

- *Strenths.* Identify the firm's current and future strengths.
- *Weaknesses.* Identify the firm's weaknesses in relation to future opportunities and what can be done to shore up these weaknesses.
- *Strategic visibility.* Identify and understand all options and the assumptions upon which the analysis was made.
- *Trend analysis.* Convert identifiable trends to future opportunities.
- *Threats.* Identify country and competitor threats and what can be done to compete against them.

Stage 3: Conduct Reality Checks

Before pushing the process to the next step, two things should be done. First, the more eyes on a piece of work the more likely it reflects reality. Get opinion checks on the reality and risks of the scenarios, but make certain the opinions are from those who care. Second, bump the scenarios against budget.

Focus group checks. Did the focus group answer the right questions in Task 2? Do you need to do another set of focus sessions? This is the time to review focus group analysis or other forecasting techniques. Play your new scenarios to the focus group. Do they agree with the risks and rewards? Focus groups can add a layer of reality to the scenarios and can be valuable assistance to prioritize opportunities.

Budget checks. You must now deal with reality. Crunch the numbers from a prioritized list of markets, countries, and products. But don't make decisions on the numbers yet. Let the entire picture be available for the final strategic

FIGURE 19–4
Global Strategic Decision Matrix

	Target countries	Country needs	Customers	Product	Suppliers	Competitors	Blocs	Trade incentives	Barriers	Harmony	Priority Go, No/go
Home country	Strong	Many	Strong	Weak	Few	Joining outsider	None	Support-ive	None or N.A.	High go	
Country 2	Weak future	Weak	Too high tech	Some	None	No	None	Many 1) Tariff 2) Non Tariff	N.A.	Low no/go	
Country 3	Strong future	Have $	Good	Yes	Many	Yes, weak outsider	Weak	None	Progress opening	Medium go	
Country 4	Growing trend	Trend up	Needs Adaptation	Some	Local only	No 1) Learn 2) insider	Several	Few tariffs	Yes, support-ive	High go	
Country 5	Great need	Yes, for our products	Great need as is	N.A.	Many	Yes insider	Many	Many: tariffs, quotas, NT, NJ	Not yet, but wants	High go	

N.A. = Not applicable.

formulation phase. Based on your final priority list, check the probable success against the budget.

Prioritize opportunities. The product of this step is a prioritized list of opportunities, country by country, which will then be transferred to the next phase of the formulation process—deciding the firm's future objectives. A summary of the priority opportunity recommendations might look like Figure 19–4.

Stage 4: Develop New Mission and Objectives

A mission statement is the credo or foundation of the firm. It establishs the values, beliefs, and guidelines for the people of your organization all over the world. Remember that this mission statement will be translated into several languages and interpreted by people in many lands with differing cultures.

Does the firm's mission as stated or defined in Task 2 still reflect what the company intends to do? If so, do not change it; but at this point the results of your work in Tasks 2 and 3 and the early steps of Task 4 will probably show where the mission may need some fine-tuning. Typically, the GFOT will see new opportunities and challenge the firm's old mission in terms of its fundamental reason for existence, its scope of operations, and the things that set it apart from other firms in its industry.

The new corporate mission statement should identify the new thrust of the firm into the global marketplace. It should also speak to the following:

- Products.
- Markets.
- Ethical aims.
- Technologies.
- R&D efforts.

The new statement must, in simple terms, provide a straightforward analysis of the direction and commitment of the firm. It should describe the dynamics or the level of risk or conservatism—whichever is your long-term intention.

Remember that the results of gap analysis could be negative; thus there are no overseas opportunities. Should this happen, obviously global strategy formulation ceases, but many of the results of the process can be used to strengthen the domestic firm and the formulation process should continue on a domestic basis. Thus your firm's revised mission and objectives would reflect this alternate strategy.

Corporate, Country, and Business Unit Mission Statements

Often there is a need to write a statement of intent for each country in the firm's global plan. This need comes about because the firm's objectives may include joint ventures and satellite businesses that are not exactly alike. These statements must be worded to integrate and support the corporate global mission statement. Similarly, business units within countries may be unique and sufficiently different that the firm's leadership may see a requirement for its own statement.

Rank and Castoff Opportunities

The list of opportunities should now be ranked in terms of country, market, and other opportunities. Cast off those which are clearly unachievable.

Revise Objectives

At the completion of Task 2 the GFOT was asked to define, based on its appreciation of the process at the time, a set of company objectives. Now is the time to review those objectives and compare them with the list of opportunities. Some goals will still be valid, but many will need revision. Rewrite the short- and long-term objectives showing differences from prior years. Objectives must now be stated in terms of accomplishment, such as annual, five-, 10-, or 20-year results. Based on gap analysis and trends, opportunities that could be exploited under various scenarios became apparent to the GFOT.

Country objectives. Each country will present different opportunities and those should be defined in terms of an objective. Country objectives might be stated in terms of total market share to be achieved in a certain period of time. Another might be a unit volume for a specific product in a country. Yet another might be to build a warehouse by a specific date.

New product/technology objectives. Some opportunities require new products and technologies for the new country markets. Explain the new products, their technologies, and from which R&D center they will come. Include human technologies that must be developed to support the new markets.

SUMMARY

Formulating a cohesive global strategy does not come easy. Each opportunity must be identified and analyzed for its risks and rewards. Then it must be aligned against operational matters and the budget. At this point do not make choices, just assign a rank and let the next step take care of the decision process.

CHECKLIST

- Has the intelligence analysis discovered new opportunities?
- Were there gaps between the results of the first and second workshop?
- Did the priority of future objectives change between workshops?
- Has the GFOT been recalled in its original form?
- Have the mission statements been reworded in light of the findings of intelligence analysis?
- Have the future objectives been defined?

Chapter 20

Matching Company Strategies to Country Strategies

I simply imagine it so, then go about to prove it.

Albert Einstein

Having defined the firm's global, country, and business missions and the objectives of the future, the firm must now formulate the means to accomplish those objectives in terms of strategies and tactics. This chapter explains the various options available to match company strategies to country strategies. Figure 20–1 shows the progression. Chapter 21 explains how to match the appropriate tactics to the selected strategy.

An expanding company does not rely on only one strategy. As Figure 20–2 shows, a firm may be an insider in one country, a risk-sharer or learner in another, and an outsider in several other countries. The strategy you use will be dependent on the strategy of the country you wish to penetrate.

Grand Strategy

By definition, the grand strategy of a global business is the world viewpoint; that is, to have an intention to go global and eventually become an insider and to have a presence in as many countries as makes good business sense. Beyond the global strategy of the firm, you now must have a set of country strategies; that is, how your firm plans to accomplish objectives must be explained country by country.

Country Strategies

Country strategies can be expressed in several ways. Major strategies are: no growth, outsider, insider, and risk-sharer/learner. Minor strategies are: speed of entry, growth supporting, and capital rationing or responsive to trade creation opportunities.

MAJOR COUNTRY STRATEGIES

Major strategies are those that dominate the expansion of markets on a global basis. They are applied on a country-by-country basis and are industry specific.

No Growth

For some organizations there may be no growth opportunities in some countries. In that case the firm's tactics may either be stable or defensive in its own country against the entry of competitors from other countries. A firm that finds itself without any globalization opportunities should go back to the drawing board in terms of R&D or product development to establish products and/or services desired in other countries.

Outsider

An outsider strategy is one in which the company prefers to do business at arm's length from certain countries because either the barriers or the economic risks and/or the political risks are too high to take an insider position. This is a low-risk strategy.

FIGURE 20–1
*Progression of Matching
Strategies and Tactics*

Insider

An insider strategy is the ultimate goal of the global business, but is usually not achievable in the short run. Another name for the insider strategy is *glocal*. It is one in which the global firm acts locally and is perceived as being a local organization. It is a high-risk strategy, but provides a high level of control with long-term survival and profits.

Risk-Sharer/Learner

For a country where the global organization feels uncomfortable and needs more time to understand culture, changing barriers, commercial codes, and business methods, the correct approach might be to take a learning strategy. This is the strategy of minimizing risk and capital by sharing with an insider. It results in loss of control, but allows the firm to enter the market a bit at a time, building market share and name recognition as the organization learns the ropes.

MINOR COUNTRY STRATEGIES

These are strategies of opportunity, generally applicable to situations that spring out of rapidly changing government strategies.

Speed of Entry

A speed-of-entry strategy is used when the firm sees a big opportunity that must be taken advantage of in the short term. Time becomes of the essence and the firm is willing to take large capital and political risks in order to achieve rapid growth of market share.

Growth Supporting

The global business must be continuously conscious of its ability to grow financially through new markets and product development. Strategies to reduce product costs by importing improved components or by acquiring new technology might be appropriate to become competitive in certain countries.

Trade Creation Opportunities

This is a strategy which searches for the best country opportunities to satisfy certain company objectives such as cost reduction or market penetration. The strategic opportunity is revealed in terms of a trade creative scheme conceived for economic development purposes.

FIGURE 20–2
Matching Strategies

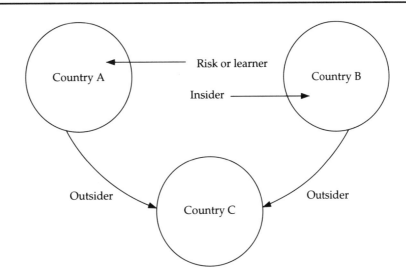

Capital Rationing

This strategy is for the firm that has limited working capital, but wishes to get started in the international marketplace as funds permit.

When to Enter Strategies

There is a right time and a wrong time to enter each country that has market potential—timing is everything. Strategy should be carefully analyzed in terms of opportunities and objectives.

SUMMARY

To accomplish formulated objectives, strategies must be thought through by line leadership. Only through collaboration, inclusion, and ownership of strategies can a successful vision be brought to fruition. Strategies have many levels and each should be considered separately and in conjunction with the others in order to ensure integration and synergy.

CHECKLIST

- Do you understand each country's strategy vis-à-vis your industry, products, and objectives?
- Has your company accepted the grand strategy of going global?
- Have you decided which strategy is appropriate for each country objective?
- Is your plan sufficiently flexible to take advantage of minor country strategies?

Chapter 21

Matching Tactics to Strategy

The only sure way to avoid making mistakes is to have no ideas.

Albert Einstein

Most nations support exporting as a national strategy because when home products are exported jobs stay at home, foreign currency is induced, and the nation's balance of payments is positively affected. From a business point of view, however, there is no best tactic. Tactics vary according to usefulness to achieve country strategy. This is the process of deciding the best method of entry and how to compete in a new country. There may be more than one method for each company or product. The process is explained in this chapter and essentially answers the question: What are the best international business entry tactics for your firm to attain its new objectives? International business tactics include: (1) Import products; (2) Export products; (3) Use intermediaries; (4) Form an association under the ETCA of 1982; (5) Start a firm; (6) Acquire a firm; (7) Merger; (8) Develop a joint venture; (9) Franchise; (10) Use market subsidiary; (11) License; (12) Use direct mail; (13) Use free zones; (14) Share production; (15) Use multilevel marketing (MLM). Table 21–1 shows how these tactics relate to the country strategies discussed in Chapter 20.

INSIDER TACTICS

Insider tactics match the insider strategy of gaining a glocal position in the market.

Start a Firm

Investment in a start-up in another country is usually the most expensive way. The benefit is control. Not every country will allow foreign ownership. In those that will, the argument for the entering global business is good knowledge and name recognition. Without knowledge and recognition, return on the investment will become extensive in terms of time and promotional costs.

Acquire a Firm

The advantage of acquisition of an already established firm should be obvious— it already has local knowledge and a name. The key is to ensure thorough research about the firm. Is it financially sound and suitable as an extension of the global business' mission? The disadvantage of acquiring an already established firm includes cost and risk of fatal flaws inherent in a particular business. Start-ups are sometimes cheaper.

Create a Merger

Like start-ups and acquisitions, mergers bring the same advantages but can have the same pitfalls. Even more dangerous is the accommodation of missions and implantation of the global strategy. It is wise to undertake a new strategic formulation process soon after any merger.

Develop a Joint Venture

Partnering is the forming of strategic alliances or joint ventures to increase long-term stability and leverage. *Control* is the key word in the joint venture. Parties must be singing the same tune from the same sheet of music. Strategy should be

TABLE 21–1
Matching Tactics to Major Strategies

Insider	Risk-sharer/learner	Outsider
Start a firm	Use marketing subsidiaries	Exporting products
Acquire a firm	Share production	Importing products
Create a merger	Joint venture (partner)	Form ETCA associations
Develop a joint venture	Free zone	Use intermediaries
Franchise		License Direct mail MLM

ironed out before moving ahead. This method of entering foreign markets has swept the world in recent years.

Franchise

Franchising is an inexpensive way to become an insider in another country. Not every product lends itself to franchising, but those that do often develop strong relationships and excellent management by competent owners.

Franchises produce new business opportunities, new jobs, and new entrepreneurs because they allow people with limited capital and experience to succeed in their own enterprise. In the United States, statistics show that about 95 percent of all franchises are still in business after five years compared to less than 20 percent of independently owned businesses.

Some say that franchising is the business phenomenon of the 20th century. Because of the success of such giants as McDonald's, Kentucky Fried Chicken, and Dunkin' Donuts, franchising will become the expansion method of the 21st century. In any case, the process can be complicated and you should get sound legal and financial advice.

GENERIC BUSINESS UNIT TACTICS

Credit is generally given to Michael Porter of Harvard University for identifying several generic business-level tactics which define how each business should compete in its respective industries in each country. There are three tactics: overall cost leadership, differentiation, and focus.

Overall Cost Leadership

The overall cost leadership tactic implies the ability to produce and deliver the product or service at a lower cost than the competition. Close attention to costs requires scale-efficient facilities, vigorous pursuit of cost-effectiveness, and avoidance of marginal customers.

Differentiation

A differentiation tactic requires creating a product or service that is perceived by the customer as unique. As a result of gaining loyalty and lowering sensitivity to price, this strategy brings the opportunity to ask higher prices. Differentiation can be accomplished in several ways: brand image, design image, quality image, special features, customer service, or any combination of these.

Focus

A firm that uses the focus tactic concentrates on a specific segment of customers. The segment may be a particular group, a geographic segment, or part of a product line. The intent of this tactic is to be able to serve a narrow market better than others in the industry that attempt to serve a broad market.

FUNCTIONAL TACTICS

Functional tactics must be integrated to match the larger grand, corporate, and business-unit strategies. Functional tactics are the development, by each business unit, of a specific short-term plan of action which supports the larger undertaking. Such tactics must be developed in the areas of marketing, finance, production/operations, R&D, human resource management, ecology, and societal concerns.

Marketing

This plan provides the guide for marketing managers and includes who will sell what, where, to whom, and how. These tactics explain the five ps: pop (responsiveness to customers), product, price, promotion, and place.

Financial

The issues developed in the finance tactic have to do with capital acquisition, long-term capital investment, debt financing, dividend allocation, and leveraging. This functional tactic guides the management of cash flow and working capital.

Production/Operations

Production operations must be coordinated with marketing and financial tactics if the firm is to succeed in accomplishing its country strategy. The production/operations tactic includes decisions about plant size, location, equipment, sourcing of raw materials and components, and scheduling.

R&D

This tactic guides the R&D function of the firm. Issues such as the time frame for R&D efforts and whether the emphasis is to be on basic research or product development are expounded in this plan.

Human Resource Management (HRM)

People make or break firms. HRM as a functional tactic has grown in importance to such an extent that no strategic plan is complete without the inclusion of the following elements: recruitment, selection, labor relations, equal employment opportunities, employee compensation, career development, empowerment, and discipline. Another major element which must be included is an assessment of the behavioral implications of major changes in grand strategy and methods to accommodate changes to corporate culture.

Ecological

Concern for the greening of production and products is a worldwide concern. No strategic plan would be complete without the inclusion of the implications of ecology as it relates to products and industry.

Societal

Crossing borders means crossing cultures and social structures. Each entry tactic should be accompanied by a discussion of tactics to become a good neighbor and societal participant.

NEW PRODUCT/ TECHNOLOGY TACTICS

In addition to the development of tactics to enter new country markets or entirely new businesses, the outcome of the strategy formulation process may well reveal new product and technology opportunities and objectives. The purpose of this section is to discuss that eventuality in terms of constraint evaluation and tactics.

Constraint Evaluation

New technology development must be programmed and included in any new R&D functional tactics of the firm, just as new product development must be included within the production/operations tactics. Paramount to inclusion in constraint evaluation tactics are decisions about the financial support needed to bring technologies and products to market. Another constraint is internal technical competence; that is, can it be developed inside the company or must the firm go outside for assistance. Related to these constraint decisions are issues about leading-edge management.

Technology Tactics

The issue of technology leads to a discussion of the value chain of any organization. Technology may not just lead to a need for new products, it may also be the inclusion of new methods of processing which improve the competitiveness of doing business across borders. Improving technology to the leading edge is costly and developing to the leading edge is even more costly. Your portfolio of technology should be analyzed to determine whether the leading edge is desired. Does the firm have the competence? What is the cost of obtaining that competence?

Product Tactics

In determining new product tactics, competition and life cycle of existing products are just two of the critical factors that must be considered. Paramount to the constraints surrounding these tactics are matching the new product to personnel, competence, and financial capacities to ensure success.

OUTSIDER TACTICS

Outsider tactics are those which keep the base company at arms' length from another country.

Export Products (International Marketing)

This is the process of selling a product or service from a manufacturing base in one country to customers in another country. The mechanics of this process include: researching and developing a marketing plan which includes a description of the marketing objective; market tactics; and a budget. This tactic is most successful when

- Home currency (exchange rate) is weak against the importing country's currency.
- Product life cycle can be extended.
- The import country has low tariff barriers.
- There is importing encouragement from a foreign government.
- There is high political risk.
- Diversification of financial risk across a broad market is important.

Import Products (Global Sourcing)

Today's customers care little about where a product is made, only that it has good quality and delivery, the right price, and stable production. This means to compete in the global marketplace, sooner than later, firms must consider a mix of foreign and domestic content. Most modern sourcing programs are complex in that they involve make-or-buy decisions that include value analysis and just-in-time processes. Success using this tactic requires lower costs of production or higher quality inputs than can be obtained in the home market.

Associations

A useful concept for every fledgling global business is to form associations to export. In the United States, a law titled the Export Trading Company Act of 1982 is extremely flexible and permits the formation of very creative organizations or associations to compete in cross-border trade. Agreement of the Department of Commerce and, in cases of bank participation, the Federal Reserve System are required. Many countries have similar laws. By joining with banks and other firms, small companies can share costs, knowledge, and other capabilities to achieve economies of scale in order to gain an international foothold. These laws also provide methods to circumvent antitrust laws.

Associations afford firms several advantages, all of which come by way of joint export activities.

- *Barriers.* Firms can end run nontariff trade barriers by sharing costs of difficult foreign government labeling, packaging, and quality requirements.
- *Bidding.* By teaming up, firms can respond to foreign orders which might exceed the capacity or capability of any single firm.
- *Capital.* Greater funds in the form of equity can be brought to export activities by bank participation.
- *Economies of scale.* Joint venture agreements between domestic companies to compete internationally bring increased efficiency.
- *Immunity.* By gaining advanced certification from the U.S. Department of Commerce, joint activities—even price setting—can gain immunity from federal and state criminal and civil prosecution.
- *Market research.* Firms can share the costs of foreign market research and travel.
- *Market entry and development.* Firms with complementary products can achieve cost reductions of advertising, trade shows, missions, and other joint activities.
- *Shipping.* Carriers will negotiate lower discounts and longer rate contracts because joint arrangements can provide needed volume and scheduling guarantees.

Intermediaries

The use of intermediaries offers several advantages. Any examination of the process of establishing a cross-border marketing operation should include the possibility of using intermediaries. They often offer the quickest way to get started with minimum outlay of capital. Equally important is the ability of the exporter to observe and learn how to do business in another country before committing to an insider strategy.

Intermediaries come in several forms: general trading companies; export trading companies; import/export management companies; and even piggybacking with a large multinational firm. Names and addresses of reputable intermediaries are typically gained through government information sources.

The primary reasons for using intermediaries are as follows:

1. They conserve financial resources that would otherwise be consumed during the years your firm took to develop its own international marketing department.
2. Export sales come more quickly because intermediaries already have agents, distributors, and customers in place.
3. You learn by observing the professionals in order to eventually develop your own international department.
4. Intermediaries save you time by concentrating their effort on your overseas sales thus allowing you to concentrate on your domestic market.

License

A licensing agreement offers the exporter the fastest entry into another country without the logistical headaches or the production pressures of exporting. Long-run profits and control are exchanged for royalties. At once, licensing reduces risk, circumvents import restrictions, and protects intellectual property rights.

Licensing is not only the fastest means of getting into a foreign market, but it is also a means of establishing a foothold with little capital outlay. It provides valuable advantages for a small- or medium-sized company to gain market entry. Most notable is the ability to gain some local knowledge before committing to your own operation. Licensing also offers a shield against political risk, because by dealing through a local firm, expropriation or other political measures are forestalled or minimized. From the foreign government's point of view licensing is often a preferred arrangement because it brings opportunities for technology transfer.

Direct Mail

Using the postal systems to market products is growing internationally. Of course, the method is no better than the postal technology of the nations involved. The method is sensitive to being able to target a specific market for a specific product. Direct mail is generally an outsider's marketing method.

RISK-SHARER/ LEARNER

In some countries the global business may feel it needs more time to learn its business methods and culture. Sharing the risk buys time.

Use Marketing Subsidiaries

Marketing subsidiaries are either wholly owned or joint ventures organized to support direct export by providing timely information about tactical entry and sales effort. Short of taking a complete insider position, the marketing subsidiary represents a physical presence and, therefore, a greater commitment than arms' length exporting. Most marketing subsidiaries are centrally located in the target country and can be a prelude to taking a permanent insider position.

Share Production

Some nations have surpluses of one factor of production or another. The United States has a surplus of management, technology, know-how, and intelligence while Mexico and other less-developed nations have a surplus of labor. To stimulate economic development, all nations formulate schemes to take advantage of their surpluses. Singapore and Mexico are among the most aggressive in the development of schemes to showcase the added value of less-expensive labor costs. The concept of production sharing is a viable tactical concept to be considered by any business that has high product labor content.

SPECIAL TACTICS

Special tactics, as opposed to major tactics, are peripheral to the spine of most country's major strategies. Special tactics are those of change and influencing change. They may lead to long-term profits, but are designed to carefully probe without major resource commitment.

Develop Business with Nonmarket and New- Market Countries

Perestroika (restructuring) and *glasnost* (openness) have brought surprising market opportunities. Needless to say restructuring from Marxism to capitalism will not happen overnight. During the shakeout many companies are carefully assessing methods of developing this eventual consumer explosion.

Influence the Government

This tactic may be the most useful in terms of reducing interstate controls which often satisfy special-interest manufacturers at the expense of the competitive process and consumers. Understanding the U.S. method of seeking remedies to unfair trade barriers is another element managers have at their disposal to try to level the playing field.

Special Financing Techniques

Forfeiting and countertrade are special techniques used to take advantage of trade creation opportunities in those countries where capital and foreign exchange are in short supply. A bank enters into a forfeiture when it buys a debt instrument from an exporter at a discount. The benefit is cash flow for the exporter. Countertrade is an umbrella term for the range of goods exchanges without using currency.

TABLE 21–2
Matching Company
Strategies to Entry Tactics

Company Strategy	Entry Tactics
All	Know the culture.
No growth	Home market or postone entry.
Outsider	Export; intermediary; license; association; direct mail.
Insider	Start a firm; aquire a firm; merger; franchise; multilevel marketing; fight unfair trade by being a change agent.
Risk-sharer	Association; joint venture; franchise; multilevel marketing.
Learner	Joint venture; market subsidiary.
Speed of entry	Intermediary.
Growth supporting	Import; production sharing; FTZ; FTA.
Trade creation opportunities	Acquire a firm; joint venture; merger; special financing techniques.
Capital rationing	Franchise.

SUMMARY

In practice there are one or more entry tactics to match company strategies. Culture reaches across every strategy and tactic. Table 21–2 shows how the various entry tactics can be matched to a country strategy.

CHECKLIST

- Has the company decided on a tactic to match each country strategy?
- Has each insider strategy been matched to both an entry tactic and a business tactic?
- Are you using an appropriate outsider tactic?
- How long will you use a risk-sharer/learner tactic in each country?
- Have you considered the applicability of special tactics?

Chapter 22

Preparing the Strategic Plan

We can't cross a bridge until we come to it; but I always like to lay down a pontoon ahead of time.

Bernard Baruch

Small organizations seldom have staff permanently assigned to write the plan. Nevertheless, the actual preparation of the written strategic plan should be placed in the hands of a special team that has the skills necessary to bring order to several diverse analyses of the organization's future. Because some or all of the material may be proprietary and sensitive in terms of competitors, the writers must be of unquestionable loyalty.

Physical security of the material can also be a factor. All papers related to the plan's formulation should be retained in a location commensurate with the level of security required by the company's line of business.

Multiple Purposes

The finished strategic plan must serve multiple purposes and multiple audiences. First, the plan must be the foundation of a presentation to the board of directors or other decision-makers for approval. Second, the plan must be a working document for the implementation process. Last, it should serve as a historical document.

Presentation

The presentation of the objectives of your global strategy to the board of directors should be a logical road map illustrating how the GFOT came to its conclusions. In summary form, the presentation should explain the entire written plan which decision-makers hold but seldom read in detail. Most important, the recommendations should be concise and get to the heart of the matter. Graphics from the written plan should also be used.

Working Document

The same graphics used to gain approval can also be used to assist top management to explain and implant the new strategy into the culture of the firm. Methods used to institutionalize strategy were explained in Chapter 3.

The implementation portion of the strategic plan should be broken into its small parts such as short-, mid-, and long-term objectives and should be accompanied with a working schedule. Each period of the working implementation plan should be broken into the specific objectives of the plan of action with milestones, including a schedule, tactics, new programs, and projects.

Instructions should be communicated effectively in the language level of the target audience. Any new or difficult terminology should be explained in accurate but easy language.

When finalized, the written plan should not go on a shelf never to be seen again until the next strategic planning session. Instead, the plan should be developed in such a form that it can be broken into small parts for distribution and use. In other words, project officers should receive their section, functional leaders should receive theirs, and working level managers should be given a short statement of their expected objectives. The master plan should be made readily available for any who wish to see the plan in its entirety.

Historical Document   The master copy of the final document should be kept in a central location available to those who must put it into action. The work of the GFOT will seldom hold up over the long haul. Because the strategic plan is a living document, over time there will be multiple changes. All changes should be included as part of the master so that the process can be historically reconstructed.

Developing the Outline   Approval of the format for the final plan should be gained early in the formulation process. One such model which has been used successfully has two main parts: formulation and implementation.

Formulation Outline   The formulation outline generally follows the outline of Tasks 2–4 of this book.

1. Executive summary.
2. Description of the formulation process.
3. Current company position.
4. Country mapping analysis.
5. Opportunities.
6. Strengths and weaknesses.
7. Expected competition.
8. New mission and objectives.
9. Strategies and tactics.
10. Alternative strategies considered but rejected.
11. Financial highlights and budgets.
12. Resource allocations.
13. Recommendations.

Executive summary. This should be a digest of the entire plan pared down to its very essentials. It should mirror the plan in its structure and fully develop the conclusions and recommendations of the study. Get to the heart of the matter quickly, because its purpose is to enlighten busy people in the shortest possible time.

Formulation process description. This section of the report should explain how and why the company went about the formulation process. A listing of the GFOT should be included along with the periods it met and where activities took place. Any guidelines or assumptions should be explained.

Fleshing out the outline. Each of the other items shown on the outline of the formulation process should provide detailed results of the mapping process. Results should explain, in summary form, the reasons for a go, no/go determination for each outline element.

Recommendations. This portion of the strategic plan should follow the logic of the outline. Each recommendation should include sufficient supporting information to link it to the key location within the document's main elements.

Implementation Outline   This outline generally follows Chapters 24–26 of this book.

1. Plan of action with milestones.
2. Policies and standard operating procedures.

3. Description of the organization.
4. Projects: entry tactics that cut across functions. A time duration must be specified.
5. Operating plans: permanent functions.
6. Budget linked to strategy.
7. Results measurement.

SUMMARY

The strategic plan should be written to serve multiple purposes. The language should be targeted to a level appropriate to be the company's working document. The plan writers should be aware of its proprietary and sensitive nature.

CHECKLIST

- Have you established security guidelines? What is proprietary and sensitive and what is not?
- How will you handle physical security?
- Does the organization use key-person confidentiality agreements?
- Do you have approval for the format?
- Are you thinking about presentation as you write the plan?
- Can the plan be broken into its parts for implementation?
- Is the executive summary a tightly written section?
- Are the recommendations clear and to the point?

Chapter 23

Strategy Approval

Everything should be made as simple as possible, but not simpler.

Albert Einstein

INFORMAL APPROVAL

If the firm is still in the entrepreneurial stage of development, decisions and approval about strategy are probably made exclusively by the top executive. The organizational structure at this stage is usually informal; even daily communications are conducted informally. If the formulation process was conducted by persons other than the top manager, the presentation would most likely be made in a conversational discussion with key company employees present.

FORMAL APPROVAL

If the firm has matured to a functional, staff-oriented stage, the approval process becomes formalized. No matter what the size or stage of organizational formality, corporate leaders and boards of directors seldom take the time to consider details even of strategic plans. Therefore, the presentation should synthesize the results of the formulation process for delivery in a crisp format.

Approval of the new strategy should precede approval of the implementation process and should be a separate presentation. Strategy approval will depend a great deal on thoroughness and logic. Less is better, but not less quality. Clarity is better, but not more time-consuming words.

Often the boards of directors of large, publicly owned firms have both inside and outside directors. Inside directors usually include the chief executive and chief operating officers. Outside directors include experienced persons from all walks of life such as bankers, attorneys, and officers of other companies.

BOARD OF DIRECTOR SUPPORT

Commonly the boards of large organizations have the chairperson act as chief executive officer, and it is he or she who concentrates on strategic planning and external operations. Day-to-day operations are left to the chief operating officer (or president) who reports to the chairperson. These more complex boards have their own organization composed of one or more standing or permanent committees. The committees serve as the board's antenna on the company, and one or more of the committees might be involved in the strategic process from the beginning. Typically the committees include audit, compensation, executive, finance, nominating, planning, and social responsibility.

Audit. The audit committee consists only of outside board members. These experts are tasked to protect the firm and its directors from problems related to legal liabilities and deficiencies in financial information. The committee recommends auditing firms and oversees internal accounting procedures and audit results.

Compensation. One or more directors is assigned to the compensation committee. It makes recommendations on the salary, bonuses, fringe benefits, and stock options for certain top employees of the firm.

Executive. The executive committee serves as a sounding board for the chief executive. It is normally granted authority to act for the full board between regular meetings.

Finance. This committee reviews and evaluates the capital expenditures and financial planning of the firm. It is responsible through its policy decisions for the financial soundness of the corporation.

Nominating. This committee's task is to nominate candidates for board membership.

Planning. This is the committee that is responsible for the strategic planning process. Its functions include reviewing mission statements, objectives, and strategies and monitoring performance feedback.

Social responsibility. The purpose of this committee is to keep tuned to the public relations aspects of managing a complex firm. For the global business this would include being tuned to cultural and national differences that relate to being a responsible insider.

In large firms, both the planning and financial committees should be involved in the formulation process from the beginning. The process, however, is best served if formulation is developed through a GFOT or other similar mechanism. Board members who have participated in the process may prefer to let others make the presentation.

PRESENTATION

Never present a strategic plan to a cold board. If you wish approval, have preliminary discussions as you go through the formulation process. Even let the decision-makers read major sections of the report in advance. Fix the board's problems before final presentation. It is important not to go into the approval process only to be sent off on another goose chase. This is where the planning and financial committees can best serve the strategic process. Get them on your side and let them persuade the other board members.

Begin the formal presentation by outlining the process used to achieve the preliminary decisions made by the GFOT. A diagram, such as provided in this book, shows the overall framework with its feedback loops. This will provide the big-picture understanding for the board of directors.

Next discuss Tasks 2–4 showing the major results. Expose those things that have been cast off, but don't dwell on them.

For Task 2 emphasize the competencies of the company, but also be open about the firm's weaknesses. It would be beneficial for Tasks 3 and 4 if the matching process, along the line of concepts presented in this book, was used. This way everyone would understand the corporate officer's recommendations. This would also give the board appropriate methods for comparison. That would also involve them in a much more significant manner in the decision-making process of strategic planning.

The matching technique should involve ranking competencies of the company and, as your research will allow, competitors at each level of the company. On the lower levels of the company, the process could actually take the form of a management audit. The result would be twofold: First, it would provide comparative input for corporate officers for all strategic areas of the company; and second, it could serve lower management levels in the role of self-evaluation, and thus continual improvement.

With the data arrayed, matched, and prioritized, state with clarity your company's new objectives and strategies so the board can come to grips with the precise approval elements. Once approval has been gained, top management can proceed to develop the implementation plan.

SUMMARY

For the small firm the approval process is usually informal. As the firm's size increases, however, so does the formality of the approval process. Understanding the makeup of the board of directors and making a straighforward, well-researched presentation of your plan will get the new strategy and objectives approved.

CHECKLIST

- Is the approval process informal or formal?
- Will the approval presentation be delivered in a crisp format?
- Has advance support from the board been obtained?
- Have you worked with the board all during the formulation process?
- Will you be precise on what you want the board to approve?
- How will you keep the board focused on policy and not on details?

5

MANAGE THE ORGANIZATION TOWARD TIME-FUTURE

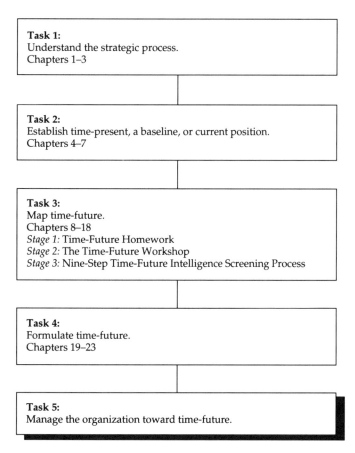

Task 1:
Understand the strategic process.
Chapters 1–3

Task 2:
Establish time-present, a baseline, or current position.
Chapters 4–7

Task 3:
Map time-future.
Chapters 8–18
Stage 1: Time-Future Homework
Stage 2: The Time-Future Workshop
Stage 3: Nine-Step Time-Future Intelligence Screening Process

Task 4:
Formulate time-future.
Chapters 19–23

Task 5:
Manage the organization toward time-future.

No matter how professionally formulated, the finest strategic plan will languish on a shelf unless it is used aggressively to steer the organization into the future. This task explains how to manage the global firm to achieve strategic objectives. It is in this phase that names, dates, and places are assigned to activities such as objectives, programs, projects, and schedules.

Chapter 24 explains how to implement the strategy by assigning milestones and adapting the organization to changing conditions. Chapter 25 reviews the key processes a project officer must understand when executing entry tactics. Chapter 26 develops the concepts of feedback controls. Chapter 27 offers four levels upon which success can be measured.

Implementing Strategy

Execution is everything.

H. Ross Perot

Implementing a global strategic plan is the action phase of the strategic process. Unlike the formulation phase which is right brain, visionary, entrepreneurial, and creative, implementation is the left brain, operational activity which executes strategy. Implementation is the process of executing strategy through a plan of action with milestones (POAM) in order to achieve the desired direction and vision.

Strategy is successful only if it produces the intended results with the levels of performance required to sustain those results. This means that people, by name, must take responsibility for seeing that the firm is suitably organized; that objective achievement is translated into daily activity; and that there is a way to measure accomplishment.

Who Implements

Obviously the chief executive officer and the chief operating officer are responsible for the overall implementation. But they cannot accomplish a single aspect of the plan themselves. Implementation takes place at all levels of the firm. Enter the word *leadership.*

It will take leadership at all levels of the firm to get the job done. For the small company, the number involved could be quite small. As the firm grows, however, implementation becomes more complex.

Besides the organization's chief officers, the heads of functional departments, business unit managers, and project officers are key players. But implementation does not stop there. Shop managers, production line supervisors, marketing managers, and R&D teams also become actors. Even support staff, such as administrative assistants, may have short-term tasks to meet certain goals.

PLAN OF ACTION WITH MILESTONES (POAM)

The POAM is not a new method of getting things done. Some call it the do list. It is simply a breakdown of all major elements of the strategy into their smallest steps, then assigning a name and a time for accomplishment of each step.

Lay out a schedule of action steps for the accomplishment of your objectives. Do this in terms of milestones. Assign a person's name to the completion of each objective. This becomes the firm's POAM and a way the organization can keep track of accomplishments. This requires collaboration with line leadership. In fact, much of strategic implementation should be left to the line for its pragmatic thinking and involvement. Let the doers develop the action schedule. Table 24–1 is an example of a simple POAM.

> Strategy formulation is the process of jumping time to decide what is to be accomplished in the future. Implementation is the process of making that strategy come true.

One of the keys to success of the POAM process is identifying a person for each action item. That identification should be a bottom-up process that allows the correct person in the organization to take ownership for the item, then establish his or her own time estimate for accomplishment. At first some will be pessimistic in their estimates and others will be optimistic. As the process unfolds, however, estimates can be adjusted for reality. Obviously institutionalization of globalism and the new strategy will play a large part in the enthusiasm of the organization toward the POAM. Make no mistake, the POAM process is a hold-their-feet-to-the-fire method. It works, but it can also be intimidating and sometimes stressful. People who are ordinarily given great freedom in their work are now asked to be limited. Even though the limits are their own, some tend to perceive completion dates as an imposition of stress. Therefore, the behavioral aspects of the POAM must be accompanied by a stress-release mechanism such as quality circles or periodic one-on-one exchanges with management.

Another key to success is matching each element of the POAM with resources and budget. Finally there must be a method of feedback that allows top management to know how the implementation process is going and, more importantly, where the problems are. This must be timely information so that solutions can be identified and implemented.

REWARD OR NOT REWARD

The philosophies of W. Edwards Deming and Kazuo Inamori rule out reward systems. Those two giants of industrial excellence believe actions should be focused toward the organization as a whole. They believe individual rewards only contribute to competition between departments and other segments of the organization. For them, if there is to be a reward, it should be a bonus for all based on the results of the total organization.

Nevertheless, the philosophy of many firms includes the concept that motivating and rewarding good performance by individuals and organizational units are key ingredients for effective strategic implementation. These organizations believe if strategy is to be given top priority, then a reward system must be linked to strategic performance.

The range of reward mechanisms in industry vary according to a wide spectrum of leadership approaches and performance appraisal objectives. These range from very positive to extremely negative.

Positive	Negative
Compensation	Less responsibility
Raises	Criticism
Bonuses	Tension
Stock options	Fear
Incentives	Demotion
Benefits	Firing
Promotion	
Recognition	
Praise	

TABLE 24–1
Plan of Action with Milestones (POAM)

Objective/action steps	Who	Complete	Resources needed anually
Outsider in Country A	Export team	1/15/95	$200,000
1. Form department	Alex	1/15/94	$95,000
2. Develop office	John	1/20/94	$30,000
3. Make contacts/travel	Margie	3/15/94	$20,000
4. Market research	John	4/15/94	$10,000
5. Check out intellectual property	Margie	4/15/94	$5,000
6. Quotations	Margie	4/15/94	
7. Market plan	Margie	6/15/94	$5,000
8. Promotion/advertising	John	7/15/94	$35,000
9. Negotiations	Alex	9/15/94	
10. First sale	Alex	11/15/94	
11. First shipment	Team success	1/15/95	

Total costs	$200,000
Income	$1,000,000
Profit	$800,000

Should your philosophy include a reward system, conventional wisdom suggests that it be structured more positively than negatively. Nevertheless, options to use the full range are seldom ruled out. Depending on the obstacles to overcome, a mixture of negative and positive rewards may be the most effective. A manager has to do more than just talk to everyone about the importance of strategy implementation. No matter how inspiring the leader's exhortations might be, they seldom command best efforts for very long. To sustain the energy and commitment that a new strategic thrust requires, leaders must be creative in developing incentives that match objectives.

POLICIES AND STANDARD OPERATING PROCEDURES

The purpose of policy is to provide a standardized framework which guides the thinking, decisions, and actions of managers. It is intended to economize managerial time and promote consistency among various operating units. Obviously, this consistency is desirable but more difficult when operating across international boundaries.

Policies are not locked in concrete and do have exceptions, but they are worded in such a way as to apply to the general situation. Strategy-implementing policies provide the guidelines for establishing and controlling ongoing operations in a manner consistent with the implementation of the strategic objectives.

Standard operating procedures (SOPs) are seen by some as synonymous with policy, but the difference lies in specificity. SOPs are often extensions of a generalized policy to explain a local situation. Often these procedures, such as preparing budgets, show a specific format which facilitates comparison of various subordinate units.

Good policy and procedures are not easy to write. The key is to capture the central element in words aimed at the average employee's reading level. Policy and procedures should be phrased in such a way that they are easily grasped by the user not the writer. Policy and procedures written in legalese or by some Ph.D. aimed at another Ph.D. are probably not written at the proper level. Keep in mind how the policy and procedures translate into other languages. Keep them as simple as possible. Remember the following:

- Write simple, clear statements.
- Write to the users' level.
- Limit discretion without destroying the concept that action should be taken at the lowest possible level within the firm.
- Double and triple check translations.
- Promote uniform handling of similar activities.
- Create policy that empowers subordinates and clears the path for quick decisions.
- Reduce conflicting practices and smooth the way for strategy to work.
- Reduce uncertainty for users regarding day-to-day activities, authorizations, and decisions.
- Reduce misunderstanding.

Information System

To implement even the most rudimentary strategic change the modern firm must have a computerized data base. It need not be expensive, but it must be sophisticated enough to include an easily accessed data information base and a method to manipulate those data to track a POAM. Linking small desktop computers for multiple access is well within the level of technology needed.

MATCHING THE ORGANIZATION

The boundaries of your global business are defined by what your firm does; that is, what its products are, what suppliers do for the company, and where you do business. In other words, what your firm makes, buys, and where it sells. For the global business these boundaries take on a new complexity because they cross international borders and are often changing rapidly. As the firm grows globally, it must continuously search for the best organization that integrates a far-flung, cross-border enterprise into a cohesive whole, yet manages the implementation of adopted strategy and tactics by exception.

The Global Business

The global business is one that takes a worldwide point of view and makes no distinction between domestic and international business. In practical terms it may favor one market region over another, but that is probably a result of early growth—emerging from the imprint of its founding country or more probably because of some tax or investment advantage. A global viewpoint eventually invades every business decision that affects the bottom line. The type of organization and people selected for it must fit this international viewpoint because their experience, the products and raw materials will be marketed and sourced on a worldwide basis. Staffs will have global responsibilities.

Strategic Boundaries

Vertical adjustments to your strategic boundaries are the what and where, and make-or-buy decisions that relate to the expansion or contraction of single functions or product lines. Horizontal adjustment relates to changes of strategic boundaries through the expansion or contraction of multiple functions or diversification into new industries.

Forward integration is a vertical adjustment synonymous with market power, that is, going on the offensive to increase sales volume. Forward integration is the theme of going global, and it can be accomplished by any of the several market entry tactics such as exporting your products or establishing an overseas subsidiary. Backward integration is the defensive strategy of reducing costs and protecting the firm against exploitation from powerful sources of raw materials and product by searching for new, less-costly sources or producing the component yourself.

Figure 24–1 visualizes business decisions to the left and right of center. Those to the left are decisions related to reducing production costs, and those to the right as those having to do with expanding markets. Integration means the consideration of what you do and what others do for you, and those decisions are made based on quality, price, delivery, and reliability.

The Changing Organization

When implementing your global business it is inevitable that you will face reorganization. There is no best method—no standard to model when the boundaries of an organization stay within a country and also when the business crosses international borders. Each global business must design the organization that brings the best results from its people, for its product line and for its global applications.

How to Choose the Right Marketing Method

Today the firm that considers entering the global market does not have to start a new department which can be expensive as well as time consuming. You can get into the international market without investing a large sum of capital. There are three forks in the road to get your products overseas.

1. Take the right fork and do it yourself. Although this is the most expensive method, you maintain the most control. This method is developed later in this chapter.
2. Take the middle road and let a trading intermediary do it for you. This is the fastest and least expensive way to start, but you give up control. This method is explained in Chapter 25.
3. Take the left fork by forming an association of firms under the Export Trading Company Act of 1982. This method allows you to share costs and control. It is also explained in Chapter 25.

Each of the methods has merit and each has limitations. Do not discard any choice until you have done a solid analysis. In fact, each target country will be different and a mix of these methods may be your best bet.

THE EXPORT MARKETING ORGANIZATION

In the early stage of developing an international marketing department, the typical company has four options:

1. Expand its own department from a domestic base.
2. Recruit an already experienced staff.
3. Use the Export Trading Company Act of 1982 to form a cooperative export organization. This law is primarily applicable in support of export operations because of its antitrust implications, but it also has useful tax implications.
4. Use a mix of organizational support including intermediaries to get the job done.

Expansion of the international department will be a function of capitalization. As a minimum the organization should have an export manager, a salesperson, and administrative support.

FIGURE 24–1
Strategic Boundaries

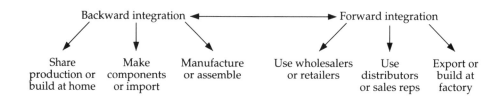

Expand from a Domestic Base

Your firm can develop from within by expanding the duties of a few personnel who show an international interest. Usually one or more members of the firm's domestic marketing organization have the inclination and ambition to begin forming the new department. Slowly, over time, allow those personnel to become the international department. The key to success is finding a leader personality who is capable of developing a plan, being responsible for training the staff, and generally functioning as the export manager. Often a firm will bring in an outside consultant at this point, one who is a seasoned manager and who has had experience with start-ups. Other duties related to export marketing, finance, and traffic are spread among the various domestic departments and integrated with their normal activities.

Advantages.   Personnel who already know the firm's products, organization, and key employees in other departments bring initial stability to the development of a new department. There is a built-in level of trust that is never there initially when outsiders are hired for a new function. This method of developing from within brings with it some cost savings in the short run. Often, only the job descriptions of experienced employees are enriched not their salaries.

Disadvantages.   The flip side to this method is that the present staff will have their time diluted and the development of the new department will often take a backseat to normal duties. Two things can suffer: (1) the current job, with the inevitability of errors, omissions, and delays that a new exporter can ill afford; and (2) the timely start-up of the new department. For the same reasons, when an outside consultant is hired, that person sometimes has a difficult time getting the attention of the current staff due to their overloaded condition.

Recruit a Staff and Form a Separate Department

The second option is the recruitment of a staff that is already trained and has developed a track record at other companies. In this case you would create a separate export department by hiring several key employees to concentrate on the development of the export business. The first to be hired would, of course, be the export manager who, with your support, would hire the remainder of the staff using the schedule developed in your strategic plan.

Advantages. By having a separate export department in charge from the beginning, management can get better data and a feel for the development process. Recruited personnel often have established contacts and relationships with support organizations. The company's image will be enhanced and employee morale within the department should not become a problem.

Disadvantages. Top management of the company must be cautious of new managers for international operations who bring with them approaches that are too optimistic and that interject utopian sales projections based on their experiences with other established firms. This method will require a period of familiarization for new employees to learn how your company operates and about its products.

Foreign Nationals

Sooner or later you will want to hire foreign personnel because they offer advantages over the exclusive use of domestic hires. For instance, foreign nationals

1. Allow you to do business. In many countries, a foreign firm cannot operate unless it uses native agents or representatives.
2. Are less expensive in terms of both salaries and travel costs.
3. Give your company a home-country identity.
4. Can help you avoid cultural and legal barriers.
5. Have a relatively easy time managing other foreign nationals.
6. Are less vulnerable to threats of terrorism.

On the other hand, foreign nationals can be difficult to shed once they become settled into a job. Some foreign laws require severance pay or specific causes prior to firing. Typically they are hired through an employment contract, which, unless carefully worded, can become binding and expensive to break.

IMPORT ORGANIZATION

Worldwide purchasing must be keyed to production flow, engineering, research and development, marketing, after-market requirements, and material selection. Worldwide purchasing plays a growing part in the optimization of an integrated manufacturing system.

Today's sourcing organization must not only have the capability to purchase materials, goods, and services to support in-house manufacturing, but it must also locate parts and assemblies from sources outside the boundaries of the business. All this is done with the intent to improve profit margins of the business unit as a whole.

ORGANIZATIONAL MODELS

There are several ways to organize your firm to accommodate changes as it grows in the international arena. While there is no rigid pattern, most global companies are organized geographically, functionally, or by product line. The best way to implement strategic change, however, is through project management, and that requires a matrix organization.

Your expansion may be in many countries on many continents with many products. When that happens you will have several organizational options available, depending on selling patterns, sales growth, and significant legal or tax advantages recommended by your lawyer or accountant. In selecting the proper organization for your firm the critical elements are to (1) avoid duplication, that is, divisions or departments doing the same function; and (2) avoid suboptimization, that is, treating international business as a separate segment of corporate business thus preventing its optimal use in the best interest of the total organization.

Start-Up Organization

The first organization will either be split off from the domestic marketing or purchasing departments or organized as a new entity. The initial effort is generally focused on one or two high-priority target countries. Typically a project officer is assigned the task of implementing the first entry into a new country. Figure 24–2 shows a typical organizational diagram for a firm that is getting started in international business.

Matrix Organization

Many of the objectives of global strategy can best be accomplished through program and project management methods; that is, assigning a person to a specific action item of the POAM which requires cutting across the functional organization. Figure 24–3 shows how a matrix organization might look. The project officer is given a charter and a POAM. Managers in the functional organization are then directed to cooperate with the project officer in the implementation. For example, a certain entry tactic, such as setting up an export program or establishing a joint venture might be best performed by a project officer.

FIGURE 24–2
Start-Up Organization

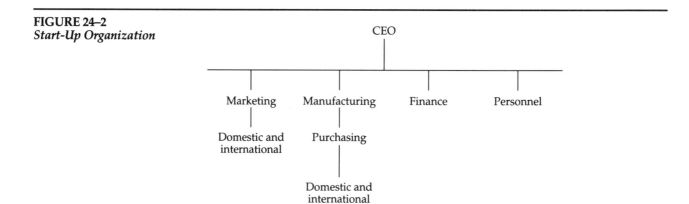

FIGURE 24–3
Matrix Organization

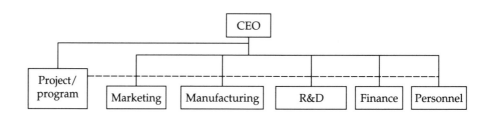

Organizing Geographically

Early on, you may find that your firm is serving several countries in regions that are close to one another yet far from your home base. This is the typical beginning of restructuring the organization by geographical area.

By organizing a headquarters or a marketing subsidiary in the region, there is a common base for management, and it becomes easier to communicate, thus optimizing marketing know-how. Figure 24–4 is an example of such a structure.

Flat Geographic Organization

The main drawback of this geographic organization is the tendency to dilute the global viewpoint. Over time regions begin to take on domestic viewpoints, and there is the danger of suboptimization. To overcome this tendency, a strong coordinational management style must be in place.

One top manager overcomes this tendency by keeping a close rein from the corporate headquarters. His or her organization is flat and tight. There are four subordinate managers in the home office with the top manager, and each has a region in which the company does business through sales representatives. The reps, in each of the 50 countries where this firm does business, are natives of that country and thus are familiar with the people, businesses and government, and their needs. The top manager believes that his or her company has pop (responsiveness) which translates to bigger sales as a result of using representatives. The flat geographic organization looks like Figure 24–5.

Functional Organization

A functional organization lends itself to a firm that has homogeneous products. Line executives have global responsibilities. Figure 24–6 shows a typical organization.

FIGURE 24–4
Organizing Geographically

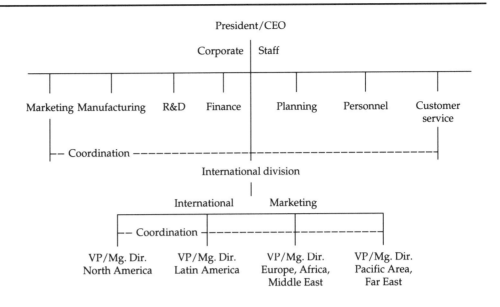

FIGURE 24–5
Flat Geographic Organization

Organization by Product   Another means of organization is shown in Figure 24–7 in which each line product has its own international sales organization. This is a world company approach where product groups are responsible for global marketing and sourcing. This method is typical for firms with several unrelated product lines for which their marketing tasks vary more by product than by region.

Integrated International Organization   Figure 24–8 shows an organization structure for an integrated manufacturing system. It shows that the worldwide sourcing manager (WWSM) is at the same level within the organization as the line purchasing managers. The WWSM is a principal assistant to the purchasing director who is responsible for developing policy and procedures and providing a vision for line purchasers. They are closely linked to the worldwide marketing manager (WWMM) and marketing counterparts in the integrated organization.

Kyocera Amoeba Organization   Earlier in Chapter 4 the Kyocera philosophy was discussed. It includes the amoeba method of organization. At the time of publication, Kyocera owned 40 companies in 11 countries. Figure 24–9 shows the complexity of this organizational concept. The corporation is managed by exception with each subordinate organization a profit center attempting to maximize its contribution to the adopted strategy.

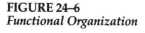

FIGURE 24–6
Functional Organization

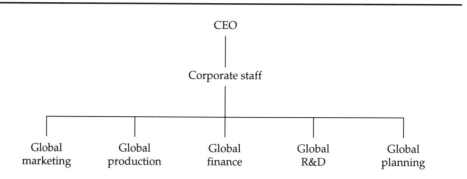

FIGURE 24–7
Organization by Product

Hierarchical Model versus Nontraditional Models

The hierarchical model came to the business world from the military. It is one which is shaped like a pyramid with each level of the organization reporting to the one above it, with horizontal units coordinating events at their own level. The span of control of each senior level is typically limited to five or six subordinate managers and each function at each level is discretely defined. The fundamentals of the hierarchical model are as follows:

- Every job assigned to a unit must be assigned to one or more persons.
- All responsibilities must be clear cut and well understood.
- Specific responsibilities should not be assigned to more than one person.
- Each unit and person within the organization must know, from top to bottom, to whom they report and who reports to them.
- Responsibility must be matched by authority.
- Do not have too many people report to one leader.
- Exercise control only at your assigned level.
- Divide the work load evenly among the units and people within the units.

Kazuo Inamori's philosophy of amoeba organization might give the impression that it is a very nontraditional model. To the contrary; there is a very distinct overlaying of hierarchical leadership to the amoeba system.

Many behavioralists argue that since all work is accomplished through people, the hierarchical model has become obsolete. Thus, it should be substituted with models where subordinate units and jobs are decentralized and less defined. These rely on collaboration and cooperation, thus reducing competition among horizontal levels.

FIGURE 24–8
Flat geographic

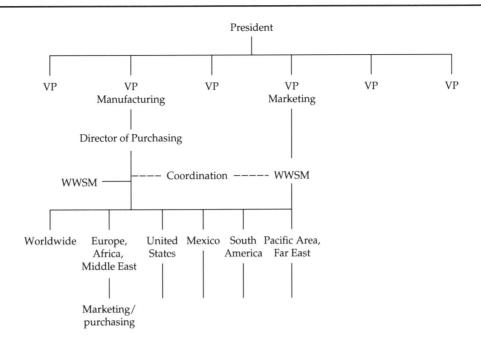

Others say the hierarchical model is still needed because it alone allows people to know where they are in the organization. Like the Gatling gun, however, which has been modified over the years to work in helicopters and as a defensive system aboard modern naval frigates, the hierarchical model needs to be qualified to lessen the competitive syndrome and strengthen teamwork.

SUMMARY

Implementation of your global strategy means assigning each action item to a person by name and obtaining a commitment for its accomplishment. This can be done using a mechanism called the plan of action and milestones (POAM). The question of reward for accomplishing strategy is one with which each organization must wrestle. Some argue that only the entire organization should be rewarded. Others believe that individuals must be stimulated by a reward system to be successful. Your organization must be tailored for your strategy, but that organization should be viewed as changeable; that is, as the company changes so must the organization.

CHECKLIST

- Have all levels of the organization been included in the implementation process?
- Have milestones been established for the accomplishment of strategic and tactical objectives?
- Is a stress-release mechanism in place?
- Has a reward system been discussed?
- Do managers have a wide range of positive and negative performance mechanisms?
- Do written policies support the new strategy?
- Are the policies consistent across international boundaries?

FIGURE 24–9
Kyocera Amoeba Organization

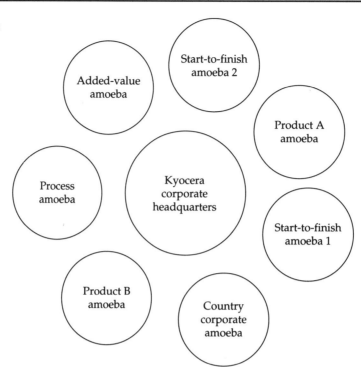

- Have standard operating procedures been adapted to local conditions?
- Have all written policies and procedures been checked for translation errors?
- Does the organization have an automated management information system suitable to support implementation?
- Does the organization support the changing implementation process?

Chapter 25

Executing Tactics

The future belongs to those who believe in their dreams.

Eleanor Roosevelt

The theme of this book is how to take advantage of opportunities beyond home borders and ultimately become an insider. This chapter is about the things a project officer should be concerned about as he or she goes about the process of executing entry tactics.

TIME-PAST

Until recently most firms have not gone on the offensive internationally. American firms in particular have been satisfied with local markets because they offered large populations with excellent purchasing power.

In the past most firms entered the global market only as a sequence of events over time. In other words, companies came to the business of importing or exporting only as an afterthought. This staged process, often taking many years, generally began only when small firms were successful in the domestic market. The literature that documents this process explains that the stages typically followed a pattern similar to the one detailed here.

• *Stage 1.* At some point in the firm's life it became engaged in extraregional expansion, widening its experience and market consciousness. For some it began with a search for cheap raw materials or components. During this period the small firm began to fill some unsolicited (over-the-transom) orders but still had not engaged in a serious international plan.

• *Stage 2.* Soon the firm began to investigate exporting. If the investigation was successful, the firm began to experiment. At first it was interested only in overseas sales of its surplus products since it was without resources to fill overseas orders on an ongoing basis.

• *Stage 3.* If the experimentation was successful the firm became an experienced exporter by actively soliciting overseas sales. Therefore, it was willing to make limited modifications to its products and marketing procedures to accommodate the requirements of overseas buyers.

• *Stage 4.* The exporting firm eventually made major modifications in its products as well as to its marketing practices in order to reach more international buyers.

• *Stage 5.* Finally, the firm developed new products for existing or new overseas markets and diversified its markets to other countries.

Today, instead of staying home and waiting for the telephone to ring, firms are on the offensive and global business strategy determines cross-border expansion. The task of implementing the chosen tactics should now be assigned to one or more project officers whose duty it is to execute the adopted global strategies.

OUTSIDER TACTICS

Outsider tactics include exporting, importing, forming associations to export, using intermediaries, licensing, and direct mail alternatives.

EXPORT MARKETING PROJECT

International marketing is, in the eyes of many small firms, an awesome thing—a major obstacle to tapping growing market opportunities. But if the activity is approached rationally there are sufficient alternatives such that any company should be able to enter.

The first step is to assign the project to a strong project officer, someone who will get the job done. That person should be oriented toward marketing and have a background of experience in that field.

As a project officer assigned to establish an export market with one or more countries, the first responsibility is to review the approved strategic plan. Your job will be to create new strategic boundaries for your firm through forward integration. Exporting requires travel to check out markets and distributors as well as sales coordination among overseas representatives. Are you enthusiastic and ready for global travel? If not, tell your boss you are not the right person for the job.

Intelligence, the Prerequisite

Organizing for international marketing is all about organizing for selling and that effort requires creativeness and determination not experienced in some aspects of business operations. The prerequisite for any successful international business venture is intelligence. Before your international effort can move forward you must invest in market research, either by your own team or with the assistance of a firm that specializes in the field. The formulation process required sufficient intelligence gathering to make strategic decisions, but now a detailed market plan must be developed and that requires additional research.

Market Plan

Keep in mind that the export market plan must be integrated into your firm's total strategic plan. The market plan should cover three to five years. There are two phases to an export marketing program. Phase 1 is the planning stage and phase 2 is the action stage.

Phase 1: Planning Stage

Your plan should be written as a distinct part of your firm's larger, overall business plan and should define your company's international policy. Realistic goals and objectives should be set and a suitable organization plan should be developed. Above all, your plan should be put on paper.

The firm's total marketing plan has three subparts: the domestic commercial plan, the government plan, and the international plan. Don't make the same mistake many firms do by making two separate plans, one for the domestic and government market and another for the international market. Certainly the approach should be a separate investigation of each market, but the total plan should include all. This way there is synergy and many commonalties. This chapter deals only with the international marketing plan. This outline explains the international market.

A. Executive summary: written only after all other parts of the plan are complete.

B. International marketing objective: leader, follower, challenger, or niche player.

C. Intelligence.
1. Target market including segmentation.
2. Players.
3. Interstate (governmental) controls.
4. Market alternatives.

D. Market subtactics.
1. Product.
2. Price.

3. Place.

4. Promotion.

E. Action Stage.

1. Budget.

2. Contingencies.

Phase 2: Action Stage

Executing the plan requires a systems approach. Then when you are finished the results can be measured. Such an approach includes budgeting, measuring results, correcting tactics, and contingency plans.

Systems Approach

The marketing process should be visualized as a system wherein a set of predetermined inputs (market tactics) are measured and acted upon in such a way that they are continually changed as conditions change. In the international marketplace these tactics are sometimes affected by external as well as internal conditions. The strongest of the firms participating in the international marketplace retain a flexibility about their efforts which allows them to react to these changing conditions.

Budgeting

An export marketing plan is a wish list developed by you and your team. It represents every method you would like to use to get the product to the target market. Few firms can satisfy all tactical elements in terms of resources. Marketing must stand alongside R&D for its fair share of the company's funds. This is why marketers must prioritize the elements of their plan in terms of results. Select from your total plan those elements that your think will bring the greatest, fastest return. Don't give up on the rest of your plan. Execute it as funds become available.

Measuring Results

From the beginning, the elements of every market plan must be developed in such a way that they can be measured in terms of actual sales success. Statistical analysis should drive every step of the marketing plan. Every advertising campaign, every trade show, and every distributor must have measurable, quantitative, statistical checkpoints that determine sales success.

Correcting Market Tactics

Keep in mind that marketing plans are never locked in concrete. In fact, the most important thing you should understand about successful exporting is that the market plan is in almost constant change.

The development of any market plan must have safety valves. That is, in case one marketing tactic doesn't work, where do you go from here? For instance, if advertising doesn't bring in the desired sales results through the media of one target market, there must be some thought to redirecting those funds to a distribution network or to the hiring of agents.

Contingency Plans

Every plan should have a set of contingencies or activities, based on a set of what-ifs. Those decisions will not be based on conjecture or emotion, but rather on hard statistical data related to income and profit over a predetermined time objective.

The Export Team

The most important aspect of the growth of your international sales effort will be the selection of the right people to carry out your plan. The dominant personal characteristic of these employees will be the ability to work on a team in a multicultural environment.

A typical international marketing department, when fully developed, would include an export manager, a traffic manager, a communications manager, an engineering services manager, credit and finance personnel, a sales manager, a promotion assistant, and sales personnel. Of course, not all of these positions are filled at once. Instead most companies let their organization develop as their sales and activities increase, hiring only as cash flow will allow expansion.

Evaluating Personnel

In as much as your sales staff is so vital to you, from the outset you should have an image of the ideal international salesperson in mind. Among other things, the ideal person should

1. Want to sell.
2. Enjoy travel.
3. Have a desire to deal in a foreign environment and language.
4. Be able to adapt to other cultures.
5. Have a track record or at least exhibit behavioral instincts for the bottom line, that is, have the ability to close.
6. Show bounce-back characteristics, the ability to regroup from rejection.

IMPORT PROJECT

The modern approach to global business seeks synergism. Just as international marketing (exporting) must be integrated with your company's total marketing strategy, so must international sourcing (importing) be integrated with your total purchasing and manufacturing strategy.

Project Officer

The assignment of a project officer to establish the tactic of importing is just as valid as it is for the exporting function. The person assigned should be well versed in the purchasing process and have an interest in international travel. Integration will again require you to redefine the boundaries of your business.

Intelligence

Good intelligence is as much a prerequisite for purchasing as it is for a successful marketing effort. Before your international effort can move forward you must invest in research, either by your own team or with the assistance of a firm that specializes in the field. You cannot assume that sources will find you or that the grapevine will get the word out to qualified international suppliers.

Purchasing Team

Experienced domestic purchasing managers who have the inclination to travel and the talent to work with people of other cultures are the best selection. The ideal selection for the position of worldwide sourcing manager (WWSM) would be a person with a purchasing background; but most important that person should have a high degree of skill at influencing behavior patterns. This job is only 10 percent buying and requires 90 percent missionary work or the selling of new ideas and approaches.

The modern international line purchaser needs the ability to relate to other cultures and understand the relationship of the buying function to macro business objectives. Purchasing represents a major reflection of the company and as such purchasers should be multilingual and culturally sensitive as well as proficient in their tasks.

ASSOCIATION PROJECT

The project officer's job is to pull together diverse organizations into a common export marketing objective. This takes the nicest sense of protocol and a collaborative approach which is capable of persuading others to work together for the common good.

To increase teamwork, manufacturers and others around the world have been joining forces to take advantage of revisions to antitrust laws to increase the number of trade-related joint ventures. For American businesses, the Export Trading Company Act of 1982 (ETCA) provides many advantages.

Public and private sector organizations have closed ranks to take several initiatives to stimulate international trade. Corporate networks link educational institutions to cooperate for R&D and for ways to streamline logistical systems or to adapt products and services to world markets.

Capital, either pooled from cooperative industries or gathered from banks, is required for this new teamwork. Capital is essential to develop the computerized information systems needed to support not only marketing information, but to bring about efficient physical distribution. Financing is even required to attract a share of the most talented people into international marketing.

Firms with like products, or even distinctly unlike products in combinations, share the costs of international trading and extend their reach to global markets. Combinations are better equipped to get the products of small firms into the market. Banks, airlines, freight companies, and other international businesses that already have networks of established offices throughout the world are well suited to associate with trading companies in order to provide global market reach.

The role of international marketing associations is complex and has at least 10 major functions:

1. *Financial services.* They extend credit, make loans, provide loan guarantees, and develop venture capital.

2. *Information services.* They have up-to-date information on clients around the world.

3. *Risk-reduction services.* They offer foreign exchange management, letters of credit, and insurance.

4. *Organization and coordination services.* They take on complex projects and pool capital to share risks.

5. *Auxiliary services.* They offer documentation, freight forwarding, and customs information. Because of economies of scale, the cost of their services is reduced. Thus, auxiliary services have great capital efficiency.

6. *Human resources.* They devote immense efforts to hiring and training the best employees.

7. *Financial resources. Sogo shoshas* amass phenomenal amounts of capital.

8. *Global commercial networks.* These provide

9. *Communications systems.* These provide excellent intelligence networks.

10. *Capital formation.* This develops incentive capital from outside the manufacturing sector, particularly in support of small- and medium-sized firms.

INTERMEDIARY PROJECT

An intermediary is a firm that acts to market or broker goods manufactured in one country to companies and governments in another. The responsibility of the project officer in this case is to find the right intermediary to serve your firm. There are several arrangements available to a small firm that decides to use the indirect method. There are five general categories of intermediaries.

1. *General trading companies (GTCs).* These firms, as their name implies, import and export a broad range of goods, cutting across many product lines and marketing to many countries. There are both international and American GTCs operating in the United States.

2. *Export trading companies (ETCs).* In the United States, these are new companies formed under the Export Trading Company Act of 1982. They can be bank- or nonbank-owned and have broad antitrust benefits. They may be creatively organized to stimulate exporting, but they may import goods as well.

3. *Import/export management companies (I/EMCs).* These are America's traditional intermediaries. Most often referred to in the literature as EMCs, they are

usually small firms that specialize by exporting or importing, product or industry, and market areas.

4. *Multinational corporations (MNCs)*. Some very large corporations that compete on a global basis take on, as an additional business unit, the exportation of goods for others.

5. *Piggybacking*. This is a method of exporting whereby a company with complementary products convinces a larger firm, often an MNC, to act as intermediary.

What Intermediaries Can Do for You

Intermediaries are independent organizations which often act as the exclusive sales department for noncompetitive manufacturers. Although there is some loss of control, these organizations come very close to behaving like your own export department. Even the loss of control can be tempered by asking for frequent performance reviews. (See Appendix E for the major elements of an agent/distributor agreement.)

Intermediaries work simultaneously for a number of manufacturers for a commission, salary, or retainer plus commission. They work through their own overseas network of distributors and market your products overseas along with other allied but noncompetitive product lines. Most intermediaries provide a wide range of services including the following:

- Strategic market planning.
- Market research.
- Shipping.
- Advertising.
- Documentation.
- Channel distribution selection.
- Insurance.
- Financing
- Exhibition of your products in trade shows.

These firms, as your export managers, will solicit orders from international clients, correspond on your stationery, and sign off on letters or telexes and invoices in the name of the principal manufacturer. The manufacturer bears the risk of nonpayment, but the intermediary assists the manufacturer with the details of the transaction and gets paid a commission on the export sale.

Most sales initiated by intermediaries need approval of their client companies. This way manufacturers retain control of the marketing of their product overseas, especially when they maintain their own brand names.

In short, an intermediary essentially domesticates your overseas sales by taking full responsibility for the export end of your business, thus relieving you of all the headaches of doing it yourself. A good intermediary takes a personal concern in your company managing the entire scope of the international marketing effort for long-term development and profit.

What the Manufacturer Wants

In the early stage, the manufacturer should search for the right intermediary, that is, one that handles similar product lines. Having narrowed the search to several that can do the job, the final selection should be based on finding the company which

1. Will develop strategic marketing plans.
2. Has international experience.
3. Possesses product knowledge.

4. Works in an overseas network.
5. Has geographic coverage.
6. Shows no conflict of interest.
7. Makes periodic progress reports showing current status based on the marketing plan.

What the Intermediary Wants

A manufacturer should not be surprised to learn that many large, successful intermediaries have more to say about who selects them than the manufacturer. What manufacturers and intermediaries want and get are two different things. Everything is negotiable and no one works for nothing. Here is a list of what intermediaries want:

1. A product that has a ready market.
2. A product that has staying power.
3. An advance, retainer, or earnest money against time spent doing research and developing a strategic market plan.
4. Sufficient margin to cover handling costs and to make a reasonable profit.
5. Freedom to develop and execute a strategic plan.
6. Products in the intermediary's area of expertise.
7. A trustful relationship with the manufacturer, that is, to be perceived as a team member.
8. Realistic expectations.
9. Free marketing support, such as, samples, advertising, and trade show participation.
10. Information about company progress, policy changes, and production delays.

Representative/ Distributor Agreement Checklist

1. The products covered.
2. The initial duration of the agreement.
3. Grounds for termination and the notification period.
4. How and when the I/EMC will be paid commissions and discounts.
5. Manufacturer support such as samples and literature.
6. Pricing policy and arrangements for future changes.
7. Terms of sale.
8. Use of patents, trademarks, and similar devices.
9. Rights to appoint subdistributors.
10. Warranty policy.
11. Returned goods policy.

LICENSING PROJECT

In this case the project officer's duty is to negotiate an arrangement wherein the the licensor gives something of value to the licensee in exchange for certain performance and payments. Commercial licensing arrangements comprise one or more of the following:

1. Know-how.
2. Patent rights.
3. Copyrights.
4. Trademark rights.
5. Technical advice including diagrams, feasibility studies, manuals, and plans.
6. Architectural and engineering designs.

In return the licensee agrees to do all or some of the following:

1. Pay some amount, usually a royalty, related to sales volume.
2. Produce the product.
3. Market the product in some specified sales territory.

Licensing Tips

1. Carefully select the licensee. Draw up a list of candidates then eliminate those who are less likely to provide the needed long-term relationship.
2 Get expert assistance in drawing up the agreement.
3. Retain control through a combination of equity in the licensee and duration of the relationship.
4. Retain know-how of key parts
5. Put a key person in charge of the arrangement; don't let it become a back-burner process.

Licensing by any company, particularly small firms, should be considered as a method of getting quickly into the market. The structure of the license is critical, however, and should be handled with the assistance of a consultant or an attorney (See Appendix F for a typical international licensing agreement.)

The principal elements of a modern comprehensive contractual agreement are

• *Product coverage.* Often the products are listed in an appendix to the main document. Define the rights and products broadly enough to take in all peripheral processes and apparatus on which you intend to receive royalties.

• *Rights.* Specify and identify by number, date of issue, and term, each patent, trademark, technological innovation, and copyright.

• *Territorial coverage.* Be specific in this definition since territorial scope may differ from distribution rights.

• *Term of contract.* Fix the tenure or period of the license.

• *Extension and renewal clauses.* Rights may be exclusive or nonexclusive and you should retain the right to extend or renew depending on the licensee's performance.

• *Protection of rights.* Retain the action to proceed against infringement. In general, licensees should not be left to retain such infringements for their own benefit.

DIRECT MAIL PROJECT

Direct mail is a medium of advertising and communicating. Marketing through the mail is fundamentally the same whether it is domestic or international. The project officer's responsibility is to identify the potential consumer universe within the target country and to solicit a response based on presentation of the written word through the postal system. Almost any product or service can be sold by direct mail, but your results depend on the mailing list, the offer, and the package.

Mailing List

The mailing list is the most important element, because in order to make sales you must send your offer to interested prospects. It is estimated that because of population mobility, most U.S. lists will deteriorate 20–25 percent in a given year due to insufficient addresses. Other countries are generally less mobile.

Offer

Make your offer simple and clear. Seldom do you get a second chance to explain your points when you are communicating by mail. No letter is too long if it tells the whole story and keeps the reader's attention. Make certain you write and rewrite your message until anybody can understand what you're selling. In this regard, let a few disinterested people read the material before you mail it.

Package

The package is the presentation of the material to the prospect. There are no hard-and-fast rules, but generally the package consists of a letter, a circular or catalog, an order form, and a return envelope.

- The letter should clearly explain your offer and entice the buyer to move and not procrastinate.
- The circular or catalog should be uncluttered and show and tell the product's uses and qualities.
- The order form should be easy to fill out and send to you in the return envelope.

INSIDER TACTICS

An insider strategy is one in which a firm wants customers to visualize it as a local company. The tactics to accomplish this are: start a firm; acquisition and merger; partnering or joint venture; and franchising.

START-A-FIRM PROJECT

The process of starting a new company in any country is essentially the same. Before committing resources, a complete business plan should be developed which projects at least three to five years into the future.

The Business Organization

Decide how your business will be organized. The three common legal forms are sole proprietorship, partnership, or corporation. Selecting the form of your business should be based on the intent, complexity, laws, tax implications, and liability requirements of the business.

The Ten Commandments of Starting an Overseas Business

1. Limit the primary participants to people who not only can agree and contribute directly to the business, but who are also experienced in some form of international business.
2. Define your market in terms of what is purchased, by whom, and why.
3. Concentrate all available resources on two or three products or objectives within a given time period.
4. Remember that the best information comes through your own industry.
5. Write down your business plan and work from it.
6. Walk on two legs. Pick a good freight forwarder or customs house broker to walk alongside your banker.
7. Translate your literature into the language of the country in which you will do business.
8. Use the services of the national commerce and treasury departments.
9. Limit the effects of your inevitable mistakes by starting slowly.
10. Communicate frequently and effectively with your international contacts, and visit the overseas markets and manufacturers.

MERGER AND ACQUISITION PROJECTS

Because of insider knowledge and a track record, acquisition of an existing business is often the preferred way to become an insider in another country. The advantages of acquiring are

- You may get existing business at a bargain price.
- You bypass start-up problems, particularly in establishing relationships with banks.
- Guesswork is minimized about location, facilities, and advertising.
- The current owners and staff can give you valuable information about competition, demand, and seasonal fluctuations.
- You get time-tested suppliers and service people.

- You inherit trained employees who will stay on and help you learn the culture, language, and country business methods.

There are also pitfalls to acquisition that you must avoid. Many firms look good on paper—the paper that the present owners show you. Trust only your own analysis and your own lawyer, because businesses all over the world can be made to look healthier than they are. Analyze carefully and use every tool suggested in Chapter 7.

PARTNERING (JOINT VENTURE) PROJECT

Businesses worldwide are forming relationships that strengthen their position. It is a modern-day tactic useful in both the forward and backward integration process. Partnering is a particularly useful tactic for small firms which have low-volume, highly differentiated products.

Joint-venture or co-investment is a foreign business arrangement wherein the foreign firm has sufficient equity to have a say in the management of the company to protect its interests. The advantages of co-investment are: It is more profitable than royalties from licensing; there is greater control; and often there are better marketing results. On the other hand, the joint venture represents a greater commitment than either licensing or franchising resulting in higher risks should there be political turmoil. Control is the vital element in the development of a joint venture, and the agreement must be carefully structured.

FRANCHISE PROJECT

The primary reason for using the franchise to enter distant markets is that foreign laws are usually not overly restrictive. In fact, franchising is encouraged by most countries because it tends to foster local ownership and increased employment.

The franchise is a system of vertical distribution. More important than that, it is a method of doing business that combines big business know-how with the dynamism of entrepreneurship. Franchising's strength comes from sharing goals.

It isn't hard to figure out why so many firms, even many of America's corporate giants, have chosen franchising as a means to grow fast or lose a market. The franchiser doesn't have to spend money to open a franchise, and it's immediately profitable because someone pays you to start one.

As the project officer to set up a franchise you will be expected to provide know-how, training, trademarks, trade names, techniques, management expertise, and market research assistance. The key to your overseas franchise success, however, will be a strong relationship developed by a careful balance of good support programs and hands-off operation. Experience has shown that motivated franchisees most often manage their businesses better than your own employees.

There are hazards on both sides of the relationship. Here are some of the things each side wants to ensure a successful partnership.

What the franchisor wants

- An operator who has local knowledge of the market.
- Someone who has adequate business experience.
- Someone who has sufficient funds to risk the capitalization costs and franchise fees and make it through the bad times.
- A dedicated manager with a stake in the enterprise.
- A team player.

What the franchisee wants

- An exclusive territory.
- To be able to transfer the franchise.
- To know if the franchisor will take the franchise back.
- To know who will pay for the training

- To know the background of the franchisor—whether he or she is a veteran or a beginner.
- To know what kind of promotion the franchisor provides.
- Financing.

The Elements of a Franchise

Of course the laws of the country in which you franchise will govern, but there are two fundamental elements to the process: the disclosure statement, sometimes referred to as the offering circular or sale prospectus, and the franchise agreement.

Disclosure statement.   Prior to any sale, the franchisor should disclose the following information to a prospective operator:

- Franchisor's identifying information.
- Franchisor's business experience, the officers, and the directors.
- Franchiser's financial information.
- Any litigation history.
- Any bankruptcy history.
- Description of the franchise.
- Obligations of the purchase.
- Site selection.
- Financing arrangements.
- Initial funds required of the operator.
- Recurring funds.
- Any persons the franchisor requires or advises the franchisee to use.
- Training.
- Restriction of sales.
- Termination, cancellation, and renewal.

Franchise agreement. This is fundamental and should include the following:

- Franchise fees and royalties.
- Location.
- Trademarks, service marks, and logos.
- Advertising.
- Training and business support.
- Protection of trade secrets.
- Maintenance and repairs.
- Accounting and records.
- The business system.
- Allowable modifications to the business system.
- Quality control and performance.
- Insurance required.
- Length of franchise agreement.
- Rights and duties of parties upon termination.
- Business start-up.
- Hours of operation.
- Transferability of interest.
- Franchisor's right of first refusal.
- Disability or death of franchisee.
- Taxes, permits, and applicable laws.
- Default and opportunity to cure.
- Disclaimers.
- Termination and renewal terms.

RISK SHARING/
LEARNING TACTICS

A firm takes a risk sharing or learning strategy when it is uncertain of itself or the target country.

PRODUCTION-
SHARING PROJECT

Offshore production provides five advantages to the global business.

1. Production/assembly plants can be close to the export market.
2. Low costs of production make products more competitive in the domestic marketplace.
3. Products can be offered at competitive prices for the export market.
4. A firm can add plant capacity without a large capital expenditure.
5. Value can be added to the product at less cost.

The term *production sharing* means manufacturing or assembly in a different country or region, not the home base of the parent company, in order to take comparative advantage of production factors, principally to lower costs. Other names commonly used for this process are the following:

- Complimentary assembly facilities.
- Co-production.
- Export factories.
- Export platforms.
- Export processing zones.
- Global factories.
- Global production zones.
- In-bond programs.
- Maquiladoras.
- Off-border production.
- Offshore production.
- Twin plants.
- Value-added processing.

Most, if not all, of the countries that offer production sharing are classified as developing or least-developed nations. Because the advantages for these countries are jobs, technology transfer, economic development, and international exchange income, attracting production-sharing opportunities has become very competitive. The most obvious benefit to the global business is the surplus of labor that translates into relatively low wage rates.

Country-of-Origin Markings

Every article of foreign origin entering a country must be legibly marked with the name of the country of origin unless an exception from marking is provided. In the case of production sharing, the parent company of the overseas organization is the ultimate consumer of the imported articles and requests a waiver from the marking requirements. Waivers are granted when the imported article is substantially transformed into a new and different product wherein the imported article is not sold or offered for sale in its imported condition either over the counter or as a replacement part.

Who Are the Labor Exporters?

Some say production sharing is the fastest growing industry in the world today. Mexico, closest to the vast U.S. domestic market, is the fastest growing of these offshore production-sharing areas. Mexico also has the greatest market share followed by Singapore, Taiwan, Hong Kong, and Malaysia.

Even the former Soviet Union is moving into the production-sharing business. Free economic zones have been authorized for areas ranging from Armenia and Estonia to the Port of Nachodka in the Soviet Far East. The foreign investment incentives for these zones include: duty-free export and import; a reduction in tax and lease payments; labor policies governed by the local zones; and application for free market prices. For instance, 50 percent of the production and assembly would be ordered by the state at state prices, the remainder at market prices.

The Decision

There are five major factors that you must consider when making the production-sharing decision:

1. *Suitability.* What is the suitability of your product for production sharing?
2. *Location.* What are the relative advantages of the various production-sharing locations for your product?
3. *Method.* What method of production sharing? Investment (long term) or shelter (short term)?
4. *Costs.* What are the comparative fully burdened costs at each location?
5. *Control.* How much must you control the production process?

Product Suitability

Do you make something or process something that has a great deal of labor content? Analyze your business. Are you operating on the edge of profitability because of high labor costs? If you reduced your manufacturing costs would your product be more competitive when exported to world markets?

Location

The distances from Mexico to most marketplaces in the United States are short. While it usually takes from three to four weeks to transport goods from the Far East to the United States, it takes only three or four days from Mexico. The high cost of Pacific Ocean transportation stands between the labor-intensive offshore production capability of Taiwan, China, India, and Malaysia. Keep in mind though that Asian, West African, and Central American locations often provide advantages when the target market is Asia, Europe, or South America.

Method

Nations with large, low-cost labor pools market their production-sharing programs as investment opportunities. Investment, however, is not the only method. Private companies have ingeniously developed processes which provide risk sheltering of foreign companies by contracting through an intermediary to rent space and employees or to subcontract for piece-rate assembly and production.

Investment. A foreign firm can invest in most production-sharing countries. You can own and operate a plant or enter into a joint venture to do so. In addition to low labor rates, each competing country offers significant investment incentives and concessions. These were discussed in Chapter 13. Some of these include the following:

1. Duty-free import of capital goods, equipment, and raw materials in one or more free zones.
2. Tax holidays, that is, exemptions from tax on profits.
3. Rent-free land.
4. Waivers of import licensing for imported capital goods and other production materials.
5. One hundred-percent ownership for export-oriented enterprises.
6. Free remittance of profits and dividends after payment of taxes.
7. Personal tax exemptions.
8. Accelerated depreciation.
9. Investment tax credits.
10. Increased deductions for business entertainment in connection with export sales.
11. Double deduction of export promotion expenses.
12. Special financial assistance such as grants for research, feasibility studies, and export marketing development.
13. Provisions for employee training.

Risk sheltering. Some of the countries which offer production sharing have unstable political systems and a history of nationalizing industries on a whim. Thus the savings brought about by investment are often outweighed by reasons to shelter the risk. Two methods have sprung up over the years which allow firms to avoid the risk of overseas investment yet to take advantage of low labor rate opportunities.

Subcontracting. Driven by local investors who offer specialized assembly and manufacturing processes on a piece-rate basis, this method has grown at a natural pace. The global firm can have the entire product manufactured or it can provide the molds, raw materials, and/or semi-assembled parts. Then the contractor returns the product, having supplied only the labor.

Subleasing. This method, principally used for the Mexican Maquiladora program, differs from subcontracting by offering space and employee rental computed at an average hourly rate instead of at a per unit basis. With this method, the global firm usually provides the materials, machinery, equipment, and management.

Control

Global factories can be characterized as captive or noncaptive. A captive facility would be one that is dedicated and controlled for the assembly or production for a single parent company's product. A noncaptive plant is typically owned by a native of the country where it is located and operated to serve many international companies on a contractual basis.

Think of investment as a movement toward autarky (self-sufficiency), with the plant at an overseas location. Also remember that subcontracting is a movement away from vertical integration.

The Project/Business Plan

In the beginning you may have only a notion of your plan tucked away in your head. The underlying concept of a project plan is to write out your thoughts. By raising, then systematically answering, basic operational questions, you force self-criticism. Once on paper others can read the plan and you can invite their opinions. Don't let your ego get in the way. Ask for constructive criticism from the most experienced people you can find. Often it is better to ask strangers because friends and relatives tend to want to shield you from hurt. Explain to your readers that you want to hear both the bad news and the good news. The more eyes that see the plan, the more likely you will identify hazards while you still can act to avoid them, and spot opportunities while you can easily act to maximize them.

A project plan can be as brief as 10 pages and as long as 50. On average, plans run about 20 pages each. Every outline is usually about the same. The following format can be used for your project plan.

COVER SHEET: Company name, address, principals, and so on.

STATEMENT OF PURPOSE: Business Plan for Fiscal Year 19xx.

TABLE OF CONTENTS (corresponds to each exhibit):

   A. Executive summary.

   B. Description of the project.

   C. Product line plan.

   D. Sales and market plan.

   E. Operations plan.

   F. Organization plan.

   G. Financial plan.

H. Supporting documents.

I. Summary.

EXHIBITS

Exhibit A: Executive Summary—Summarizes the entire plan in global terms; succinct expression of long- and short-term goals; written last.

Exhibit B: Description of the project.

1. Goals: long and short term; financial; nonfinancial.

2. Product line strategies.

   a. Sales and marketing.

   b. Product development operations.

   c. Financial organization.

3. Location and reasons for it.

Exhibit C: Product line plan.

1. Product line and products: description; price; costs; historical volume; future expectations.

2. Competition's product line and product position: pricing; advertising; promotion.

Exhibit D: Sales and marketing plan.

1. Person(s) responsible for generating product line and product sales.

2. Competition's approach to sales and marketing.

Exhibit E: Operations plan.

1. Production and operations function: production scheduling; inventory (product line and product).

2. Capital expenditures (if required).

Exhibit F: Organization plan—includes organization's structure; organization chart; resumes of key personnel; managerial style.

Exhibit G: Financial plan.

1. Summary of operating and financial schedules.

2. Schedules.

3. Capital equipment.

4. Balance sheet.

5. Cash flow (break-even analysis).

6. Income projections.

7. Pro forma cash flow.

8. Historical financial reports for existing business; balance sheets for past three years; income statements for past three years; tax returns.

Exhibit H: Supporting documents.

1. Personnel resumes.

2. Cost-of-living budget.

3. Letters of reference.

4. Copies of leases.

5. Anything else of relevance to the plan.

Exhibit I: Summary.

Implementation

Your business plan is a road map, but the acid test is whether it will work. You may have to detour to get where you are going, so don't put the map on the shelf and forget about it. Use it as an operating document. Review it and revise it as experience dictates.

SUMMARY

The three broad categories of entry tactics are outsider, insider, and risk sharing. Each has several subcategories. Each tactic has its corresponding set of action steps which, when taken in careful consideration, can avoid mistakes to the new global company.

CHECKLIST

- Are you the ideal project officer? Is someone else better suited to the job?
- Has intelligence been developed to support your project?
- Has a project plan been written?
- Has the supporting action plan been developed and funded?
- Is the firm aware of the potential of using the Export Trade Act of 1982?
- Has the decision to do direct exporting been weighed against the use of a trading intermediary?
- Have you carefully prepared a representative/distributor agreement?
- If the organization's strategy is to be an insider, has a business plan been written?
- Does the labor content of your product warrant production sharing?

Chapter 26

Results Measurement

The way we control the future at Apple [Computers] is to invent it [ourselves].

John Scully

Feedback is an essential part of any management system. Because the implementation of strategy may take five or more years, a feedback loop is even more important. In the case of global strategy, developing a control system is significantly more complex because of the possibility of multiple companies serving multiple countries.

To this point you have set the objectives for future strategic achievement. The purpose of this chapter is to discuss what should be measured and the methods to continuously and proactively measure results.

Management Information System (MIS)

The intent of any control system is to compare actual results against objectives, then feed the results back to management for action at the appropriate levels in the organization. Today, with the low cost of computer hardware and software, there is no excuse for any company not to have the capability to track the information needed to measure these results. Keep in mind that management needs only the exceptions, trends, and problems. Whatever MIS is installed, it must provide this kind of alerting process so that hot spots are brought to top management's immediate attention. The MIS must not mire managers with volumes of unneeded information.

CONTROLS

Management has the responsibility for two types of controls: process and strategic.

Process controls. Process controls are those that tell management if the global strategic management process has been installed correctly. These controls also provide feedback designed to improve the strategic formulation and implementation process. Table 26–1 shows the feedback information needed.

Strategic controls. Management must also track the implementation of the approved strategy to ensure that the intended thrust into the future is achieved. Such a tracking system must provide evaluated information in a sufficiently timely manner that leaders can fine-tune the strategy, change strategic direction, or abort the strategy altogether. The methodology of attaining tracking lead time is through the development and monitoring of key result indicators.

KEY RESULT INDICATORS

Key result indicators (KRIs) are a limited number of areas selected from the plan of action with milestones (POAM) in which high performance will ensure success and/or will allow early detection of strategic problems. These areas should be both external and internal as well as nonfinancial and financial. External matters

219

TABLE 26–1
Process Control Feedback

Feedback purpose	Information needed
To improve the next iteration.	How to improve the process.
To understand the firm.	Better ways to analyze the firm's current position. Better ways to visualize the future (the ad hoc process).
To improve data gathering and analysis.	How to get better data. How to get more timely data. How to better disseminate data. How to gain better trust in data and the analysis.
To improve the formulation task.	How to tell if strategy is consistent and feasible. Better definition of nonfinancial objectives. Better financial predictors. How to improve plan preparation. How to improve decision making. How to improve the approval process. How to improve matching. How to improve the institutionalization process.
To improve the firm's operations.	How to improve implementation. How to improve execution. How to improve the monitoring and measurement process.

are those related to cross-border strategy and industrial competition. Internal matters are those related to the production and marketing processes. How these controls are set up depends a great deal on how the firm is organized. The corporate organization needs information about the entire organization; however, data collection will be different if the firm is decentralized or centralized in its cross-border operations.

External KRIs.   Strategy is about the external prediction factors that allow the firm to thrust into the future. Therefore, some of the most important KRIs are those designed to focus on the major elements of globalization of the firm.

Nonfinancial external KRIs. These bring focus to such aspects of global strategy as changes in country governments and success of market entry tactics or if the firm is adjusting well to new country cultures. Table 26–2 provides several factors for developing nonfinancial KRIs.

Financial external KRIs. These are related to the attainment of strategic objectives. In the case of global business strategy, the underlying objective is to increase sales through cross-border territorial expansion such as growth in sales and market share. The expansion, however, is not without short-term costs, and those must be monitored closely.

The financial KRI targets should be stated in the strategic plan, the annual business plan, the project plan, and the budget. Companies post audit results by comparing actual to target for major items. Of course, the nonfinancial KRI of market share also has financial implications.

Budgets should be designed to correlate with the POAM and should include revenue budgets, capital budgets, and expenditure budgets. Revenue budgets provide management insight into the attainment of the sales targets which match strategic objectives. Monitoring of capital budgets provides insight into the firm's allocations for growth, while expenditures watch spending growth against targets.

TABLE 26–12 *External Nonfinancial KRIs*	Factors	Information required
	Economic	Inflation; interest rates; currency fluctuations; exchange rates; market share.
	Political	Government changes; political leadership changes.
	Opportunistic	Trade creation.
	Industrial	New competitors; product/technology changes; customer needs.
	Scheduling	Meeting nonfinancial milestones.

Internal KRIs.   Internal strategy controls are those which monitor, company by company and business unit by business unit, the internal operational costs and revenues to attain strategic objectives. These KRIs should also be selected from the POAM at each organizational level.

Nonfinancial internal KRIs.   These provide indications of progress, such as the implantation of the global strategic planning process in each business unit and the attainment of production schedules. Just as important are key indicators such as employee turnover, absenteeism, tardiness, and grievances.

Financial internal KRIs.   These monitor such items as dividend payments, earnings per share, net profit, profit-to-sales ratios, return on investment, and stock price. Management may wish to supplement the MIS with periodic audits.

SUMMARY

A business without controls to measure results is like a ship without a rudder. A simplistic computerized management information system is a must for any company pressing into the future. Key result indicators must be established and monitored frequently to ensure that the firm is using the correct strategy and that it is being implemented.

CHECKLIST

- Has the organization installed an MIS to track the feedback controls?
- Do the firm's process controls provide methods to improve the strategic management process?
- Does the MIS track the implementation of the formulated strategy through a series of KRIs?
- Are both financial and nonfinancial KRIs included in the feedback process?
- Are both internal and external KRIs included?

Chapter 27

Keys to Success

As we enter the 21st century, I believe that globalization will progress to a point much further than any of us can foresee.

Jong-Hyon Chey, chairman of the Sunkyong Group

More firms are adopting a strategic approach in order to cope in the new economic age. For them it is the key to the incredible opportunities of the 21st century. They see strategy as an anchor to windward, because if nothing else, it forces executives to face up to the hard questions of where they are going and how will they survive over the long haul. It forces companies to do things they would not do otherwise. Yet the use of strategy to manage companies has not always been popularly adopted. Some executives still argue, "My world changes too quickly." Others drone, "We don't have the time." Yet others put it off by saying, "Think 10, 20, or 30 years into the future? I can hardly think about tomorrow."

This chapter is designed to discuss the key elements of attaining offensive management success through the use of global business strategy. Success is often in the eye of the beholder. One company's definition of success may be an arm's length away from another. For purposes of this book there are four levels upon which success can be measured: formulation, institutionalization, implementation, and operational.

FORMULATION SUCCESS

Success of strategy formulation focuses on the vision process. The mechanics of jumping time to establish objectives five or more years into the future are mighty obstacles for some, but can be easily overcome with the right preparations.

Attitude

Firms that are most successful using global strategic managment are those that have a positive attitude for business. They believe in eternal growth. They don't look back at past accomplishments but continue to challenge the future. They keep the company on the offensive because they know that a defensive company is heading downhill. They have leaders who want to know how to make the paradigm shift from local to global.

Risk

Firms that have had success with formulating an achievable strategy have been those willing to take the risk of learning from the grass roots of their own company as well as learning about new countries and cultures. They have a high drive for collaboration.

Timing

The formulation of global strategy is not a process that can be hurried. Top management should think through the process well in advance of establishing it as new company force. Scheduling the process well in advance of its start date wins converts. Some companies have even had dry runs which do nothing more than get the company into the concept and work out the bugs of conceptual thinking and paperwork headaches. The dry run can even be a significant part of the institutionalization process. On the other hand, some companies use excuses to delay getting started, always finding some new obstacle. There may never be a perfect time—get on with it!

Time Horizon

Those firms most successful in formulating achievable strategies are those who are not intimidated by a shift in their time frame from the here-and-now, short-term profit motive to long-term thinking. That type of thinking brings survival in the open competition of the new economic age.

INSTITUTIONALI-ZATION SUCCESS

Institutionalization may be the most important aspect of developing a global strategy, because successful companies achieve what has been called a mental and spiritual state for the future. Institutionalization of a company philosophy becomes the basis for a new company culture and effective, creative research and invention.

Challenge

Successful firms have found that institutionalizing the strategic process inevitably begets the concept of challenging the future. It becomes a normal thought pattern from top to bottom. Ideas begin to erupt that have been unintentionally subverted. The leaders of these successful firms are secure enough in their own intellect that they can accept the risks to the firm's original foundation, which challenging the future always brings.

Confidence

Once the strategic process takes hold, firms that have been successful in the institutionalization process take on a new confidence. Workers feel good about themselves because they know their firm will survive as a result of their individual and collective efforts and not just those of top management.

IMPLEMENTATION SUCCESS

Firms that have been most successful using strategy as a management process have been those that have not let the process die after formulation. Strategy does not implement itself, and those who cry foul and state that strategy does not work are inevitably those who did not carry through the implementation task.

Will

The word *will* is used in the context that strategic success rests in an underlying spirit within the firm that any odds can be overcome. To successfully implement strategy, the firm's leaders must have the will to overcome obstacles.

Resources

Implementation success is dominated by the resources of the firm. The strategy formulation process is not infallible and often underestimates resource needs, even though the strategic thrust might have been correct. Success is gained by those firm which not only discover resource deficiencies but also find ways to generate whatever is needed to implement what otherwise is a good strategy.

Tenacity

More than anything else, the firm that is successful has tenacity. Different than will, tenacity is the discipline to see the implementation through to its logical conclusion. Once the strategic process has been institutionalized as part of the company culture tenacity becomes a part of the philosophy.

Monitoring

Monitoring the strategic plan as a matter of routine is a major reason firms gain success with the strategic process. They select a set of KRIs that in short bites of time show management the trends, problems, and exceptions.

> Never change a winning game, but always change a losing game.

Flexibility

Firms that experience success in implementing their strategy are those that maintain a flexibility about it. That is, strategy is not rigid and adjusts to global changes.

OPERATIONAL SUCCESS

Operational success is still measured in the traditional ways. Yet for the global organization operational success takes on new dimensions.

Customer

The successful company is one that focuses on the customer. Its key strategy driver is product or service oriented. To be otherwise is to be defensive and reactive. Proactivity vaults the company into the marketplace searching for ways to support customer needs.

Profit

The word *profit* remains the good word of the capitalistic notion, and free enterprise depends on it. Yet for operational success in the new economic age, longer time horizons require new approaches to defining profits. Cross-border offensive strategies require long-term patience with regard to profits and return on investment.

Presence

Landed presence is the best long-term operational objective, and the most successful global firms triumph when this is achieved. But should there be occupation forever? Operational success may sometimes be served best by using the withdrawal strategy; that is, pulling out from a country in trouble politically or where your product has lost significant market share because of government intervention.

Getting Help

Some executives are the kind who tough it out at all cost. But the most successful at attaining strategic operational objectives are those who are secure enough in their own capabilities that they can seek help from within the company or outside of it. If high-level corporate help is available, the successful executive asks for it. If a specific consultant has the answer, he or she is brought in.

Nonfinancials

The firm that gains operational success is not the firm that thinks only about the financials. Improved productivity, high employee morale, and improved product and service quality have proven to be at least equal to, if not in a superior position to, the financials.

Financials

Of course, the measurement of operational success is still dominated by the financials. Such highly important elements as increasing earnings per share and growth of market share remain at the top of the list.

FINAL SHOT

If you are a manager and believe you get paid for solving today's problems you have probably accepted the wrong calling. Leaders/managers earn their salaries for their ability to look ahead.

Appendix A

Generic Corporate-Level Strategic Alternatives

As a follow-on to its country strategies, the global business should consider four generic corporate strategies: offensive, stable, defensive, and combination. Attributed to Michael Porter and others, these strategies identify which businesses the firm intends to be in and how resources are allocated among the businesses. These decisions are driven by the market.

OFFENSIVE STRATEGIES

Offensive strategies promote growth or expansion. They include the substrategies of concentration, integration, and diversification.

Concentration.   A concentration strategy is one that focuses the expansion on a single product or service. Companies that have used this strategy include: WD-40, Coca-Cola, and McDonald's.

Vertical integration.   This occurs when a firm moves into areas currently served by its customers or suppliers. Vertical integration has two components—forward and backward. An example of forward integration is a manufacturing company, which previously relied on distributors to market its products and now begins to market its own products. Forward integration is the offensive component of vertical integration. Conversely, backward integration is the defensive component because it is most often an attempt to reduce costs by moving into an area served by suppliers.

Horizontal integration.   This is also an offensive-growth strategy, but it is a thrust to expand one or more of the firm's existing businesses or product lines. Horizontal integration is almost always done by buying another organization in the same business.

Diversification.   Diversification is the strategy of expanding into areas clearly different than the firm's current business. Diversification has two subsets: concentric and conglomerate.
   Concentric diversification is investment into a business area related or similar to the firm's current business. *Conglomerate* diversification occurs when the firm ventures into a totally unrelated business area.

STABLE STRATEGIES

A stable strategy is neutral to growth; it may or it may not grow. This is a retrenchment, don't-rock-the-boat strategy of doing the same old thing. In most cases it is the strategy of a declining industry. Some executives call this the *endgame strategy* because all growth potential has been taken out of the technology, and the firm is left wondering what to do. There are four subsets to this condition: leadership, niche, harvest, and divestment.

Leadership.   Some firms attempt to stay with the industry in its dying condition in order to become one of the few remaining companies.

Niche.   This firm tries to find a segment of the industry that has favorable characteristics and can increase stability.

Harvest. With this strategy the firm cuts costs and decreases investments in order to improve cash flow.

Divestment. This is the situation in which the firm sells assets in the early stages of a declining industry.

DEFENSIVE STRATEGIES

A defensive strategy, sometimes referred to as *retrenchment*, is used during difficult periods such as when a firm has financial problems, when new competitors enter the market, or when the owner's motivation changes. Most executives classify defensive strategies into four subsets: turnaround, withdrawal, divestiture, and liquidation.

Turnaround. This strategy is designed to get the firm back on its feet by reversing a negative trend. Typically the turnaround strategy is intended to be a temporary process and includes the following: reducing costs by cutting employee compensation and/or benefits; replacing higher-paid employees; reducing low-margin or unprofitable products; and selling unnecessary capital assets.

Withdrawal. There may be circumstances that warrant consideration of withdrawal from a given country. This strategy, like each of the other defensive strategies, should be undertaken only as a last resort because it means giving up presence and loss of employment for valuable workers.

Divestiture. Divestiture happens when a firm sells or divests itself of a business or part of a business. This typically happens when the stable or turnaround strategies fail. It is also used when diversification is not successful.

Liquidation. A liquidation strategy is one which terminates the firm's existence. It includes shutting down operations and selling assets. This is the strategy of last resort.

Combination Strategies

The leadership of most companies are not hidebound to only one of the generic strategies. Instead, after gathering all the data, most strategic teams elect to simultaneously or sequentially employ different strategies for different organizational units and situations.

Number Crunching

There are no shortcuts to understanding the current position of the company. One of the most important methods for understanding an organization is an analysis of its financial statements. Financial data must be manipulated into the traditional ratios that explain the financial success of the firm. It should be noted that the rules of thumb offered in this appendix have been generalized. Dun and Bradstreet or your local bank should be consulted for industry differences.

Traditional Ratios

There are four traditional ratio groupings, which explain a great deal about a firm. Developed from balance sheets, income statements, and other financial records these ratio groups are liquidity, leverage, activity, and profitability

Liquidity Ratios

This is the extent to which a firm can meet its short-term obligations. Current liabilities include maturing long-term debt as well as short-term payables. Two ratios are used: (1) *Current ratio* is the ability to cover short-term debt as it comes due; and (2) *Quick ratio* expresses the degree to which current liabilities can be covered by most liquid assets.

Rule of Thumb

$$\text{Current ratio} = \frac{\text{Current assets}}{\text{Current liabilities}^1}$$

A healthy ratio is 3 to 2, but varies from industry to industry.

$$\text{Quick ratio} = \frac{\text{Current assets} - \text{inventory}^2}{\text{Current liabilities}}$$

A 1 to 1 ratio is typical, but many firms operate safely at less than 1.

Leverage (or Debt) Ratios

Leverage ratios measure the relative amount of long-term debt the company carries. Five ratios explain the firm's ability to cover its long-term debt: (1) *Debt to total assets* is the extent to which funds are provided by creditors; (2) *Long-term[3] debt to equity* is the extent to which funds are provided on a long-term basis by creditors versus owners; (3) *Debt to capital* is the percentage of long-term debt in the capitalization package; (4) *Short-term liabilities to total debt* is the percent of total debt borrowed from short-term creditors; and (5) *Times interest earned* is the extent to which earnings can fall before being unable to meet interest obligations.

Rule of Thumb

$$\text{Debt to total assets} = \frac{\text{Total liabilities}}{\text{Total assets}}$$

Industry average

$$\text{Long-term debt to equity} = \frac{\text{Long-term debt}}{\text{Stockholders equity}}$$

40–60% of equity

Debt to capital $= \dfrac{\text{Long-term liabilities}}{\text{Long-term debt} + \text{stockholders equity}}$ Industry average

Short-term liabilities to total debt $= \dfrac{\text{Current liabilities}}{\text{Total liabilities}}$ Industry average

Times interest earned $= \dfrac{\text{Earnings before interest and taxes}}{\text{Interest}}$ At least 2 to 1

Activity Ratios

This is the measure of how effectively the firm uses its resources. There are five indicators: (1) *Inventory turnover* indicates the liquidity or activity of the inventory; (2) *Fixed assets turnover* is the extent to which fixed assets are used to generate sales; (3) *Total assets turnover* indicates how efficiently the company is utilizing its assets to generate sales; (4) *Accounts receivable turnover* is the percentage of the average collection period on sales; and (5) *Average collection period* is the average number of days it takes a firm to collect on credit sales.

Rule of Thumb

Inventory turnover[4] $= \dfrac{\text{Cost of sales}}{\text{Inventory of finished goods}}$ Industry average

Fixed assets turnover $= \dfrac{\text{Sales}}{\text{Fixed assets}}$ The higher the number, the more productive use.

Total assets turnover $= \dfrac{\text{Sales}}{\text{Total assets}}$ Industry average

Accounts receivable turnover $= \dfrac{\text{Annual credit sales}}{\text{Accounts receivable}}$ Industry norm

Average collection period $= \dfrac{\text{365 days}}{\text{Accounts receivable turnover}}$ Industry average

Profitability Ratios

Profitability ratios indicate management's overall effectiveness to generate profit. Typically six ratios are useful: (1) *Gross profit margin* is the amount of gross profit generated per sales dollar; (2) *Operating profit margin* is the amount of profit from operations generated without regard for taxes and interest; (3) *Net profit margin* is the after-tax profits per sales dollar; (4) *Return on total investment (ROI)*, also known as *return on assets (ROA)*, is the rate of return on total assets employed; (5) *Return on stockholders equity (ROE)* is the after-tax profits per dollar of investment; and (6) *Earnings per share (EPS)* is the profits available to the owners of common stock.

Rule of Thumb

Gross profit margin $= \dfrac{\text{Sales cost of goods sold}}{\text{Sales}}$ Industry average

Operating profit margin $= \dfrac{\text{Earnings before interest and taxes}}{\text{Sales}}$ Industry average

Net profit
margin $= \dfrac{\text{Net income}}{\text{Sales}}$ Industry average

Return on investment $= \dfrac{\text{Net income}}{\text{Total assets}}$ Equal to or higher than
market rate on treasury
bills.

Return on equity $= \dfrac{\text{Net income}}{\text{Total stockholders equity}}$ Higher than ROI

Earnings per share $= \dfrac{\text{Net income}}{\text{Number of shares of common stock outstanding}}$

Other Financial Analyses

In addition to the traditional ratios there are several other analyses that are useful in establishing the firm's current position. *Growth ratios* are rates based on historical data. *Working-capital analysis* is the ability of the firm to meet short-term debt obligations and finance current operations.

Growth Ratios

These are percentages that indicate past performance and provide insight for prediction purposes. *Sales ratio* is the annual percentage growth in total sales and provides the firm's rate of growth in sales. *Earnings per share* is the growth of EPS as an annual percentage of total growth. *Dividends per share* is the annual growth rate of dividends per share.

Rule of Thumb

Price-Earnings Ratio $= \dfrac{\text{Market price per share}}{\text{Earnings per share}}$ Fast-growing firms
tend to have high
price-earnings ratios.

Working-Capital Analysis

Working capital is computed by subtracting current liabilities from current assets. It provides an index for the short-run solvency of the firm. Neither the income statement nor the balance sheet explains current transactions during any given period; therefore, accounting departments typically develop what are called statements of changes in net working capital or financial position. These list the sources and uses of funds for a specific period. This examination is particularly useful to the analyst who is interested in projecting the potential for future expansion and the sources from which this may be met. Table B–1 shows the format of a typical statement. This analysis should be used in conjunction with other ratios, particularly liquidity ratios.

TABLE B–1
Statement of Cash Flow
Analysis

Sources	Uses
Earnings after taxes	Increase in cash and equivalents
Depreciation	Increase in plant and equipment
Decrease in other assets	Decrease in other liabilities
Increase in long-term debt	Common stock dividends
Increase in common stock	Preferred stock dividends
Increase in paid-in capital	Changes in net working capital
Total	Total

Notes:

1. Includes current liabilities falling due within one year.

2. Defined as cash and cash equivalents plus current accounts receivable. Prepaid expenses are not included.

3. Long-term defined as greater than one year and short-term less than one year.

4. Turns are best computed separately for raw materials, work in process, finished goods, and total.

Time-Future Analysis

- What are the changes in the future that will have the greatest impact on your company?
    —Qualitative?
    —Global?
    —Behavioral?
    —Technological?
    —Competitive?
    —Quantitative?
- What key factors should dictate your strategy?
- What should be your scope in the future?
    —Countries?
    —Products?
    —Markets?
    —Technologies?
    —Customers?
    —Users?
- Where should your future emphasis be?
- Who will be your future competitors?
- What are the best areas of the company to grow?
- What weaknesses should you correct in the future?
- What strengths should you emphasize in the future?
- Where are the global markets of the future?
- What are the technologies of the future?
- What are the products of the future?
- Is your company properly organized for the future?
- Should your firm be a matrix organization?
- Should your firm be integrated and cross-functional?
- Is your firm a flat, empowered organization?
- Is it a networked organization?
- Are you vision directed?
- Is your firm information- and technology-based?
- Are you customer-driven?
- Are you stakeholder focused?
- Is your firm a value-added, quality organization?
- Is it a time-based organization?
- Is it an innovative, entrepreneurial organization?
- Is your firm a flexible, adaptive, and learning organization?

Forecasting Techniques

The following list, excerpted from *The Manager's Guide to Strategic Planning Tools and Techniques*, provides a comprehensive listing of forecasting methods. This article is reprinted from *Planning Review*, (November/December 1989), with permission from The Planning Forum, The International Society for Strategic Management and Planning.

Benchmarking

This establishes reference points for the formulation of objectives based on analysis of competitor programs. See L. J. Mennon and D. W. Landers, *Advanced Techniques for Strategic Analysis*, (Hindsale, Ill.: Dryden Press, 1987).

Critical Success Factors/Strategic Issues Analysis

This is the identification and analysis of a limited number of areas in which high performance will ensure a successful competitive position. See A. C. Boynton and R. W. Zmud, "An Assessment of Critical Success Factors," (*Sloan Management Review*, Summer 1984, pp. 17–24).

Delphi Technique

This is a method of soliciting, in writing, points of view on a particular subject from a cross-section of experts. By collating the answers, then asking opinions of the same group about the collated responses, an answer can eventually be extrapolated. See A. L. Delbecq, A. H. Van de Ven, and D. H. Gustafson, *Group Techniques for Program Planning: A Guide to Nominal Group and Delphi Processes*, (Glenview, Ill.: Scott Foresman, 1975).

Dialectic Inquiry

This is the development and evaluation of conflicting points of view. The result is a synthesis of the points of view. See R. O. Mason and I. I. Mitroff, *Strategic Assumptions Surfacing and Testing*, (New York: John Wiley & Sons, 1981).

Environmental Scanning, Forecasting, and Trend Analysis

This is a method of monitoring external factors, events, situations, and projections for forecasting trends. It is usually computer based. See F. Fahey, William R. King, and V. K. Narayanan, "Environmental Scanning, Forecasting, and Planning—The State of the Art," (*Long-Range Planning*, February 1981, pp. 32–39).

Experience Curves

These provide a framework for organizing dynamic cost and price for a product, company, or industry over an extended period of time. See P. Ghemawat, "Building Strategy on the Experience Curve," (*Harvard Business Review*, March–April 1985, pp. 143–149).

Focus Groups

This is a method of bringing together qualified and recognized experts to develop, evaluate, and synthesize their points of view. See D. L. Johnson and A. H. Mendelson, *Using Focus Groups in Marketing Planning*, (St. Paul, Minn.: West Publishing, 1982).

Future Studies

These are the development of future factors based on agreement of a group of experts often from a variety of functional areas within the firm. See S. W. Edmonds, "The Role of Futures Studies in Business Strategic Planning," (*Journal of Business Strategy*, Fall 1982, pp. 40–46).

Market Opportunity Analysis

This is an analysis of the factors that affect the demand and marketing of a product or service. See D. Silverman, "Consultants' Concepts—Field Analysis: A 3-D Look at Opportunities," (*Planning Review*, September 1984, pp. 22–24).

Metagame Analysis   This is strategic decision making through a series of viewpoints in terms of every competitor and every combination of competitive responses. See B. K. Dutta and William R. King, "Metagame Analysis of Competitive Strategy," (*Strategic Management Journal*, October 1980, pp. 357–370).

Multiple Scenarios   These express a sequence of time frames and snapshots through narratives. See K. Nair and R. Sarin, "Generating Future Scenarios—Their Use in Strategic Planning," (*Long-Range Planning*, June 1979, pp. 57–61).

Nominal Group   Using the interactive setting of a group process, this technique evaluates and synthesizes
Technique   individual points of view. See A. L. Delbecq, A. H. Van de Ven, and D. H. Gustafson, *Group Techniques for Program Planning: A Guide to Nominal Group and Delphi Processes*, (Glenview, Ill.: Scott Foresman, 1975).

PIMS Analysis   This is the application of diverse experiences of firms. See S. R. Schoeffler, R. D. Buzzell, and D. F. Heaney, "Impact of Strategic Planning on Profit Performance," (*Harvard Business Review*, March–April 1974).

Portfolio Classification   This is the classification and display of the present and prospective positions of firms and
Analysis   products according to the attractiveness of the market, and the ability of the firms and products to compete within that market. See G. S. Day, *Analysis for Strategic Market Decisions*, (St. Paul, Minn.: West Publishing, 1986).

Product Life Cycle   In this analysis of market dynamics, a product is reviewed according to its position with-
Analysis   in distinct stages of its sales history. See G. S. Day, *Analysis for Strategic Market Decisions*, (St. Paul, Minn.: West Publishing, 1986).

Simulation Technique   This is a computer-based technique used to simulate future situations and then forecast courses of action. See G. D. Craig, "A Simulation System for Corporate Planning," (*Long-Range Planning*, October 1980, pp. 43–56).

Situational Analysis   This is the systematic development and evaluation of past, present, and future data to identify internal strengths and weaknesses and external threats and opportunities. See H. Weihrich, "TOWS Matrix—A Tool for Situational Analysis," (*Long-Range Planning*, April 1982, pp. 54–66).

SPIRE   SPIRE, or the Systematic Procedure for Identification of Relevant Environments, is a computer-assisted, matrix-generating tool for forecasting environmental changes that can have a dramatic impact on operations. See H. Klein and W. Newman, "How to Use SPIRE: A Systematic Procedure for Identifying Relevant Environments for Strategic Planning," (*Journal of Business Strategy*, Summer 1980, pp. 32–45).

Strategic Gap Analysis   This examines the difference between the extrapolation of current performance levels, such as the current sales, and the projection of desired performance objectives, such as a desired sales level. See H. I. Ansoff, *Corporate Strategy*, (New York: McGraw-Hill, 1972).

Sustainable Growth   This is the financial analysis of the sales growth rate that is required to meet market share
Model   objectives and the degree to which capacity must be expanded to achieve that growth rate. See P. Varadarajan, "The Sustainable Growth Model: Tool for Evaluating the Financial Feasibility of Market Share Strategies," (*Strategic Management Journal*, October 1984, pp. 353–367).

Appendix E

Political Risk Forecast Chart

TABLE E–1 *Sample Political and Economic Forecast Chart*

Next to each country name is the date of our last update or report, followed by the 18-month (2nd line) and five-year (3rd line) political forecasts; the Regimes most likely to hold power and their probabilities, risk rating for Turmoil (low to very high), and risk rating (A+ the least to D- the most) for financial Transfer, direct Investment, and Export to the country. Parentheses indicate a changed forecast. An asterisk means a non-incumbent regime. The list of Economic indicators contains our our most recently issued economic data and forecasts, including a previous five-year average, a one-year forecast or estimate, and a five-year forecast average. Real Growth of GDP and Inflation are expressed as percentages, and Current Account figures are in billions of U.S. dollars.

Country / Regimes & Probabilities		Turmoil	Transfer	Investment	Export		Real GDP Growth	Inflation	Current Account
Algeria	9/91					1987–1991	2.0	11.7	–0.43
Bendjedid 45%		High	C	C	D+	1992	5.5	22.5	+0.60
Bendjedid 40%		Very High	C–	D	D+	1993–1997	4.0	20.0	+0.50
Argentina	10/91					1987–1991	0.2	1103.1	–1.35
Menem 60%		High	B–	B–	C	1992	5.0	150.0	–2.00
*Menemista 50%		Very High	D+	D+	D	1993–1997	2.5	100.0	–1.00
Australia	10/91					1987–1991	2.5	7.1	–12.62
*Hewson 45%		Low	A–	A	A–	1992	1.5	3.5	–12.00
*Hewson 45%		Low	A–	B+	B	1993–1997	2.5	5.0	–8.00
Austria	6/91					1987–1991	3.5	2.6	+0.09
Grand Coalition 85%		Low	A+	A+	A+	1992	3.0	4.0	+0.50
Grand Coalition 60%		Low	A+	A	A	1993–1997	3.3	3.7	+0.20
Belgium	11/91					1987–1991	3.4	2.5	+3.42
Center Left 45%		Low	A–	A+	A	1992	2.3	3.5	+5.00
Center Left 40%		Low	B+	A	A–	1993–1997	3.0	4.0	+4.00
Bolivia	6/91					1986–1990	1.4	67.8	–0.31
ADN-MIR 80%		Moderate	B	A	B	1991	2.8	15.0	–0.25
Center Right 50%		High	C	B+	C	1992–1996	2.5	20.0	–0.30
Brazil	10/91					1987–1991	0.3	1158.7	+0.16
Collor & Center Right 45%		High	C–	C+	C–	1992	1.0	400.0	+0.50
Center-Right 45%		Very High	D+	D+	D+	1993–1997	2.2	200.0	+1.50
Bulgaria	11/91					1987–1991	–2.5	26.1	–0.66
*Center Right 60% (55%)		Moderate	C	B+	C+	1992	–4.5	50.0	–0.30
*Center Right 60% (50%)		Low	B	A	B+	1993–1997	2.0	10.0	–0.45
Cameroon	6/91					1987–1991	–5.1	3.7	–0.48
*Prime Minister 40%		High	C	B	C	1992	–4.0	3.0	–0.01
*Nationalist 40%		Moderate	C	B	C–	1993–1997	–2.0	4.0	+0.10
Canada	11/91					1987–1991	2.5	4.9	–11.08
PC Majority 65%		Low	A–	A	A+	1992	3.2	3.5	–12.00
PC 50%		Moderate	A–	B+	B+	1993–1997	3.0	2.5	–10.00
Chile	6/91					1987–1991	5.9	19.5	–0.85
Center Left 75%		Moderate	B	A–	B	1992	5.0	20.0	–1.00
Center Left 55%		Moderate	B	A–	B	1993–1997	5.0	18.0	–0.75
China	11/91					1987–1991	6.8	11.1	+2.04
Pragmatists 65% (60%)		Moderate	B+ (B–)	B+ (B)	B (C+)	1992	6.5	8.0	+3.00
Pragmatists 55%		Low	A– (B)	B (B–)	B (B–)	1993–1997	6.0	9.0	+2.00
Colombia	11/91					1987–1991	4.2	27.6	+0.21
Gaviria 75%		High (V. High)	A (B–)	A– (B)	A– (B–)	1992	4.0	25.0	+0.60
Liberals 60%		High	B– (C)	C+	C (C–)	1993–1997	5.0	25.0	+0.70
Costa Rica	8/91					1987-1991	4.0	18.6	–0.40
Calderon 85%		Low	B-	A-	B-	1992	3.5	25.0	–0.25
*PLN 60%		Low	B-	A+	B-	1993–1997	3.2	17.0	–0.20

Political Risk Letter, Volume 111, Number 11, November 1, 1991, pp. 5. Published with the consent of Political Risk Services of Syracuse, NY, Tel: 315-472-1224, and *Planning Review*.

235

Elements of an Agent/Distributor Agreement

I. Basic components.

  A. Parties to the agreement.

  B. Statement that contract supersedes all previous agreements.

  C. Duration fixation—perhaps after a three-to-six month trial agreement.

  D. Territory.

    1. Exclusive.

    2. Nonexclusive.

    3. Manufacturer's right to sell directly at reduced prices or without commission to local government and old customers.

  E. Products covered.

  F. Expression of intent to comply with government regulations.

  G. Clause limiting sales forbidden by U.S. Export Control Act.

II. Manufacturer's rights.

  A. Arbitration:

    1. If possible in manufacturer's country.

    2. If not, before the International Arbitration Association.

    3. Define rules to be applied (e.g., in selecting arbitrational panel).

    4. Make sure award will be binding in distributor's country.

  B. Jurisdiction should be that of manufacturer's country (e.g., complete the signing at home).

  C. Termination conditions (e.g., manufacturer need not indemnify if contract is cancelled after due notice).

  D. Clarification of tax liabilities.

  E. Payment and discount terms.

  F. Conditions for delivery of goods.

  G. Nonliability for late delivery beyond manufacturer's reasonable control.

  H. Limitation on manufacturer's responsibility to provide information.

  I. Waiver of manufacturer's responsibility to keep lines manufactured outside the United States (e.g., by licensees) outside of covered territory.

  J. Right to change prices, terms, and conditions at any time.

  K. Right of manufacturer or its agent to visit territory and inspect books.

  L. Right to repurchase stock.

  M. Option to refuse or alter distributor's orders.

  N. Training of distributor personnel in the United States subject to the following:

    1. Practicability.

      2. Costs to be paid by the distributor.

      3. Waiver of manufacturer's responsibility to U.S. immigration approval.

III. Distributor's limitations and duties.

    A. No disclosure of confidential information.

    B. Limitation of distributor's right to assign contract.

    C. Limitation on distributor's position as legal agent of manufacturer.

    D. Penalty clause for late payment.

    E. Limitation on right to handle competing lines.

    F. Responsibility for obtaining customs clearance.

    G. Publicization of distributor's designation as authorized representative in defined area.

    H. Requirement to remove all signs or evidence identifying distributor with manufacturer if relationship ends.

    I. Acknowledgment of manufacturer's ownership of trademark, trade names, and patents.

    J. Information supplied by distributor:

      1. Sales reports.

      2. Names of active prospects.

      3. Government regulations dealing with imports.

      4. Competitive products and competitors' activities.

      5. Price at which goods are sold.

      6. Complete data on other lines carried, if requested.

    K. Information on purchasers.

    L. Accounting methods.

    M. Requirement to appropriately display products.

    N. Duties concerning advertising and promotion.

    O. Limitation on distributor's right to grant unapproved warranties, make excessive claims.

    P. Clarification of responsibility arising from claims and warranties.

    Q. Responsibility to provide repair and other services.

    R. Responsibility to maintain suitable place of business.

    S. Responsibility to supply all prospective customers.

    T. Requirement that certain sales approaches and literature be approved by manufacturer.

    U. Prohibition of manufacture or alteration of products.

    V. Requirement to maintain adequate stock and spare parts.

    W. Requirement that inventory be surrendered in event of a dispute which is pending in court.

International Licensing Agreement

T his agreement, made on this _____ day of _____, 19___, by and between ABC Corporation, a [state] corporation having its principal place of business at [city], [state], United States of America ("Licensor"), and XYZ Corporation, a [state] corporation having its principal place of business at [city], [state] ("Licensee");

WITNESSETH THAT:
Whereas Licensor is now and has been in the business of manufacturing and selling [product] identified as models [alpha/numerics], all of which are referred to hereinafter as "Licensor [product]"; and Whereas Licensor possesses engineering data and technical information on all of the Licensor [product] that he or she is willing to release to Licensee so that Licensee may itself manufacture and operate such [product]; and Whereas Licensor is the owner of certain Letters Patent in the licensed territory pertaining to certain of said Licensor [product], which patents are listed and identified in Exhibit "A" hereto attached; and Whereas Licensee is desirous of profiting from Licensor's information and data, entering into this agreement for the manufacture, use, and sale of the Licensor [product], and securing a license under said Letters Patent in the territory hereinafter specified.

NOW, THEREFORE:
In consideration of the premises and of the mutual covenants of the parties to be faithfully performed, the parties hereby covenant and agree as follows:

Section 1. Term

This agreement shall be effective for a period of [ ] years computed from the date of its execution.

Section 2. Grant

Licensor hereby grants to Licensee the exclusive right to manufacture, sell, and use Licensor [product] on the terms and conditions hereinafter set forth. The right to manufacture that is granted applies only to models [alpha/numerics]. Licensor agrees not to license third parties to manufacture, use, and sell embodiments of the above-mentioned patents in the licensed territories so long as Licensee's license to manufacture, use, and sell the Licensor [product] is in full force and effect. The license granted shall include a license to manufacture, use, and sell the Licensor [product] under any applicable patent listed in Exhibit "A" and any additional patent of the licensed territory issued to Licensor during the term hereof.

Section 3. Territory

The license to manufacture, use, and sell granted in Section 2 shall be exclusive as to the countries listed in Exhibit "B" hereof, except when noted in said Exhibit as nonexclusive.

Section 4. Terms of Payment

In consideration of the furnishing by Licensor to Licensee of the technical know-how, information, and data, Licensee hereby agrees to pay Licensor as a fixed royalty a total sum of [XXXX] thousand dollars ($XXX,XXX) in lawful currency of the United States of America, in addition to periodic royalties as hereinafter specified. This sum of [XXXX] thousand dollars ($XXX,XXX) shall be payable by Licensee to Licensor as follows:
a. [XXXX] thousand dollars ($XXX,XXX) within thirty (30) days following the execution of this agreement;
b. [XX] thousand dollars ($XX,XXX) at the end of the first twelve (12) months following the execution of this agreement;

c. [XX] thousand dollars ($XX,XXX) at the end of twenty-four (24) months following the execution of this agreement.

The initial payment provided herein shall be made before Licensor supplies Licensee with any technical information concerning the Licensor [product].

Section 5. Obligations of Licensor

a. Immediately following the first payment required in Section 4, Licensor shall supply Licensee with drawings and technical information, including, to the extent available, all drawings necessary for the production of the Licensor [product], including drawings of each part, drawings of assembled products, and drawings of jigs, tools, and testing and inspection apparatus, and data necessary for working, including processes, bills of material, working hours, and tolerances, in accordance with the following schedule, subject, however, to the continuation of payments by Licensee to Licensor as herein provided:

Model [alpha/numerics]—on or before _____

Model [alpha/numerics]—on or before _____

Model [alpha/numerics]—on or before _____

Model [alpha/numerics]—on or before _____

It is understood and agreed that these drawings and technical data shall be furnished by Licensor to Licensee in accordance with the foregoing schedule and without further payments to Licensor other than those herein specified.

b. Until Licensee shall be able to manufacture and supply the demand for Licensor [product] within the licensed territory, Licensor agrees that, at the request of Licensee, Licensor [product] shall be sold by Licensor to Licensee, in completed or "knock down" form, in accordance with the attached Exhibit "C," subject to the maximum discounts listed therein. Payment for these Licensor [product] shall be by irrevocable letter of credit.

c. In the event any improvement of the Licensor [product], in relation to its manufacture or use, is made by either of the parties, technical information with respect thereto shall be furnished to the other party without payment. These improvements, if made by Licensee and if patentable, shall be filed and registered as patents under the joint ownership of both parties, and may be used by either party for any machine other than the Licensor [product] even after the termination of this agreement.

d. In furtherance of the program for the development of the Licensor [product] by Licensee, Licensor grants to Licensee permission at any time to send to Licensor's plant, at Licensee's expense, a reasonable supply to enable Licensee to manufacture the Licensor [product]. If requested by Licensee, Licensor will send to Licensee's plant at Licensee's expense one of Licensor's technicians at such time and for such period as may be agreed. Also upon the request of Licensee, Licensor will help and cooperate, at Licensee's expense, in Licensee's purchase of any parts necessary for the production of the Licensor [product]. The cost of these parts and their testing shall be at the expense of Licensee.

e. Licensor will furnish literature, mats of artwork advertising, films, slides, and other promotional and training materials to Licensee at cost.

Section 6. Obligations of Licensee

a. Licensee agrees to bear all costs and expenses necessary to change the specifications and drawings from American units to metric units, when necessary.

b. Licensee agrees to use its best efforts to exploit and promote the increasing demand for Licensor [product] to the greatest extent possible throughout the licensed territory. To this end, Licensee agrees to maintain a competent sales, engineering, and service organization, satisfactory manufacturing facilities, and adequate factory space in good repair.

c. Licensee agrees to apply to every licensed Licensor machine, whether manufactured to Licensor's or Licensee's specifications, the trademark "ABC" in the following manner: "ABC-XYZ." Licensee agrees that, upon termination of this Agreement, it will cease using the trademark "ABC" in any way except on [product] manufactured by it prior to such termination, and that it will voluntarily cancel any registration of any trademark, including the mark "ABC," which it may have secured during the life of this Agreement.

d. Licensee agrees to permit Licensor to send a technician to Licensee's plant at any time to ascertain that the Licensor [product] are manufactured strictly in accordance with the specifications of Licensor. The cost of that inspection shall be borne by Licensor. While Licensor represents that it has made and sold commercially acceptable models of the Licensor [product], it is understood and agreed that, despite such inspections by Licensor, the operability, workmanship, and material of the licensed [product] shall be the sole responsibility of Licensee, and Licensor shall not be responsible for any damage caused by faulty or improper operation of the Licensor [product].

e. Licensee agrees that it will not do or permit any act or thing that would endanger any proprietary rights to use any trademark, trade name, or design of Licensor, and that it will not claim any proprietary interest in the trademark "ABC" except as a Licensee under that mark, and then only during the life of this Agreement and subject to the control by Licensor of the nature and quality of the Licensor [product]. Licensee will, if required at any time, assign to Licensor any registration of the trademark "ABC" that it may acquire within the licensed territory, and execute any and all proper papers necessary to the protection of the trademark.

f. Licensee agrees to keep strictly confidential all technical information, drawings, specifications, manufacturing instructions, and other information relating to the Licensor [product], whether furnished by Licensor or developed or in any way acquired by Licensee in connection with the exploitation of the Licensor [product]. Licensee will not, without first obtaining the written consent of Licensor, communicate this confidential information and matters to anyone other than its employees, agents, or representatives, and then only to the extent necessary for the proper exploitation of the Licensor [product] in accordance with the provisions of this agreement.

Section 7. Royalties, Minimum Royalties, and Reporting Procedures

a. In consideration of the license herein granted and in addition to the fixed royalty payments specified in Section 4, Licensee further agrees to pay Licensor periodic royalties at the rate of four percent (4%) of Licensee's ex-factory price on each of the Licensor [product] or variations of the said models manufactured and sold hereunder. The same percentage rate shall apply on Licensee's ex-factory price for replacement parts and accessories manufactured and sold by Licensee. [Product], replacement parts, and accessories are considered sold when they are either billed out, shipped, or delivered, whichever is earliest. The ex-factory price does not include transportation, packing, insurance, service, and optional costs.

b. Periodic royalties due and accrued hereunder shall be paid by Licensee to Licensor within sixty (60) days after the close of each fiscal quarterly period of each fiscal year of this Agreement, the term "fiscal year" being defined as the twelve (12)-month period following the execution of this Agreement.

c. Royalties and minimum royalties shall be payable to Licensor in United States dollars at its address in [city], [state].

d. Licensee agrees that at all times during the existence of this Agreement, it will keep accurate books of account and other records that shall contain all details relating to the manufacture and sale of the Licensor [product] and parts thereof, including the names and addresses of each purchaser of each Licensor machine. Licensee agrees that these books of account and other records shall be kept in accordance with the legal regulations in existence in country and carefully preserved for at least ten (10) years.

e. Licensee agrees that it will furnish Licensor with a written statement within thirty (30) days following the close of each fiscal quarterly period showing the amount of periodic royalties due for that period. The statement shall show in detail sales of the Licensor [product] and accessories and parts therefore and the names and addresses of the customers to whom they were made. Licensee further agrees to pay Licensor within sixty (60) days after the close of each fiscal quarterly period the amount shown to be due according to the statement.

f. Licensee hereby grants to Licensor or its duly accredited representative, including any accredited certified public accountant, the right to inspect and make copies of the books of account of Licensee for the purpose of ascertaining or confirming the accuracy of the statements rendered hereunder. The cost of these inspections shall be borne by Licensor.

g. Licensee hereby agrees to pay Licensor royalties in the minimum amount of [XXXX] thousand dollars ($XX,XXX) per year beginning eighteen (18) months after the execution of this Agreement. It is understood and agreed that the minimum royalties shall be paid by Licensee to Licensor within sixty (60) days following the end of the fiscal year, it being further understood and agreed that credit may be taken by Licensee against the minimum due for actual royalties already paid during the previous fiscal quarters of the year.

h. When the royalties paid by Licensee to Licensor during a particular year, calculated as hereinabove provided, exceed the minimum guaranteed yearly royalty, then the excess earned royalty of that year may be applied to one or both of two succeeding fiscal years in which the earned royalty did not amount to the guaranteed yearly minimum royalty for that particular year.

i. The total amount of royalties to be paid to Licensor by Licensee shall be calculated for each fiscal year as hereinabove defined as of the first day of the fiscal year until the last day of that fiscal year, and when the period of accounting does not reach one year, the minimum royalty shall be calculated at a daily rate as prorated according to the amounts due.

j. Licensee shall withhold from the payments required to be remitted to Licensor the proper amount of [Country] income tax applicable thereto as required by the [Country] government at the time of payment.

Section 8. Patent Rights

Licensor makes no representation or warranty that the Licensor [product] licensed herein are free from any charge of infringement of any patent reasonable modifications in its specifications suggested to it by Licensee for the purpose of avoiding any charge of infringement that may be made.

Section 9. Termination

a. If either party breaches any of the provisions of this Agreement, the other party may give notice of the default by registered air mail to the other party at the address stated hereinafter. If the defaulting party does not cure the breach or default within ninety (90) days from the date of receipt of the notice, then this Agreement shall terminate, subject to the terms and conditions hereinafter set forth.

b. A party shall not be deemed to be in breach or default of any provision of this Agreement by reason of delay or failure in performance due to force majeure. However, if performance becomes impossible for more than one twelve (12)-month period by reason thereof, the injured party may terminate this Agreement by giving notice as provided above.

c. This Agreement shall terminate automatically in the event that Licensee is adjudicated to be or becomes bankrupt or places any of its property in liquidation for the purpose of meeting claims of its creditors.

d. In the event that either party undergoes an important change in managing operations tending to alter or decrease the benefits of this Agreement to it, the period of the Agreement provided in Section 1 may be changed by mutual consent.

Section 10. Cessation of Operations on Termination

Upon termination or expiration of this Agreement, Licensee agrees to cease all manufacture and sale of the Licensor [product] and to return to Licensor drawings, designs, literature, and written technical information relating to the Licensor [product]. Licensee further agrees to prepare immediately upon termination or expiration of this Agreement a final accounting, which shall include all the Licensor [product] in process that Licensee shall be licensed thereafter to sell, providing royalties in respect thereto then due and payable are immediately paid. Upon termination or expiration of this Agreement, Licensee will make no further use of any technical information, drawings, specifications, manufacturing instructions, or other information relating to the Licensor [product], whether furnished by Licensor or developed or in any way acquired by Licensee in connection with the exploitation of the Licensor [product].

Section 11. Arbitration

Should there be any difference of opinion between the parties or if any dispute arises as to any of the matters provided for herein, the parties shall endeavor to settle the differences or dispute in an amicable manner through mutual consultation. In case the difference or dispute cannot be mutually settled, the matter shall be submitted for arbitration to the [Country] Commercial Arbitration Association, whose award shall be final and binding upon both parties.

Section 12. Applicable Law

The law applicable to this agreement shall be the law of [Country].

Section 13. Notices

a. Notices required to be given under this Agreement shall be sent by registered air mail and addressed as follows:

ABC Corporation

XYZ Corporation

b. Notice of any change of mailing address of either party shall be given promptly to the other by registered air mail.

Section 14. Force Majeure

No party to this Agreement shall be responsible to the other party for nonperformance or delay in performance of any terms or conditions of this Agreement due to the acts of God, acts of governments, wars, riots, strikes, accidents in transportation, or other causes beyond the control of the parties.

Section 15. Renewal

This Agreement is subject to renewal on mutually agreeable terms. A declaration of intent to renew shall be given by either Licensor or Licensee to the other party no later than one hundred and eighty (180) days prior to the expiration of this Agreement.

Section 16. Severability

Should any part or portion of this Agreement be held invalid, illegal, or void, the remainder of the Agreement shall continue in full force and effect as if the void, illegal, or invalid provision had been deleted or never included.

Section 17. Benefits

This Agreement and all rights granted persuant to its terms shall be personal to the parties and shall be incapable of assignment, sublicense, or transfer without consent, however, shall not be withheld unreasonably.

In Witness Whereof, the parties hereto have caused this Agreement to be executed by their proper officers, duly authorized, on this ____ day of _____, 19___.

ABC Corporation (Licensor)

By_____.

Its _____.

Attest:

_____.
Its Secretary

XYZ Corporation (Licensee)

By _____.

Its _____.

Attest:

_____.
Its

Organizations Involved in International Trade

Agency for International Development (AID). The unit within the U.S. government responsible for the administration of U.S. bilateral development assistance programs. AID also actively participates in the development of other U.S. policies and programs related to third world economic development.

Coordinating Committee for Multilateral Export Controls (COCOM). A committee established in 1951 by NATO-member countries to coordinate their policies relating to the restriction of exports of products and technical data of potential strategic value to the former Soviet Union and certain other countries. To date, it consists of NATO countries plus Japan and excluding Iceland.

Customs Cooperation Council (CCC). An intergovernmental organization created in 1953 and headquartered in Brussels, through which customs officials of participating countries seek to simplify, standardize, and conciliate customs procedures. The council has sponsored a standardized product classification, a set of definitions of commodities for customs purposes, a standardized definition of value, and a number of recommendations designed to facilitate customs procedures.

European Community (EC). A popular term for the European communities that resulted from the 1967 Treaty of Fusion, which merged the secretariat (the commission) and the intergovernmental executive body (the council) of the older European Economic Community (EEC) with those of the European Coal and Steel Community (ECSC) and the European Atomic Energy Community (EURATOM). The EEC first came into operation on January 1, 1958, based on the Treaty of Rome, with six participating member states—France, Italy, the Federal Republic of Germany, Belgium, Netherlands, and Luxembourg.

From the beginning, a principal objective of the community was the establishment of a customs union, other forms of economic integration, and political cooperation among member countries. The Treaty of Rome provided for: the gradual elimination of customs duties and other internal trade barriers; the establishment of a common external tariff; and guarantees of free movement of labor and capital within the community. The United Kingdom, Denmark, and Ireland joined the community in 1973, Greece in 1981, and Spain and Portugal in 1986.

The community is headquartered in Brussels. The council meets several times a year at the foreign ministere level, and occasionally at the heads of state level. Technical experts from community capitals meet regularly to deal with specialized issues in such areas as agriculture, transportation, and trade policy.

European Free Trade Association (EFTA). A regional grouping established in 1960 by the Stockholm Convention, headquartered in Geneva, now comprising Austria, Iceland, Norway, Sweden, and Switzerland. Finland is an associate member. Denmark, Portugal, and the United Kingdom are former members, but they withdrew from EFTA when they joined the EC. EFTA member countries have gradually eliminated tariffs of manufactured goods originating and traded within the association. For the most part, agricultural products are not included on the EFTA schedule for internal tariff reductions. Each member country maintains its own external tariff schedule and each has concluded a trade agreement with the EC that provides for the mutual elimination of tariffs for most manufactured goods except for a few sensitive products. As a result, the EC and EFTA form a de facto free trade area.

Export-Import Bank of the United States (Eximbank).   A public corporation created by executive order of the president in 1934 and given a statutory basis in 1945. The bank makes guarantees and insures loans to help finance U.S. exports, particularly for equipment to be used in capital improvement projects. The bank also provides short-term insurance for both commercial and political risks, either directly or in cooperation with U.S. commercial banks.

Foreign Credit Insurance Association (FCIA).   An agency established in the United States in 1961 to offer insurance facilities in partnership with Eximbank for U.S. exporters.

General Agreement on Tariffs and Trade (GATT).   A multilateral trade agreement aimed at expanding international trade as a means of raising world welfare. GATT rules reduce uncertainty in connection with commercial transactions across national borders. Ninety-two countries accounting for approximately 80 percent of world trade are contracting parties to GATT, and some 30 additional countries associated with it benefit from the application of its provisions to their trade.

The designation GATT also refers to the organization headquartered in Geneva through which the general agreement is enforced. This organization provides a framework within which international negotiations—known as rounds—are conducted to lower tariffs and other trade barriers, and a consultative mechanism that may be invoked by governments seeking to protect their trade interests.

The GATT was signed in 1947 as an interim agreement. It has been internationally recognized around the world as the key international institution concerned with trade negotiations since it became clear that the United States would not ratify the Havana Charter of 1948. That accord would have created an International Trade Organization (ITO) as a specialized agency of the United Nations system, similar to the International Monetary Fund and the World Bank. The Interim Commission of the ITO (ICITO), which was established to facilitate the creation of the ITO, subsequently became the GATT secretariat. The cornerstone of the GATT is the most-favored-nation clause (Article I of the General Agreement).

For the United States, the GATT came into existence as an executive agreement, which, under the U.S. Constitution, does not require Senate ratification. Part Four of the General Agreement (Articles XXXVI, XXXVII, and XXXVIII), adopted in 1965, contains explicit commitments to ensure appropriate recognition of the development needs of developing countries which are GATT contracting parties.

International Monetary Fund (IMF).   An international financial institution established in 1946 that seeks to stabilize the international monetary system as a sound basis for the orderly expansion of international trade. Specifically, the fund monitors exchange rate policies of member countries, lends them foreign exchange resources to support their adjustment policies when they experience balance of payments difficulties, and provides them financial assistance through a special compensatory financing facility when they experience temporary shortfalls in commodity export earnings.

International Trade Administration (ITA).   The trade unit of the U.S. Department of Commerce, ITA carries out the U.S. government's nonagricultural foreign trade activities. It encourages and promotes U.S. exports of manufactured goods, administers U.S. statutes and agreements dealing with foreign trade, and advises on U.S. international trade and commercial policy.

North American Free Trade Agreement (NAFTA).   A treaty that commits three nations—Canada, Mexico, and the United States—to promote employment and economic growth in each country. This is done through the expansion of trade and investment opportunities in the free trade area and by enhancing the competitiveness of North American firms in the global market in a manner that protects the environment.

Organization for Economic Cooperation and Development (OECD). An organization based in Paris with a membership of 24 developed countries. OECD's basic aims are to achieve the highest sustainable economic growth and employment while maintaining financial stability, and to contribute to sound economic expansion worldwide and to the expansion of world trade on a multilateral, nondiscriminatory basis. The OECD succeeded the Organization for European Economic Corporation (OEEC) in 1961, after the post-World War II economic reconstruction of Europe had been largely accomplished.

Organization of Petroleum Exporting Countries (OPEC). A cartel comprising 13 leading oil-producing countries that seek to coordinate oil production and pricing policies.

United Nations Conference on Trade and Development (UNCTAD). A subsidiary organ of the U.S. General Assembly that seeks to focus international attention on economic measures that might accelerate third world development. The conference was first convened (UNCTAD-I) in Geneva in 1964.

U.S. International Trade Commission (USITC). Formerly the U.S. Tariff Commission, which was created in 1916 by an act of Congress. Its mandate was broadened and its name changed by the Trade Act of 1974. USITC is an independent fact-finding agency of the U.S. government that studies the effects of tariffs and other restraints to trade on the U.S. economy. It conducts public hearings to assist in determining whether certain U.S. industries are injured or threatened with injury by dumping, export subsidies in other countries, or rapidly rising imports. USITC also studies the probable economic impact on specific U.S. industries of proposed reductions in U.S. tariffs and nontariff barriers to imports. USITC's six members are appointed by the president with the advice and consent of the U.S. Senate for nine-year terms.

United States Trade Representative (USTR). A cabinet-level official with the rank of ambassador who is the principal advisor to the U.S. president on international trade policy. The USTR is concerned with the expansion of U.S. exports, U.S. participation in GATT, commodity issues, east-west and north-south trade, and direct investment related to trade. As chairperson of the U.S. Trade Policy Committee, the USTR is also the primary official responsible for U.S. participation in all international trade negotiations. Prior to the Trade Agreements Act of 1979, which created the Office of the USTR, the comparable official was known as the president's special representative for trade negotiations, a position first established by the Trade Expansion Act of 1962.

World Bank. The International Bank for Reconstruction and Development (IBRD), commonly referred to as the World Bank, is an intergovernmental financial institution located in Washington, D.C. Its objectives are to help raise productivity and incomes and to reduce poverty in developing countries. The World Bank was established in December 1945. It loans financial resources to creditworthy developing countries. It raises most of its funds by selling bonds in the world's major capital markets. Its bonds have, over the years, earned a quality rating enjoyed only by sound governments and leading corporations. Projects supported by the World Bank normally receive high priority within recipient governments and are usually well planned and supervised. The World Bank earns a profit, which is plowed back into its capital.

World Intellectual Property Organization (WIPO). A specialized agency of the United Nations system that seeks to promote international cooperation in the protection of intellectual property. WIPO administers: the International Union for the Protection of Industrial Property (the Paris Union), which was founded in 1883 to reduce discrimination in national patent practices; the International Union for the Protection of Literary and Artistic Works (the Bern Union), which was founded in 1886 to provide analogous functions with respect to copyrights; and other treaties, conventions, and agreements concerned with intellectual property.

Glossary of Antidumping Terms and Phrases

The Tariff Act of 1930, as currently amended, provides for the imposition of antidumping duties on imported merchandise found to have been sold in the United States at less than fair value, if these sales have caused or are likely to cause material injury to, or materially retard the establishment of, U.S. industry. The following is a list of terms and phrases commonly used in connection with proceedings under this act. This appendix is not intended to provide an authoritative explanation of antidumping procedures, only a simplified overview. Accordingly, the information set forth cannot be read to vary from the act itself or from its implementing regulations.

Administrative review. If requested by an interested party, each year, beginning on the anniversary of the publication date of an antidumping duty order, the U.S. Department of Commerce will review and determine the amount of any antidumping duty. The results of this review are published in the *Federal Register* noting any antidumping duty assessed, estimated duty deposited, or suspended investigation to be resumed.

Antidumping duty. A duty assessed on imported merchandise which is subject to an antidumping duty order. The antidumping duty is assessed on an entry-by-entry basis. It is an amount equal to the difference between the U.S. price of that entry and the foreign market value of such or similar merchandise at the time the merchandise was sold to the United States.

Antidumping hearing. A hearing held at the request of an interested party in antidumping proceedings for the purpose of allowing interested persons to orally express their views to officials of the U.S. Commerce Department. The hearing may be requested and held prior to the assistant secretary for import administration's final determination, or before the final results of an administrative review are published.

Antidumping investigation notice. The notice published in the *Federal Register* announcing the initiation of an antidumping investigation, which must be initiated within 20 days of the filing of a valid petition.

Antidumping order. A notice issued following final determination of sales at less than fair value and material injury, or threat of material injury. This order provides for the imposition of antidumping duties where sales are made at less than foreign market value.

Antidumping petition. A petition filed on behalf of an affected U.S. industry alleging that foreign merchandise is being sold in the United States at less than fair value, and that such sales are causing or threatening material injury to, or materially retarding the establishment of, a U.S. industry. Commerce regulations (19CFR353) and International Trade Commission's regulations (19CFR207) specify the information a petition should contain.

Assessment. The imposition of antidumping duties on imported merchandise.

Class or kind of merchandise. A term defining the scope of an antidumping investigation. Included in the class or kind of merchandise is that sold in the home market which is such or similar to the petitioned product. Such or similar merchandise is that which is identical to or like the petitioned product in physical characteristics.

Constructed value. A means of determining fair or foreign market value when sales of such or similar merchandise do not exist or, for various reasons, cannot be used for comparison purposes. The constructed value consists of: the cost of materials and fabrication or other processing employed in producing the merchandise; general expenses of not less than 10 percent of material and fabrication costs; and profit of not less than 8 percent of the sum of the production costs and general expenses. The cost of packing for exportation to the United States is then added to the constructed value.

Cost of production. A term employed in the Tariff Act of 1930 to refer to the sum of the cost of materials, fabrication, and/or other processing employed in producing the merchandise sold in a home market or to a third country, together with appropriate allocations of general administrative and selling expenses. The cost of production is based on the producer's actual experience and does not include any mandatory minimum general expense or profit as in constructed value.

Critical circumstances. The assistant secretary for import administration determines whether there is a reasonable basis to believe or suspect that there is a history of dumping in the United States or elsewhere. The secretary also determines whether the importer knew or should have known that the exporter was selling merchandise at less than fair value, and that there have been massive imports of this merchandise over a relatively short period. This determination is made if an allegation of critical circumstances is received from the petitioner.

Deposit of estimated duties. Estimated antidumping duties shall be deposited upon entry of merchandise which is the subject of an antidumping duty order for each manufacturer, producer, or exporter. These estimated duties are determined in the affirmative final determination of the assistant secretary for import administration or the latest administrative review of such determination.

Disclosure meeting. An informal meeting at which the U.S. Commerce Department discloses to an interested person the methodology used in determining the results of an antidumping investigation or administrative review. A disclosure meeting is generally held after publication of a preliminary determination or preliminary results of a review and before the antidumping hearing.

Dismissal of petition. A determination made by the assistant secretary for import administration that the petition does not properly allege the basis on which antidumping duties may be imposed; that it does not contain information deemed reasonably available to the petitioner supporting the allegations; or that the petition is not filed by an appropriate interested party. This dismissal terminates the proceeding.

Dumping margin. Amount by which the imported merchandise is sold in the United States below the home market value, third-country price, or the constructed value. Thus, if the U.S. purchase price is $200 and the fair value is $220, the dumping margin is $20. The margin is expressed as a percentage of the U.S. price. In this example the margin is 10 percent.

Exclusion of particular firms. One or more foreign manufacturers, producers, or exporters may be excluded from either an affirmative preliminary or an affirmative final determination if the assistant secretary for import administration determines that all examined exports of the merchandise to the United States by these firms were made at prices not less than fair value. Usually information on 100 percent of the exports will be required. In exceptional cases the assistant secretary may determine that a lesser percentage (never less than 75 percent) is adequate.

Exporter's sales price. A statutory term used to refer to the U.S. sales price of imported merchandise when it is imported by or for the account of the exporter. It is based on the price at which the merchandise is sold or agreed to be sold, after importation, by the exporter to an unrelated U.S. purchaser. Certain statutory adjustments are made to permit a meaningful comparison with the foreign market value of such or similar merchandise; for example, import duties, U.S. selling and administrative expenses, and freight are deducted from the U.S. resale price.

Fair value. The reference against which U.S. sale prices of imported merchandise are compared during an investigation. It is generally expressed as the weighted average of the exporter's home-market prices or prices to third countries during the period of investigation. In some cases fair value is the constructed value. Constructed value is used if there are no home-market or third-country sales or if the number of such sales made at prices below the cost of production is so great that remaining sales above the cost of production provide an inadequate basis for comparison.

Final determination. This is done by the assistant secretary for import administration after the investigation of sales at less than fair value and the receipt of comments from interested parties. This determination usually is made within 75 days of the date a preliminary determination is made. If the preliminary determination was affirmative, however, the exporters that account for a significant proportion of the merchandise under consideration may request, in writing, a postponement of this determination. If the preliminary determination was negative, the petitioner may likewise request a postponement. In neither case can this postponement be more than 135 days after the date of the preliminary determination. If the final determination is affirmative and follows a negative preliminary determination, the matter is referred to the U.S. International Trade Commission for a determination of the injury caused by the sales at less than a fair value. (Had the preliminary determination been affirmative, the commission would have begun its investigation at that time.) Not later than 45 days after the date the assistant secretary for import administration has made his or her affirmative final determination, in a case where the preliminary determination was also affirmative, the commission must render its decision on injury. Where the preliminary determination was negative, the commission must render its decision not later than 75 days after the affirmative final determination. A negative final determination by the assistant secretary terminates an antidumping investigation.

Foreign market value. The price, as defined in the Tariff Act of 1930, at which merchandise is sold, or offered for sale, in the principal markets of the country from which it is exported. If foreign home-market sales are not useable, the foreign market value is based on prices to third countries or a constructed value. Adjustments for quantities sold, circumstances of sale, and differences in the merchandise can be made to those prices to ensure a proper comparison with the prices to the United States.

Home-market price. See *foreign market value.*

Period of investigation. The period, usually six months, beginning at least 1,150 days before, and continuing 300 days after the first day of the month when an antidumping petition is filed, during which an exporter's home-market (or third country) and U.S. prices and other appropriate facts are investigated to determine whether sales to the United States have been at less than fair value.

Preliminary determination. The determination by the assistant secretary for import administration announcing the results of the investigation conducted within 160 days (or, in extraordinarily complicated cases, 210 days) after a petition is filed or an investigation is self-initiated by the secretary. If the assistant secretary determines that there is a reasonable basis to believe or suspect that the merchandise under consideration is being sold or is likely to be sold at less than fair value, liquidation of all affected entries is suspended, and the matter is referred to the U.S. International Trade Commission. Preliminary determination also refers to the decision by the commission whether there is a reasonable indication that an industry in the United States is materially injured, or threatened with material injury, or establishment of an industry in the United States is materially retarded by reason of the imports of the merchandise which is the subject of the petition. The commission must make its decision within 45 days after the date on which the petition is filed, or an investigation is self-initiated by the assistant secretary. If this determination is negative, the investigation is terminated.

Protective order.   The order under which most business proprietary information is made available to an attorney or other representative of an interested party.

Purchase price.   A statutory term used to refer to the U.S. sales price at which imported merchandise is purchased or agreed to be purchased, before importation, by or for the account of an importer. Certain statutory adjustments are made, if appropriate, to permit a meaningful comparison with the foreign market value of such or similar merchandise (for example, import duties, commission, and freight).

Revocation of antidumping duty order and termination of susupended investigation. An antidumping duty order may be revoked or a suspended investigation may be terminated upon application from a party to the proceeding. Ordinarily this application will be considered only if there have been no sales at less than fair value for at least two of the most recent years. The assistant secretary for import administration may, on his or her own initiative, revoke an antidumping duty order or terminate a suspended investigation if there have not been sales at less than fair value for a period of three years.

State-controlled-economy country.   A country whose economy is centrally planned and in which the free market forces of supply and demand do not operate to establish prices and costs that can readily and meaningfully be compared to prices in a free market economy.

Summary investigation.   A 20-day investigation conducted by the assistant secretary for import administration immediately following the filing of an antidumping petition.

Suspension of investigation.   A decision to suspend an antidumping investigation if the exporters who account for substantially all of the imported merchandise agree to stop exports to the United States within six months after the date on which the investigation is suspended or agree to revise their prices promptly to eliminate any dumping margin. An investigation may be suspended at any time before a final determination is made. No agreement to suspend an investigation may be made unless effective monitoring of the agreement is possible and it is determined to be in the public's interest.

Suspension of liquidation.   If affirmative, the preliminary determination, or final determination after negative preliminary determination, shall provide for suspension of liquidation of all entries of merchandise subject to the determination which are entered, or withdrawn from warehouse, for consumption on or after the date of the publication of the notice in the *Federal Register*. Each district director of customs is told to require a cash deposit, or the posting of a bond or other security, for each entry equal to the estimated amount by which the fair value exceeds the U.S. price. When an administrative review is completed, each of the district directors of customs is told to require for each entry thereafter, a cash deposit equal to the estimated amount by which the foreign market value exceeds the U.S. price.

Tariff Act of 1930, Title VII or the act.   Authorizes antidumping duties to be assessed against imported merchandise being sold in the United States at less than fair value if such sales cause or threaten material injury to, or materially retard establishment of, a U.S. industry. The assistant secretary for import administration is responsible for making the fair value determination and the International Trade Commission is responsible for making the injury determination.

Termination of antidumping investigation.   A decision to close an investigation after withdrawal by the petitioner of the complaint. This decision may be made at any time. An investigation is also terminated upon publication of any negative final determination, including a negative determination by the International Trade Commission with regard to injury.

U.S. price.   The price compared to foreign market value in order to determine whether imported merchandise is sold at less than fair value. The U.S. price is either the purchase price or the exporter's sale price.

Glossary of International Trade Terms

International trade, like other specialized fields, has developed its own distinctive vocabulary which often mystifies laypersons—even importers and exporters. Many businesspeople stumble over terms commonly used in trade and the acronyms that represent the United States and international organizations that guide, regulate, and facilitate trade. This impreciseness in language impedes communication, causes misunderstandings, and delays transactions. Undoubtedly it results in lost sales for many companies.

The source for this glossary, frequently used in the international trading system, was prepared by the U.S. Information Agency, which consulted experts in the U.S. Departments of Commerce, State, and Treasury, the U.S. International Trade Commission, the Office of the U.S. Trade Representative, and with experts in the GATT and UNCTAD secretariats in Geneva. The glossary also includes other terms I have researched and found particularly applicable to the scope of this book.

ad valorem tariff A tariff calculated as percentage of the value of goods cleared through customs. For example, 15 percent ad valorem means 15 percent of the value.

adjustment assistance Financial, training, reemployment, and technical assistance to workers, and technical assistance to firms and industries, to help them cope with adjustment difficulties arising from increased import competition. The objective of the assistance is usually to help an industry become more competitive in the same line of production or to move into other economic activities. The aid to workers can take the form of training (to qualify the affected individuals for employment in new or expanding industries); relocation allowances (to help them move from high unemployment areas to those where employment may be available); or unemployment compensation (to tide them over while they are searching for new jobs). The aid to firms can take the form of technical assistance through Trade Adjustment Assistance Centers located throughout the United States. Industrywide technical assistance also is available through the Trade Adjustment Assistance Program.

   The benefits of increased trade to an importing country generally exceed the costs of adjustment, but the benefits are widely shared and the adjustment costs are sometimes narrowly—and some would say unfairly—concentrated on a few domestic producers and communities. Both import restraints and adjustment can be designed to reduce these hardships; but adjustment assistance—unlike import restraints—allows the economy to enjoy the full benefits of lower-cost imported goods. Adjustment assistance can also be designed to facilitate structural shifts of resources from less productive to more productive industries, contributing further to greater economic efficiency and improved standards of living.

ATA carnet A customs document that is recognized as an internationally valid guarantee and may be used in lieu of national customs documents and as security for import duties and taxes to cover the temporary admission of goods and sometimes the transit of goods. The ATA (*admission temporaire* or temporary admission) Convention of 1961 authorized the ATA carnet to replace the ECS (*echantillons commerciaux* or commercial samples) carnet that was created by a 1956 convention sponsored by the Customs Cooperation Council. ATA carnets are issued by national chambers of commerce affiliated with the International Chamber of Commerce, which also guarantees payment of duties in the event of failure to re-export. A carnet does not replace an export license.

balance of payments A tabulation of a country's credit and debit transactions with other countries and international institutions. These transactions are divided into two broad groups: current account and capital account. The current account includes exports and imports of goods, services (including investment income), and unilateral transfers. The capital account includes financial flows related to international direct investment, investment in government and private securities, international bank transactions, and changes in official gold holdings and foreign exchange reserves.

balance of trade A component of the balance of payments; the surplus or deficit that results from comparing a country's expenditures on merchandise imports and receipts derived from its merchandise exports.

barrier As used in this book, a barrier is a law, rule, or business practice imposed at and within the borders of one nation to restrict the success of businesses of another nation. The intent of barriers is sometimes innocent, but more often they are designed to keep global businesses out in order to protect domestic businesses.

barter The direct exchange of goods without the use of money as a medium of exchange and without the involvement of a third party.

beggar-thy-neighbor policy A course of action through which a country tries to reduce unemployment and increase domestic output by raising tariffs and instituting nontariff barriers. Anything that impedes imports through competitive devaluation. Countries that pursued such policies in the early 1930s found that other countries retaliated by raising their own barriers against imports, which, by reducing export markets, tended to worsen the economic difficulties that precipitated the initial protectionist action. The Smoot-Hawley Tariff Act of 1930 is often cited as a conspicuous example of this approach.

bilateral trade agreement A formal or informal agreement involving commerce between two countries. Such agreements sometimes list the quantities of specific goods that may be exchanged between the participating countries within a given period.

bounty or grant Payment by governments to goods producers often to strengthen their competitive position.

boycott A refusal to deal commercially or otherwise with a person, firm, or country.

business strategy One that focuses on how to manage a business.

chonghap-mooyeok-sangsa In Korea, the term *general trading company* is generally used to describe the companies designated as *chonghap-mooyeok-sangsa*, the official Korean name.

CIF An abbreviation used in some international sales contracts when the selling price includes all costs, insurance, and freight for the goods sold. CIF can also stand for *charge in full,* which means that the seller arranges and pays for all relevant expenses involved in shipping goods from its point of exportation to a given point of importation. In import statistics, CIF value means that all figures are calculated on this basis, regardless of the nature of individual transactions.

codes of conduct An international instrument that indicates standards of behavior by nation states or multinational corporations deemed desirable by the international community. Several codes of conduct were negotiated during GATT's Tokyo round that liberalized and harmonized domestic measures that might have impeded trade. These are considered legally binding for the countries that choose to adhere to them. Each of these codes is monitored by a special committee that meets under GATT auspices and encourages consultation and settlement of disputes arising under the code. Countries that are not contracting parties to GATT may adhere to these codes. GATT Articles III and XXIII also contain commercial policy provisions that have been described as GATT's code of good conduct in trade matters. The United Nations has also encouraged the negotiation of several voluntary codes of conduct, including one that seeks to specify the rights and obligations of transnational corporations and of governments.

commodity Broadly defined, any article exchanged in trade, but most commonly used to refer to raw materials, including such minerals as tin, copper, and manganese, and bulk-produced agricultural products such as coffee, tea, and rubber.

common external tariff (CXT) A tariff rate uniformly applied by a common market or customs union, such as the European Community, to imports from countries outside the union. For example, the European Common Market is based on the principle of a free internal trade area with a common external tariff (sometimes referred to in French as the *Tarif Exterieur Commun*—TEC), applied to products imported from nonmember countries. Free trade areas do not necessarily have common external tariffs.

comparative advantage A central concept in international trade theory which holds that a country or a region should specialize in the production and export of those goods and services that it can produce efficiently and should import those goods and services in which it has a comparative disadvantage.

This theory was first propounded by David Ricardo in 1817 as a basis for increasing the economic welfare of a population through international trade. The comparative advantage theory normally favors specialized production in a country based on intensive utilization of those factors of production in which the country is relatively well endowed (such as raw materials, fertile land, or skilled labor), and perhaps also the accumulation of physical capital and the pace of research.

corporate strategy That which addresses the firm as a multiple business unit.

countertrade A reciprocal trading arrangement. Countertrade transactions include the following:

A **counterpurchase** obligates the foreign supplier to purchase from the buyer goods and services unrelated to the goods and services sold, usually during a one- to five-year period.

A **reverse countertrade** contract requires the importer to export goods equivalent in value to a specified percentage of the value of the imported goods. This obligation can be sold to an exporter in a third country.

A **buyback** arrangement obligates the foreign supplier of plant, machinery, or technology to buy from the importer a portion of the resultant production during a five- to 25-year period.

A **clearing** agreement specifies that two countries agree to purchase certain amounts of each other's products over a predetermined period of time, using a designated clearing currency in the transactions.

A **switch** arrangement permits the sale of an unpaid balance of a clearing account to be sold to a third party, usually at a discount, that may be used for producing goods in the country holding the balance.

A **swap** scheme allows trading of products from different locations to save transportation costs. For example, Soviet oil may be swapped for oil from a Latin American producer, so the Soviet oil is shipped to a country in South Asia, while the Latin American oil is shipped to Cuba.

A **barter** arrangement allows two parties to directly exchange goods deemed to be of approximately equivalent value without any flow of money taking place.

countervailing duty A special duty imposed on imports to offset the benefits of subsidies to producers or exporter. GATT Article VI permits the use of such duties. The executive branch of the U.S. government has been legally empowered since the 1890s to impose countervailing duties in amounts equal to any bounties or grants reflected in products imported into the United States. Under U.S. law and the GATT Tokyo Round Agreement on Subsidies and Countervailing Duties, a wide range of practices are recognized as constituting subsidies that may be offset through the imposition of countervailing duties. The Trade Agreement Act of 1979, through amendments to the Tariff Act of 1930, established rigorous procedures and deadlines for determining the existence of subsidies in response to petitions filed by interested parties, such as domestic producers of competitive products and their workers. In all cases involving subsidized products from countries recognized by the United States as signatories to the Agreement on Subsidies and Countervailing Duties, or countries which have assumed obligations substantially equivalent to those under the agreement, U.S. law requires that countervailing duties may be imposed only after the U.S. International

Trade Commission has determined that the imports are causing or threatening to cause material injury to U.S. industry.

culture In its simplest definition, culture is a set of meanings or orientations for a given society or social setting.

current account That portion of a country's balance of payments that records current (as opposed to capital) transactions, including visible trade (exports and imports), invisible trade (income and expenditures for services), profits earned from foreign operations, interest, and transfer payments.

customs classification The particular category in a tariff nomenclature in which a product is classified for tariff purposes, or the procedure for determining the appropriate tariff category in a country's nomenclature system used for the classification, coding, and description of internationally traded goods. Most important trading nations classify imported goods in conformance with the Customs Cooperation Council Nomenclature (CCCN).

Customs Cooperation Council Nomenclature (CCCN) A system for classifying goods for customs purposes. Formerly known as the Brussels Tariff Nomenclature (BTN).

customs harmonization International efforts to increase the uniformity of customs nomenclatures and procedures in cooperating countries. The CCC has developed an up-to-date and internationally accepted harmonized commodity coding and description system for classifying goods for customs, statistical, and other purposes.

devaluation The lowering of the value of a national currency in terms of the currency of another nation. Devaluation tends to reduce domestic demand for imports in a country by raising prices in terms of the devalued currency. Devaluation also raises foreign demand for the country's exports by reducing its prices in terms of foreign currencies. Therefore, devaluation can help to correct a balance-of-payments deficit and sometimes can provide a short-term basis for economic adjustment of a national economy.

developed countries A term used to distinguish the more industrialized nations from developing or less-developed countries. The developed countries are sometimes collectively designated as the North, because most of them are in the Northern Hemisphere. They include all OECD member countries as well as the former Soviet Union and most of the socialist countries of Eastern Europe.

developing country A country that generally lacks a high degree of industrialization, infrastructure and other capital investment, sophisticated technology, widespread literacy, and advanced living standards among its population. The developing countries are sometimes collectively designated as the South, because most of them are in the Southern Hemisphere. All of the countries of Africa (except South Africa), Asia, and Oceania (except Australia, Japan, and New Zealand), Latin America, and the Middle East are generally considered developing countries. A few European countries, such as Cyprus, Malta, Turkey, and countries of former Yugoslavia, are also considered developing countries. Some economic experts differentiate four subcategories of developing countries as having different economic needs and interests.

1. A few relatively wealthy OPEC countries—sometimes referred to as oil-exporting developing countries—share a particular interest in a financially sound international economy and open capital markets.
2. Newly industrializing countries have a growing stake in an open international trading system.
3. A number of middle-income countries—principally commodity exporters—have shown interest in commodity stabilization schemes.
4. More than 30 very poor countries—the least developed countries—are predominantly agricultural, have sharply limited development prospects during the near future, and tend to be heavily dependent on official development assistance.

development The process of improving the quality of all human lives. Three equally important aspects of development are: (1) raising people's living levels, (2) creating conditions conducive to the growth of people's self-esteem, and (3) increasing people's freedom to choose by enlarging the range of their choice variables.

dispute settlement Resolution of conflict, usually through a compromise between opposing claims, sometimes facilitated through the efforts of an intermediary. GATT Articles XXII and XXIII set out consultation procedures a contracting party may follow to obtain legal redress if it believes its benefits under GATT are impaired.

domestic international sales corporation Also called interest charge DISC. It's a special U.S. corporation. To qualify, the corporation must derive 95 percent of its income from U.S. exports; also, at least 95 percent of its gross assets, such as working capital, inventories, and building and equipment, must be export-related. Such a corporation can buy and sell independently, or it can operate as a subsidiary of another corporation. It can maintain sales and service facilities outside the United States to promote and market its goods.

drawback Import duties or taxes repaid by a government, in whole or in part, when the imported goods are re-exported or used in the manufacture of exported goods.

dumping Under U.S. law, the sale of an imported commodity in the United States at less than fair value, which is usually considered to be a price lower than that at which it is sold within the exporting country or to third countries. Fair value can also be the constructed value of the merchandise, which includes a mandatory 8 percent profit margin plus cost of production.

Dumping is generally recognized as an unfair trade practice that can disrupt markets and injure producers of competitive products in the importing country. Article VI of GATT permits the imposition of special antidumping duties against dumped goods equal to the difference between their export price and their normal value in the exporting country. The U.S. Antidumping Law of 1921, as amended, considered dumping as constituting sales at less than fair value, combined with injury, the likelihood of injury, or the prevention of the establishment of a competitive industry in the United States. The Trade Act of 1974 added a cost of production provision, which required that dumping determinations ignore sales in the home market of the exporting country or in third-country markets at prices that are too low to "permit recovery of all costs within a reasonable period of time in the normal course of trade." The Trade Agreements Act of 1979 repealed the 1921 act, but reenacted most of its substance in Title VII of the Tariff Act of 1930.

economic growth The steady process by which the productive capacity of the economy is increased over time to bring about rising levels of national income.

embargo A prohibition upon exports or imports, either with respect to specific products or specific countries. Historically, embargoes have been ordered most frequently in time of war, but they may also be applied for political, economic, or sanitary purposes. Embargoes imposed against an individual country by the United Nations, or a group of nations, in an effort to influence its conduct or its policies are sometimes called sanctions.

escape clause A provision in a bilateral or multilateral commercial agreement permitting a signatory nation to suspend tariff or other concessions when imports threaten serious harm to the producers of competitive domestic goods. GATT Article XIX sanctions such safeguard provisions to help firms and workers adjust to the rising levels of import competition.

Section 201 of the U.S. Trade Act of 1974 requires the U.S. International Trade Commission to investigate complaints, formally known as petitions, filed by domestic industries or workers claiming that they have been injured or are threatened with injury as a consequence of rapidly rising imports. Any such investigation must be completed within six months. Section 203 of the act provides that if the ITC finds that a domestic industry has been seriously injured or threatened with serious injury, it may recommend that the president grant relief to the industry in the form of adjustment assistance or temporary import restrictions in the form of tariffs or quotas. The president must then take action pursuant to the commission's recommendations within 60 days, but may accept, modify, or reject recommendations according to his or her assessment of the national interest. Congress can, through majority vote in both the Senate and the House of Representatives within 90 legislative days, override a presidential decision not to implement the commission's recommendations. The law permits the president to impose import restrictions for an initial period of five years and to extend them for a maximum additional period of three years.

exchange controls The rationing of foreign currencies, bank drafts, and other instruments for settling international financial obligations by countries seeking to ameliorate acute balance-of-payments difficulties. When such measures are imposed, importers must apply for prior authorization from the government to obtain the foreign currency required to bring in designated amounts and types of goods. Since such measures have the effect of restricting imports, they are considered nontariff trade barriers.

exchange rate The price at which one currency is exchanged for another currency, for gold, or for special drawing rights.

excise tax A selective tax, sometimes called a consumption tax, on certain goods produced within or imported into a country.

export quota A specific restriction or ceiling imposed by an exporting country on the value or volume of certain imports, designated to protect domestic producers and consumers from temporary shortages of the goods or to bolster their prices in world markets. Some international commodity agreements explicitly indicate when producers should apply such restraints. Export quotas are also often applied in orderly marketing agreements and voluntary restraint agreements, and to promote domestic processing of raw materials.

export restraints A quantitative restriction imposed by exporting countries to limits exports to specified foreign markets, usually pursuant to a formal or informal agreement concluded at the request of the importing countries.

export subsidy A government payment or other financially quantifiable benefit provided to domestic producers or exporters contingent on the export of their goods or services. GATT Article XVI recognizes that subsidies in general, and especially export subsidies, distort normal commercial activities and hinder the achievement of GATT objectives. The Agreement on Subsidies and Countervailing Duties strengthened the GATT rules on export subsidies and provided for an outright prohibition of export subsidies by developed countries for manufactured and semimanufactured products. The agreement also established a special committee, serviced by signatories. Under certain conditions, the agreement allows developing countries to use export subsidies on manufactured and semimanufactured products, and on primary products as well, provided that the subsidies do not result in more than an equitable share of world exports of the product for the country.

export trading company A corporation or other business unit organized and operated principally for the purpose of exporting goods and services, or of providing export-related services to other companies. The Export Trading Company Act of 1982 exempts authorized trading companies from certain provisions of U.S. antitrust laws.

factors of production (endowments) The factors of production, also known as factors of endowments, are: (1) natural resources, (2) capital, (3) management, (4) technology, (5) labor, and (6) intelligence. Classical economists of the 19th century believed these factors had perfect mobility within a country, but perfect immobility between nations. Today, due to increased modern transportation and communications and the lessening of trade barriers, the international mobility of factors closely approximates the mobility within a given nation.

fair trade Fair trade has two definitions. The first is explained as a distortion of the international trade market between two or more nations which causes disagreement. One nation imposes reciprocal rules on the businesses of another nation with whom the first nation could not get agreement. The unilateral implications are protectionist.

   The same definition is the idea that all nations should operate under the same set of international trade rules.

FAS In international trade, the term *free alongside ship* refers to the point of embarkation from which the vessel or plane selected by the buyer will transport the goods. Under this system, the seller is obligated to pay the costs and assume all risks for transporting the goods from his or her place of business to the FAS point. In trade statistics, *FAS value* means that the import or export figures are calculated on this basis, regardless of the nature of individual transactions reflected in the statistics.

FOB An abbreviation used in some international sales contracts, when imports are valued at a designated point, as agreed between buyer and seller, that is considered *free on board*. In such contracts, the seller is obligated to have the goods packaged and ready for shipment from the agreed point, whether his or her own place of business or some intermediate point, and the buyer normally assumes the burden of all inland transportation costs and risks in the exporting country, as well as all subsequent transportation costs, including the costs of loading the merchandise on the vessel. If the contract stipulates FOB vessel, however, the seller bears all transportation costs to the vessel named by the buyer, as well as the costs of loading the goods onto that vessel. The same principle applies to the abbreviations FOR (free on rail) and FOT (free on truck).

foreign sales corporation (FSC) A firm incorporated in Guam, the U.S. Virgin Islands, the Commonwealth of the Northern Mariana Islands, American Samoa, or any foreign country that has a satisfactory exchange-of-information agreement with the United States. A FSC elects to be taxed as a U.S. corporation, except for the fact that it exempts from taxable income a portion of the combined net income of the FSC and its affiliated supplier on the export of U.S. products.

free trade A theoretical concept that assumes international trade unhampered by government measures such as tariffs or nontariff barriers. The objective of trade liberalization is to achieve freer trade rather than free trade, since it is generally recognized among trade policy officials that some restrictions on trade are likely to remain in effect for the foreseeable future.

   Often attributed to Adam Smith, an 18th-century economist, free trade implies no regulation by governments. It is a utopian idea. Those who espouse it believe that market forces by themselves should determine the outcome of business success. Most business managers see free trade as a goal. Realistic thinkers understand that pure laissez-faire cross-border business activity is unattainable.

free trade area A group of two or more countries that have eliminated tariff and most nontariff barriers affecting trade among themselves, while each participating country applies its own independent schedule of tariffs to imports from nonmember countries. The best-known examples are the European Free Trade Association (EFTA) and the free trade area for manufactured goods that has been created through the trade agreements among EC members and the individual EFTA countries. Article XXIV spells out the meaning of a free trade area in GATT and specifies the applicability of other GATT provisions to free trade areas.

free zone An area within a country (a seaport, airport, warehouse, or any other designated area) regarded as being outside the country's customs territory. Therefore, importers may bring goods of foreign origin into such an area without paying customs duties and taxes, pending their eventual processing, transhipment, or re-exportation. Free zones were numerous and prosperous when tariffs were high. Some still exist in capital cities, transport junctions, and major seaports, but their number and prominence have declined as tariffs have fallen in recent years. Free zones may also be known as free ports, free warehouses, and foreign trade zones.

functional strategy That which deals with the funtional areas of a business such as: finance, marketing, production, human resources, and so on.

generalized system of preferences (GSP) A concept developed within UNCTAD to encourage the expansion of manufactured and semimanufactured exports from developing countries by making goods more competitive in developed country markets through tariff preferences. The GSP reflects international agreement, negotiated at UNCTAD-II in New Delhi in 1968, that a temporary and nonreciprocal grant of preferences by developed countries to developing countries would be equitable and, in the long term, mutually beneficial.

government procurement policies and practices The means and mechanisms through which official government agencies purchase goods and services. Government procurement policies and practices are nontariff trade barriers, if they discriminate in favor of domestic suppliers when competitive imported goods are cheaper or of better quality. The United States pressed for an international agreement during the Tokyo round of GATT to ensure that government purchase of goods entering into international trade should be based on specific published regulations that prescribe open procedures for submitting bids, as had been the traditional practice in the United States. Most governments had traditionally awarded such contracts on the basis of bids solicited from selected domestic suppliers, or through private negotiations with suppliers that involved little, if any, competition. Other countries, including the United States, gave domestic suppliers a specified preferential margin as compared with foreign suppliers. The government procurement code negotiated during the Tokyo round sought to reduce, if not eliminate, the buy-national bias underlying such practices by improving transparency and equity in national procurement practices and by ensuring effective recourse to dispute settlement procedures. The code became effective January 1, 1981.

graduation The presumption that individual developing countries are capable of assuming greater responsibilities and obligations in the international community—within GATT or the World Bank, for example—as their economics advance through industrialization, export development, and rising living standards. In this sense, graduation implies that donor countries may remove the more advanced developing countries from eligibility for all or some products under the GSP. Within the World Bank, graduation moves a country from dependence on concessional grants to nonconcessional loans from international financial institutions and private banks.

harmonization All nations have interstate controls; however, the laws, regulations, procedures, and practices vary among the states making it difficult for businesses to operate on a global basis. Harmonization is the process of defining, and the peacefully negotiating of, a common set of rules and procedures so that international trade can be progressive. Interstate controls cause conflict when they restrain free trade to the extent that there are major distortions. This leads toward protectionism, depression, and war. Therefore, there is a need for harmonization.

import substitution An attempt by a country to reduce imports, and hence foreign exchange expenditures, by encouraging the development of domestic industries.

industrial policy Encompasses traditional government policies intended to provide a favorable economic climate for the development of industry in general or specific industrial sectors. Instruments of industrial policy may include tax incentives to promote investments or exports, direct or indirect subsidies, special financing arrangements, protection against foreign competition, worker training programs, regional development programs, assistance for research and development, and measures to help small business firms. Historically, the term *industrial policy* has been associated with at least some degree of centralized economic planning or indicative planning, but this connotation is not always intended by its contemporary advocates.

infant industry argument The view that temporary protection for a new industry or firm, through tariff and nontariff barriers to imports, can help it to become established and eventually competitive in world markets. Historically, new industries that are soundly based and efficiently operated have experienced declining costs as output expands and production experience is acquired. Industries that have been established and operated with heavy dependence on direct or indirect government subsidies, however, have sometimes found it difficult to relinquish that support. The rationale underlying the GSP is comparable to that of the infant industry argument.

intellectual property Ownership conferring the right to possess, use, or dispose of products created by human ingenuity, including patents, trademarks, and copyrights.

interstate controls These are laws, regulations, procedures, and practices between nations or economic unions of nations that inhibit or stimulate free trade. Some controls are barriers while others are stimulants in the form of incentives. Thus controls may be visualized as having a torquing effect on economic development and can cause significant distortions to free trade. All sovereign nations, to some extent, control the flow of goods, thought, services, funds, and freedom of movement across their borders. Not all barriers are bad; not all stimulants are good. For instance, public health conditions in one nation may dictate certain barriers to free trade that may differ from another.

investment performance requirements Special conditions imposed on direct foreign investment by recipient governments, sometimes requiring commitments to export a certain percentage of the output, to purchase given supplies locally, or to ensure the employment of a specified percentage of local labor and management.

joint venture A form of business partnership involving joint management and the sharing of risks and profits as between enterprises based in different countries. If joint ownership of capital is involved, the partnership is known as an equity joint venture.

least developed countries (LDCs) Some 36 of the world's poorest countries, considered by the United Nations to be the least developed of the less-developed countries. Most of them are small in terms of area and population, and some are landlocked or small island countries. They are generally characterized by low per capita incomes, literacy levels, and medical standards; subsistence agriculture; and a lack of exploitable minerals and competitive industries. Many suffer from aridity, floods, hurricanes, and excessive animal and plant pests, and most are situated in the zone 10 to 30 degrees north latitude. These countries have little prospect of rapid economic development in the foreseeable future and are likely to remain heavily dependent upon official development assistance for many years. Most are in Africa, but a few, such as Bangladesh, Afghanistan, Laos, and Nepal, are in Asia. Haiti is the only country in the Western Hemisphere classified by the United Nations as least developed. Also see *developing country.*

liberal When referring to trade policy, liberal usually means relatively free of import controls or restraints and/or a preference for reducing existing barriers to trade, often contrasted with the protectionist preference for retaining or raising selected barriers to imports.

long-range objectives In pursuing the firm's mission, these are the objectives that extend beyond the current operational year.

mixed credits Exceptionally liberal financing terms for an export sale, ostensibly provided for a foreign-aid purpose.

mercantilism A prominent economic philosophy in the 16th and 17th centuries that equated the accumulation and possession of gold and other international monetary assets, such as foreign currency reserves, with national wealth. Although this point of view is generally discredited among 20th-century economists and trade policy experts, some contemporary politicians still favor policies designated to create trade surpluses, such as import substitution and tariff protection for domestic industries, as essential to national economic strength.

most-favored-nation treatment (MFN) The policy of nondiscrimination in trade policy that provides to all trading partners the same customs and tariff treatment given to the so-called most-favored nation. This fundamental principle was a feature of U.S. trade policy as early as 1778. Since 1923 the United States has incorporated an unconditional most-favored-nation clause in its trade agreements, binding the contracting governments to confer upon each other all the most favorable trade concessions that either may grant to any other country. The United States now applies this provision to its transactions with all of its trading partners except for those specifically excluded by law. The MFN principle has also provided the foundation of the world trading system since the end of World War II. All contracting parties to GATT apply MFN treatment to one another under Article I of GATT.

multifiber arrangement regarding international trade in textiles (MFA) An international compact under GATT that allows an importing signatory country to apply quantitative restrictions on textiles imports when it considers them necessary to prevent market disruption. The MFA provides a framework for regulating international trade in textiles and apparel with the objectives of achieving orderly marketing of such products and of avoiding market disruption in importing countries. The MFA provides a basis on which major importers, such as the United States and the EC, may negotiate bilateral agreements or, if necessary, impose restraints on imports from low-wage producing countries. The MFA provides, among other things, standards for determining market disruption, minimum levels of import restraints, and equal growth of imports. Since an importing country may impose such quotas unilaterally to restrict rapidly rising textiles imports, many important textile-exporting countries consider it advantageous to enter into bilateral agreements with the principal textile-importing countries.

The MFA went into effect on January 1, 1974, was renewed in December 1977, in December 1981, and again in July 1986 for five years. It succeeded the Long-term Agreement on International Trade in Cotton Textiles (LTA), which had been in effect since 1962. Whereas the LTA applied only to cotton textiles, the MFA now applies to wool, synthetic fiber, silk blend, and other vegetable fiber textiles and apparel.

multilateral agreement An international compact involving three or more parties. For example, GATT has been, since its establishment in 1947, seeking to promote trade liberalization through multilateral negotiations.

multilateral trade negotiations (MTN) Seven rounds of multilateral trade negotiations have been held under the auspices of GATT since 1947. Each round represents a discrete and lengthy series of interacting bargaining sessions among the participating contracting parties in search of mutually beneficial agreements toward the reduction of barriers to world trade. The agreements ultimately reached at the conclusion of each round became new GATT commitments and thus amounted to an important step in the evolution of the world trading system.

nation A nation is an ethnic or social entity. Also called nation-state.

nationalism Nationalism is the emotionalism that bonds people to their nation. Nationalism is also a cultural phenomenon exalting loyalty, devotion, and duty to ethnic and tribal groups as well as territory.

newly industrializing countries (NICs) A relatively advanced developing country whose industrial production and exports have grown rapidly in recent years. Examples include Brazil, Hong Kong, Korea, Mexico, Singapore, and Taiwan.

nonmarket economy (NME) A national economy or a country in which the government seeks to determine economic activity largely through a mechanism of central planning, as in the former Soviet Union. Contrast NME with a market economy that depends heavily upon market forces to allocate productive resources. In a nonmarket economy, production targets, prices, costs, investment allocations, raw materials, labor, international trade, and most other economic aggregates are manipulated within a national economic plan drawn up by a central planning authority; hence the public sector makes the major decisions affecting demand and supply within the national economy.

nontariff barrier (NTB) A government measure other than a tariff that restricts imports. Such measures have become relatively more conspicuous impediments to trade as tariffs have been reduced since World War II.

orderly marketing agreement (OMA) An international agreement negotiated between two or more governments in which the trading partners agree to restrain the growth of trade in specified sensitive products usually through the imposition of import quotas. OMAs are intended to ensure that future trade increases will not disrupt, threaten, or impair competitive industries or their workers in importing countries.

organizational culture The collection of attitudes, assumptions, and beliefs that shape the behavior of an organization.

organizational mission This is the statement that defines an organization's line(s) of business. It identifies the firm's products and services and specifies the market it serves.

organizational philosophy Guidelines, agreed to by all, that establish the values and beliefs by which the organization will conduct its business.

par value The official fixed exchange rate between two currencies or between a currency and a specific weight of gold or a basket of currencies.

Paris club A popular designation for meetings between representatives of a developing country that wishes to renegotiate its official debt and representatives of the relevant creditor governments and international institutions. (Official debt normally excludes debts owned by and to the private sector without official guarantees.) Such meetings normally take place at the initiative of a debtor country that wishes to consolidate all or part of its debt service payments falling due over a specified period. The meetings are traditionally chaired by a senior official of the French Treasury Department. Comparable meetings occasionally take place in London and in New York for countries that wish to renegotiate repayment terms for their debts to private banks. Such meetings are sometimes called creditors' clubs.

peril point A hypothetical limit beyond which a reduction in tariff protection would cause injury to a domestic industry.

protectionism The deliberate use or encouragement of restrictions on imports to enable inefficient domestic producers to compete successfully with foreign producers.

quantitative restriction (QR) An explicit limit, or quota, on the physical amounts of commodities that can be imported or exported during a specific time period, usually measured by volume but sometimes measured by value. The quota may be applied on a selective basis, with varying limits set according to the country of origin, or on a quantitative global basis that only specifies the total limit and thus tends to benefit more efficient suppliers. Quotas are frequently administered through a system of licensing.

GATT Article XI generally prohibits the use of quantitative restrictions, except under conditions specified by other GATT articles Article XIX permits quotas to safeguard certain industries from damage by rapidly rising imports; Articles XII and XVIII provide that quotas may be imposed for balance of payments reasons under circumstances laid out in Article XV; Article XX permits special measures to apply to public health, gold stocks, items of archaeological or historic interest, and several other categories of goods; and Article XXI recognizes the overriding importance of national security. Article XII provides that quantitative restrictions, whenever applied, should be nondiscriminatory.

reciprocity The practice by which governments extend similar concessions to each other, as when one government lowers its tariffs or other barriers impeding its imports in exchange for equivalent concessions from a trading partner; thus, a balance of concessions is maintained. Reciprocity has traditionally been a principal objective of negotiators in GATT rounds. Reciprocity is also defined as mutuality of benefits, quid pro quo, and equivalence of advantages. GATT Part IV (especially Article XXXVI) and the enabling clause of the Tokyo round framework agreement exempt developing countries from the rigorous application of reciprocity in their negotiations with developed countries.

retaliation Action taken by a country to restrain its imports from a country that has increased a tariff or imposed other measures that adversely affect its exports in a manner inconsistent with GATT. The GATT, in certain circumstances, permits such reprisal, although this has very rarely been practiced. The value of trade affected by such retaliatory measures should, in theory, approximately equal the value affected by the initial import restriction.

round of trade negotiations A cycle of multilateral trade negotiations under the aegis of GATT, culminating in simultaneous trade agreements among participating countries to reduce tariff and nontariff barriers to trade. Seven rounds have been completed thus far: Annecy, France, 1949; Torquay, England, 1950–1951; and Geneva, 1947–1948, 1956, 1960–1962 (the Dillon round), 1963–1967 (the Kennedy round), and 1973–1979 (the Tokyo round).

Section 301 of the Trade Act of 1974 Provision of U.S. law that enables the president to withdraw concessions or restrict imports from countries that discriminate against U.S. exports, subsidize their own exports to the United States, or engage in other unjustifiable or unreasonable practices that burden or discriminate against U.S. trade.

services Economic activities—such as transportation, banking, insurance, tourism, space launching, telecommunications, advertising, entertainment, data processing, consulting, and the licensing of intellectual property—that are usually of an intangible character and often consumed as they are produced. Service industries have become increasingly important since the 1920s. Services now account for more than two thirds of the economic activity of the United States and about 25 percent of world trade. Traditional GATT rules have not applied to trade in services.

short-range objectives In pursuing the firm's mission, there are the objectives that extend beyond the current operational year.

Smoot-Hawley Tariff Act of 1930 U.S. protectionist legislation that raised tariff rates on most articles imported by the United States triggering comparable tariff increases by U.S. trading partners. Also known as the Tariff Act of 1930.

sovereignty The notion that governing must be accomplished in small pieces of specific territories called states. The characteristics of states vary. Some are kingdoms, some have specific religions, all have politics and boundaries, but their economics seem to vary widely. The borders of these states serve as barriers to the free movement of people, goods, services, and capital.

special drawing right (SDR) Created in 1969 by the International Monetary Fund (IMF) as a supplemental international monetary reserve asset. SDRs are available to governments through the IMF and may be used in transactions between the IMF and member governments. IMF member countries have agreed to regard SDRs as complementary to gold and reserve currencies in settling their international accounts. The unit value of an SDR reflects the foreign exchange value of a basket of currencies of several major trading countries (the U.S. dollar, the German mark, the French franc, the Japanese yen, and the British pound). The SDR has become the unit of account used by the IMF and several national currencies are pegged to it. Some commercial banks accept deposits denominated in SDRs, although they are unofficial and not the same units transacted among governments and the IMF.

state trading nation Countries such as the Soviet republics, the People's Republic of China, and Eastern Europeon nations that rely heavily on government entities, instead of the private sector, to conduct trade with other countries. Some of these countries, such as Czechoslovakia and Cuba have long been contracting parties to GATT, whereas others, such as Poland, Hungary, and Rumania, became contracting parties later under special protocols of accession. The different terms and conditions under which these countries acceded to GATT were designed in each case to ensure steady expansion of the country's trade with other GATT countries, taking into account the relative insignificance of tariffs on imports into state trading nations.

strategic business unit (SBU) The operating unit in an organization which sells a distinct product or service in a well-defined market and which has well-defined competitors.

strategic management Using strategy as a management tool in a home corporation that does not serve a global market.

strategy A method that uses the paradigm of jumping time to set future goals, then managing to achieve those objectives.

strategy emplantation The process of absorption of the concept and acceptance of specific strategies into a firm's culture.

strategy formulation Based on the organization's mission and philosophy, it is the analysis and selection of objectives to be achieved in the future.

strategy implementation This is the execution of strategy by means of matching appropriate tactics, organization, budgets, functional strategies, and monitoring devices.

subsidy An economic benefit granted by a government to goods producers, often to strengthen their competitive position. The subsidy may be direct—a cash grant—or indirect—low-interest export credits guaranteed by a government agency.

tariff A duty or tax levied upon goods transported from one customs area to another. Tariffs raise the prices of imported goods, thus making them less competitive within the market of the importing country. After seven rounds of GATT trade negotiations that focused heavily on reductions, tariffs are less important measures of protection than they used to be. The term *tariff* often refers to a comprehensive list or schedule of merchandise with the rate of duty to be paid to the government for the importing products listed.

terms of trade The volume of exports that can be traded for a given volume of imports. Changes in the terms of trade are generally measured by comparing changes in the ratio of export prices to import prices. The terms of trade are considered to have improved when a given volume of exports can be exchanged for a larger volume of imports. Some economists have discerned an overall deteriorating trend in this ratio for developing countries as a whole. Other economists maintain that whereas the terms of trade may have become less favorable for certain countries during certain periods—and even for all developing countries during some periods—the same terms of trade have improved for other, and perhaps most, developing countries in the same periods.

tied loan A loan made by a government agency that requires a foreign borrower to spend the proceeds in the lender's country.

trade creation (stimulants, schemes, and incentives) For purposes of explanation, stimulants or incentives are the various laws and rules, exceptions to laws and rules, and financial carrots offered by governments to create international trade. These schemes are designed to encourage foreign businesses to operate in a given country for purposes of economic development and growth.

trade policy committee (TPC) A senior interagency committee of the U.S. government, chaired by the U.S. Trade Representative, that provides broad guidance to the president on trade policy issues. Members include the secretaries of commerce, state, treasury, agriculture, and labor.

transfer of technology The movement of modern or scientific methods of production or distribution from one enterprise, institution, or country to another. This transfer is through foreign investment, international trade licensing of patent rights, technical assistance, or training.

transparency Visibility and clarity of laws and regulations. Some of the codes of conduct negotiated during the Tokyo round sought to increase the transparency of non-tariff barriers.

trigger price mechanism (TPM) A U.S. system for monitoring imported steel to identify imports that are possibly being dumped in the United States or subsidized by the governments of exporting countries. The minimum price under this system is based on the estimated landed cost at a U.S. port of entry of steel produced by the world's most efficient manufacturers. Imported steel entering the United States below that price may trigger formal antidumping investigations by the U.S. Department of Commerce and the U.S. International Trade Commission. The TPM was in effect from early 1978 to March 1980. It was reinstated in October 1980 and suspended for all products except stainless steel wire in January 1982.

turnkey contract A compact under which the contractor assumes responsibility to the client for constructing productive installations and ensuring that they operate effectively before turning them over to the client. By centering responsibility for the contributions of all participants in the project in his or her own hands, the contractor is often able to arrange more favorable financing terms than the client could. The responsibility of the contractor ends when the completed installation is turned over to the client.

unfair trade practice Unusual government support to particular firms that result in competitive international trade advantages for the firms. Examples of unfair trade practices include export subsidies and certain anticompetitive practices by the firms themselves, such as dumping, boycotts, or discriminatory shipping arrangements.

valuation The appraisal of imported goods' worth by customs officials for the purpose of determining the amount of duty payable to the importing country. The GATT Customs Valuation Code obligates governments that sign it to use the transaction value of imported goods—or the price actually paid or payable for them— as the principal basis for valuing the goods for customs purposes.

value-added tax (VAT) An indirect tax on consumption that is levied at each discrete point in the chain of production and distribution, from the raw material stage to final consumption. Each processor or merchant pays a tax proportional to the amount by which he or she increases the value of the goods purchased for resale after making his or her own contribution. The VAT is imposed throughout the EC and EFTA countries, but the tax rates have not been harmonized among those countries.

voluntary restraint agreement (VRA) An informal arrangement through which exporters voluntarily restrain certain exports, usually through export quotas, to avoid economic dislocation in an importing country, and to avert the possible imposition of mandatory import restrictions. Such arrangements do not normally entail compensation for the exporting country.

Bibliography

CHAPTER 1

Espey, James. "When Global Markets Get Tough." *Chief Executive*, October 1991.

"The History of an Unlikely Buzzword." *Fortune*, September 23, 1991, p. 140.

Nelson, Carl A. *Global Success: International Business Tactics for the 1990s.* Blue Ridge Summit, Pa.: TAB Books, a division of McGraw-Hill, 1990(a).

———. *Import/Export: How to Get Started in International Trade.* Blue Ridge Summit, Pa.: TAB Books, a division of McGraw-Hill, 1990(b).

Ohmae, Kenichi. *The Borderless World: Power and Strategy in the Interlinked Economy,* New York: Harper Business, a division of HarperCollins, 1990.

Spaeth, Anthony. "'Superbrat' Strives to Expand UB Group." *The Wall Street Journal*, May 9, 1990.

Thurow, Lester C. "The Coming Global Economy," a keynote speech presented as part of the San Diego in the Global Economy Series, San Diego, November 1990.

CHAPTER 2

Abell, D. *Defining a Business: The Starting Point of Strategic Planning.* Englewood Cliffs, N.J.: Prentice-Hall,1980.

Ansoff, H. Igor. *Corporate Strategy.* New York: John Wiley & Sons, 1965.

———. *Implanting Strategy Management.* Englewood Cliffs, N.J.: Prentice-Hall, 1984.

———. *The New Corporate Strategy.* New York: John Wiley & Sons, 1988.

Barnard, Chester. *The Function of the Executive.* Cambridge, Mass.: MIT Press, 1938.

Byers, Lloyd L. *Strategic Management: Formulation and Implementation.* 3rd ed. New York: HarperCollins, 1991.

Chandler, A. D., Jr. *Strategy and Structure.* Cambridge, Mass.: MIT Press, 1962.

Clausewitz, Karl Von. *On War.* Michael Howard and Peter Paret, eds. Princeton, N.J.: Princeton University Press, 1975.

Drucker, Peter F. *Managing in Turbulent Times.* New York: Harper and Row, 1979.

———. *The Age of Discontinuity.* New York: Harper and Row, 1985(a).

———. *Innovation and Entrepreneurship, Practice and Principles.* New York: Harper and Row, 1985(b).

Griffin, Samuel B. *Sun Tzu: The Art of War.* London: Oxford University Press, 1963.

Johnson, Chalmers. *MITI and the Japanese Miracle: The Growth of Industrial Policy, 1925–1975.* Stanford, Calif.: Stanford University Press, 1982.

———. "The Institutional Foundations of Japanese Industrial Policy." *California Management Review* 27, no. 4 (Summer 1985).

Kotobe, Masaaki. "The Roles of Japanese Industrial Policy for Export Success: A Theoretical Perspective." *Columbia Journal of World Business* 20, no. 3 (Fall 1985).

Lamont, Douglas. *Winning Worldwide: Strategies for Dominating Global Markets.* Homewood, Ill.: Business One Irwin, 1991.

Mintzberg, Henry. *Structuring the Organization.* Englewood Cliffs, N.J.: Prentice-Hall, 1979.

———. *The Nature of Managerial Work.* Englewood Cliffs, N.J.: Prentice-Hall, 1983.

———. "Crafting Strategy." *Harvard Business Review* 65, no.4 (July–August 1987), pp. 66–75.

Pearce, John A. and Richard B. Robinson, Jr. *Strategic Managment: Formulation, Implementation, and Control.* Homewood, Ill.: Business One Irwin, 1991.

Perkins, Edwin J. *The World Economy in the Twentieth Century.* Cambridge, Mass.: Schenkman Publishing, 1983.

Peters, Thomas J. and Robert H. Waterman. *In Search of Excellence: Lessons from America's Best-Run Companies.* New York: Harper and Row, 1982.

Porter, Michael E. *Competitive Strategy: Techniques for Analyzing Industries and Competitors.* New York: The Free Press, 1980.

———. *Competitive Advantage: Creating and Sustaining Superior Performance.* New York: The Free Press, 1985.

———. *Competition in Global Industries.* Boston, Mass.: Harvard Business School Press,1986.

———. "From Competitive Advantage to Corporate Strategy." *Harvard Business Review,* May–June 1987, pp. 17–22.

———. *The Competitive Advantage of Nations.* New York: The Free Press, 1990.

Quinn, Bryan. *Strategies for Change: Logical Incrementalism.* Homewood, Ill.: Business One Irwin, 1980.

Rue, Leslie W. and Phylllis G. Holland. *Strategic Managment: Concepts and Experiences.* 2nd ed. New York: McGraw-Hill, 1989.

Sloan, Alfred P., Jr. *My Years with General Motors.* Garden City, N.Y.: Doubleday Publishing, 1964.

Smith, Adam. *An Inquiry in to the Nature and Concept of the Wealth of Nations.* New York: Random House, 1937.

Thompson, Arthur A., Jr. and A. J. Strictland, III. *Strategic Management: Concepts and Cases.* 5th ed. Homewood, Ill.: Business One Irwin, 1990.

Tregoe, Benjamin B.; John W. Zimmerman; Ronald A. Smith; and Peter M.Tobia. *Vision in Action: Putting a Winning Strategy to Work.* New York: Simon & Schuster, 1989.

Whalen, Richard J. "Politics and the Export Mess." In *The Export Performance of the United States: Political, Strategic and Economic Implications,* ed. Center for Strategic and International Studies. New York: Praeger, 1981.

Yip, George S. *Total Global Strategy.* Englewood Cliffs, N. J.: Prentice-Hall, 1992.

CHAPTER 3

Everitt, William L., vice president of communications, Kyocera. Interview with author. San Diego, California, 11 December 1990.

Inoue, Michael S., vice president of corporate technology and planning, Kyocera. Interview with author. San Diego, California, 13 August 1991.

Owens, James W., president of Solar Turbines. Interview with author. San Diego, California, 30 September 1991.

CHAPTER 4

Backaitis, Nida and Harold H. Rosen, eds. *Readings on Managing Organizational Quality.* San Diego: Navy Personnel Research and Development Center, 1990.

Barnet, Richard and Ronald Muller. *Global Reach: Power of Multinational Corporations.* New York: Simon & Schuster, 1974.

Bylinsky, Gene. "The Hottest High-Tech Company in Japan." *Fortune,* January 2, 1990.

Deming, W. Edwards. *Out of the Crisis.* Cambridge, Mass.: Massachusetts Institute of Technology for Advanced Engineering Study, 1986.

Inamori, Kazuo. *Kyocera: A Bond of Human Minds.* San Diego: Kyocera International, 1987.

Walton, Mary. *The Deming Management Method.* New York: The Putnam Publishing Group, 1986.

CHAPTER 5

Parkes, Christopher. "Consumer Trends: 'In the End We Are Big Brand People.'" *Financial Times,* January 16, 1989, p. 8.

CHAPTER 6

Cramer, Richard, founder and former president of IVAC and IMED. Interview with author. San Diego, California, September 1990.

CHAPTER 7

Barry, John S. Chairman of WD-40. Interview with author. 8 December 1990.

CHAPTER 8

Webster, J; W. Reif; and J. Braker. "The Manager's Guide to Strategic Planning Tools and Techniques." *Planning Review*, November–December 1989, pp. 4–13.

CHAPTER 9

Burwell, Helen. *Directory of Fee-Based Information Services*. Houston: Burwell Enterprises, 1990.

Eells, Richard and Peter Nehemkis. *Corporate Intelligence and Espionage: A Blueprint for Executive Decision Making*. New York: Macmillan, 1984.

Fuld, Leonard M. *Monitoring the Competition: Finding Out What's Really Going On Over There*. New York: John Wiley & Sons, 1988.

———. "How to Gather Foreign Intelligence Without Leaving Home." *Marketing News*, January 4, 1988.

———. "A Recipe for Business Intelligence Success." *The Journal of Business Strategy*, January/February 1991.

King, W. R. and D. I. Cleland. "Environmental Information Systems for Strategic Market Planning." *Journal of Marketing*, October 1974, pp. 35–40.

King, W. R.; B. K. Dutton; and J. T. Rodriguez. "Strategic Competitive Information Systems." *Omega*, April 1978, pp. 123–132.

King, W. R. and J. T. Rodriguez. "Participative Design of Strategic Design Support Systems: An Empirical Assessment." *Management Science*, June 1981, pp. 717–726.

Glossbrenner, Alfred. *How to Look it Up Online: Get the Information Edge with Your Personal Computer*. New York: St. Martin's Press, 1987.

McGrane, James. "Using On-Line Information for Strategic Advantage." *Planning Review*. November/December 1987.

Montgomery, D. B. and C. E. Weinberg, "Toward Strategic Intelligence Systems." *Journal of Marketing*, Fall 1979.

O'Brien, Virginia F. and Leonard M. Fuld. "Business Intelligence and the New Europe." *Planning Review* 19, no. 4. (July/August 1991).

Prescott, John. "How Business Uses Intelligence." *The Journal of Commerce*, August 2, 1991.

Roush, Gary B. "A Program for Sharing Corporate Intelligence." *The Journal of Business Strategy*, January/February 1991.

CHAPTER 10

Drucker, Peter F. "The Transnational Economy." *The Wall Street Journal*, August 25, 1987, p. 30.

"Economic Growth Trends and Effect on Government Policies." *United Nations Annual Report*. New York: United Nations, 1983, 1984, 1985, 1986, 1987, 1988, 1989.

Mun, Thomas. *England's Treasure by Forraign Trade*. Oxford: Basil Blackwell & Mott, 1949.

Ohlin, Bertil. *Interregional and International Trade*. Cambridge, Mass.: Harvard University Press, 1952.

Rabushka, Alvin. *From Adam Smith to the Wealth of America*. 2nd ed. New Brunswick, N.J.: Transaction Books, 1985.

Ricardo, David. *On the Principals of Political Economy and Taxation*. 1817. New York: E. P. Dutton, 1948.

Smith, Adam. *An Inquiry into the Nature and Causes of the Wealth of Nations*. 1776. New York: Random House, 1937.

United Nations. Conference on Trade Development. USSR: *New Management Mechanism in Foreign Economic Relations*. 1988.

United Nations. Department of International Economic and Social Affairs. *Crisis or Reform: Breaking the Barriers to Development (Views and Recommendations of the Committee for Development Planning)*. 1984.

United Nations. Department of International Economic and Social Affairs. Development *Under Siege: Constraints and Opportunities in a Changing Global Economy (View and Recommendations of the Committee for Development Planning)*. 1987.

United Nations. Department of International Economic and Social Affairs. *Modeling of World Economic Development*. 1988.

United Nations. Uncitral Secretariat. *Uncitral: The United Nations Commission on International Trade Law*. 1986.

United Nations Economic Commission for Europe. Committee on the Development of Trade. *Marketing Management in East-West Trade*. 1985.

United Nations University. *Transforming the World Economy: Nine Critical Essays on the New International Economic Order*. Tokyo: The United Nations University, 1984.

Whalen, Richard J. "Politics and the Export Mess." In *The Export Performance of the United States: Political, Strategic and Economic Implications*, ed. Center for Strategic and International Studies. New York: Praeger, 1981.

CHAPTER 11

Porter, Michael E. "The Competitive Advantage of Nations." *Harvard Business Review* 68, no. 2 (March–April 1990), p. 85.

CHAPTER 14

Barndt, Walter D., Jr. "Profiling Rival Decision-Makers." *Journal of Business Strategy*, January–February 1991.

Garsombke, Diane J. "International Competitor Analysis." *Planning Review* 17, no. 3 (May/June 1989).

CHAPTER 15

Balassa, Bela. *The Theory of Economic Integration*. Homewood, Ill.: Business One Irwin, 1961.

"Bank to Pump Loans into E. Europe." *The San Diego Union*, April 16, 1991, p.

Behbehani, Mustafa. "The Gulf Cooperation Council's Intratrade: A Regional Integration Perspective," a paper presented at the United States International University, San Diego 1989.

"IDB Approves $3.8 Billion for Latin America, Caribbean." *The Journal of Commerce*, December 28, 1990.

Ohmae, Kenichi. "Planting for a Global Harvest." *Harvard Business Review* 67, no. 4 (July–August 1989), pp. 137–138.

Root, Franklin R. *International Trade & Investment*. 6th ed. Cincinnati: South-Western Publishing, 1990.

Roson, Peter. *The Economics of International Integration*. London: Allen and Unwin, 1980.

United Nations. Conference on Trade and Development. *Export Processing Free Zones in Developing Countries: Implications for Trade and Industrialization Policies*. 1985.

United Nations. Department of Public Information. *Basic Facts: about the United Nations*. 1987.

United Nations. Department of Public Information. *Charter of the United Nations and Statute of the International Court of Justice*. 1989.

United Nations. Department of Public Information. *Everyone's United Nations*. 1986.

U.S. Department of State. Bureau of Public Affairs. *U.S. Foreign Economic Policies 1990*. September 1990.

CHAPTER 16

Allende-Vera, Baltasar. *Political Risk Analysis: Review, Issues, and Assessment*. Houston: University of Houston, 1990.

Boyer, Edward. "How Japan Manages Declining Industries." *Fortune*, February 10, 1983.

Johnson, Chalmers. *MITI and the Japanese Miracle: The Growth of Industrial Policy*. Stanford, Calif: Stanford University Press, 1982.

———. "The Institutional Foundations of Japanese Industrial Policy." *California Management Review* 27, no. 4 (Summer 1985).

Kotobe, Masaaki. "The Roles of Japanese Industrial Policy for Export Success: A Theoretical Perspective."*Columbia Journal of World Business* 20, no. 3 (Fall 1985).

Leone, Robert A. and Stephen P. Bradley. "Toward an Effective Industrial Policy." *Harvard Business Review* 59, no. 6 (November/December 1981).

Lindblom, Charles E. *Politics and Markets: The World's Political-Economic Systems*. New York: Basic Books, 1977.

Nielsen, Richard P."Government-Owned Businesses: Market Presence, Advantages, Rationales." *The American Journal of Economics and Sociology* 41, no. 1 (January 1982).

———."Should a Country Move Toward International Strategic Market Planning?" *California Management Review* 25, no. 2 (January 1983).

———. "Industrial Policy: The Case for National Strategies for World Markets." *Long-Range Planning* 17, no. 5 (October 1984).

Perkins, Edwin J. *The World Economy in the Twentieth Century*, Cambridge, Mass.: Schenkman Publishing, 1983.

Tsurumi, Yoshi. "The Case of Japan: Price Bargaining and Controls on Oil Products." *Journal of Comparative Economics* 2, 1978.

———."Japan's Challenge to the U.S.: Industrial Policy and Corporate Strategies." *Columbia Journal of World Business*, (Summer 1982).

"The State in the Market." *The Economist*, December 1978.

CHAPTER 17

General Agreement on Tariffs and Trade (GATT). *Basic Instruments and Selected Documents*. Geneva, 1969.

Levi, Maurice. *International Finance: Financial Management and the International Economy*. New York: McGraw-Hill, 1983.

Sheth, Jagdish and Abdolreza Eshghi, eds. *Global Macroeconomic Perspectives*. Cincinnati: South-Western Publishing, 1990.

U.S. Department of Commerce. *Subsidies and Countervailing Measures: The Tokyo Round Agreements*. Vol. 1. Washington, D.C.: GPO, May 1980.

U.S. Department of Commerce. *Government Procurement: The Tokyo Round Agreements*. Vol. 2. Washington, D.C.: GPO, July 1981.

U.S. Department of Commerce. *Trade in Civil Aircraft: The Tokyo Round Agreements*. Vol. 3. Washington, D.C.: GPO, August 1981.

U.S. Department of Commerce. *Technical Barriers to Trade: The Tokyo Round Agreements*. Vol. 4. Washington, D.C.: GPO, September 1981.

U.S. Department of Commerce. *Anti-Dumping Duties: The Tokyo Round Agreements*. Vol. 5. Washington, D.C.: GPO, December1982.

U.S. Department of Commerce. *Agreement on Import Licensing Procedures: The Tokyo Round Agreements*. Vol. 6. Washington, D.C.: GPO, November 1982.

U.S. Department of Commerce. *Customs Valuation: The Tokyo Round Agreements*. Vol. 7. Washington, D.C.: GPO, November 1983.

U.S. Departments of Agriculture and Commerce. Office of the U.S. Trade Representative. *The 1987 National Trade Estimate Report on Foreign Trade Barriers*. Washington, D.C.: GPO, 1987.

CHAPTER 18

Customs Cooperation Council. *Brief Guide to the Customs Valuation Code*. 2nd ed. Brussels, 1988.

———. *The Customs Cooperation Council (In Brief)*. Brussels, 1988.

————. *Introducing the Kyoto Convention: Simplification and Harmonization of Customs Procedures Background, Benefits, and Procedure for Accession.* Brussels, 1989.

Drucker, Peter. "Peter Drucker's 1990's: The Futures that Have Already Happened." *Economist*, October 21, 1989, p. 19.

"GATT's Seven Rounds of Trade Talks Span More Than Thirty Years." *Business America.* June 23, 1986.

Morrison, Ann V. "Tokyo Round Agreement Set Rules for Nontariff Measures." *Business America*, July 7, 1986.

Morrison, Ann V. and Robin Layton. "GATT...A Look Back as the Ministerial Meeting Approaches." *Business America.* June 23, 1986.

Pen, Jan. *A Primer of International Trade.* New York: Random House, 1967.

Searing, Majory E. "The Uruguay Round-Up and Running." *Business America*, May 8, 1989.

Sek, Lenore. "Trade Negotiations: The Uruguay Round." *CRS Issue Brief*, December 20, 1988.

United Nations. Conference on Trade and Development. *Uruguay Round: Papers on Selected Issues.* 1989.

U.S. Department of Commerce. *Uruguay Round Update.* Washington, D.C.: GPO, February, May, September 1988; January, May, September 1989; February 1990; February 1991.

U.S. Department of the Treasury. *Customs Tomorrow, Final CCC Reports.* Washington, D.C.: GPO, November 1989.

CHAPTER 19
Blumer, Herbert. *Symbolic Interactionism: Perspective and Method.* Englewood Cliffs, N.J.: Prentice Hall, 1969.
Porter, Michael. *Competitive Strategy: Techniques for Analyzing Industries and Competitors.* New York: The Free Press, 1980.

CHAPTER 21
Nelson, Carl A. "Matching Tactics to Strategy." In *Proceedings of the 1992 Conference.* New Orleans: Association for Global Business, 1992.
Particelli, Marc C. "A Global Arena." *The Journal of Consumer Marketing* 7, no. 4 (Fall 1990).

CHAPTER 23
Ohmae, Kenichi. "Planting for a Global Harvest." *Harvard Business Review* 67, no. 3 (July–August 1989), p. 140.

CHAPTER 24
Nelson, Carl A. *Global Success: International Business Tactics for the 1990s.* Blue Ridge Summit, Pa.: TAB Books, a division of McGraw-Hill, 1990.
Ohmae, Kenichi. "Planting for a Global Harvest." *Harvard Business Review* 67, no. 4 (July–August 1989), pp. 137–140.

CHAPTER 25
Hellebust, Karsten G. and Joseph C. Krallinger. *Strategic Planning Workbook.* New York: John Wiley & Sons, 1989.
Melcher, Bonita H. and Harld Kerzner. *Strategic Planning: Development and Implementation.* Blue Ridge Summit, Pa.: TAB Books, a division of McGraw-Hill, 1988.

Index

Total quality management (TQM), 24, 42–45
Total sales volume, 96
Trade
  cross-border boom in, 5, 6–9
  explosion in, 5, 7
  organizations involved in, 245–47
Trade Act (1979), 156
Trade barrier mapping, 137–50
  industrial policy in, 149
  and international debt, 148–49
  nontariff barriers in, 140–46
  tariff barriers in, 138
  trade as political weapon in, 146–48
Trade bloc mapping, 114–24
  economic integration in, 114
  forms of cooperation in, 114–17
  issues in, 117–19
  major trade blocs in, 119–22
  minor trade blocs in, 122–23
Trade creation opportunities strategy, 174–75
Trade creative incentives, 125–36
  artificial comparative advantage in, 125–26
  financial capital in, 126–31
  human capital in, 131
  mapping trade creation in, 126
  schemes in, 135–36
  technology in, 132–35
Trade theories
  government intervention in, 91–92
  import substitution in, 90
  infant industry argument in, 90–91
  inward orientation in, 89–90
  outward orientation in, 90
Traditional ratios, 227
Transaction, definition of, 15
Transportation, and trade boom, 8
Trend analysis, and strategic visibility, 73–74
Trends, examples of, 74
Turnaround strategy, 226

U

UB Group of India, 13
Underdeveloped nations, 87

Union of Japanese Scientists and Engineers (JUSE), 42
United Distillers, 12
United Nations Conference on Trade and Development (UNCTAD), 7, 157–58, 247
United Nations Development Program (UNDP), 129
United Nations Industrial Development Organization (UNIDO), 134, 158
U.S. data bases, 82
U.S. dollar, value of, 152–53
U.S. International Trade Commission (USITC), 247
U.S. Tariff Act (1789), 138
U.S. Trade Representative (USTR), 160, 247
Uruguay Round, 139, 156–57

V

Value analysis (VA), 108
Values
  and attitudes, 97
  and cultures, 96–97
Venture capitalists (VCs), 128
Vertical integration, 225
Voluntary restraint agreements (VRAs), 146, 160

W

War, 148
Waterman, 22
WD-40, 59–64, 225
Weaknesses, identifying internal, 56–59
West African Economic Community (CEAO), 115
Whalen, Richard, 19
Will, as key to success, 223
Windfall profit, 152
Withdrawal strategy, 226
Worker training, 135
Working-capital analysis, 229
World Bank, 7, 87, 128, 247
World-class product, development of, 104
World Corp., 73
World Intellectual Property Organization (WIPO), 134, 159, 247
Worldwide purchasing, 107
Worldwide sourcing manager (WWSM), 206

Other books of interest to you from Irwin Professional Publishing...